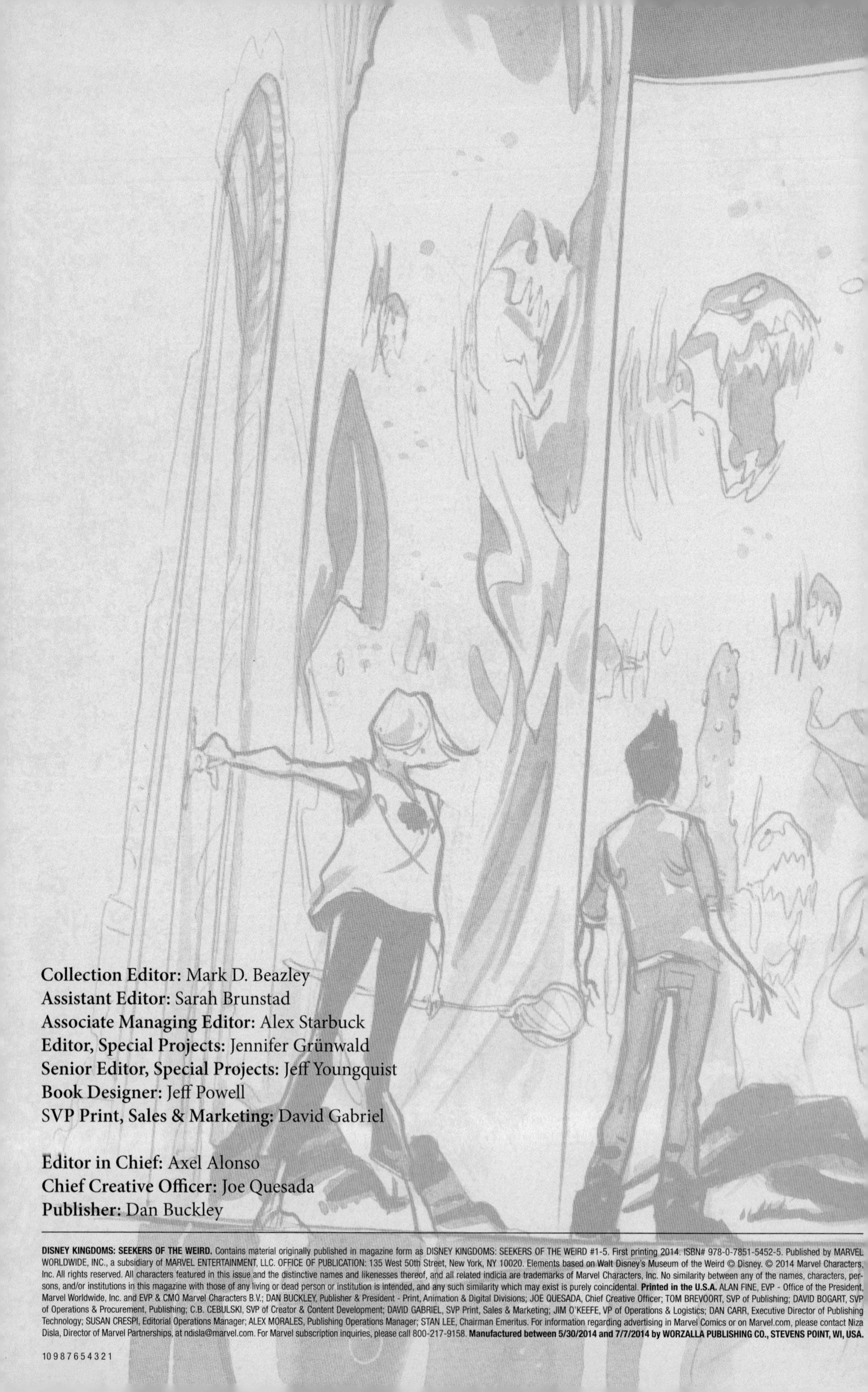

Collection Editor: Mark D. Beazley
Assistant Editor: Sarah Brunstad
Associate Managing Editor: Alex Starbuck
Editor, Special Projects: Jennifer Grünwald
Senior Editor, Special Projects: Jeff Youngquist
Book Designer: Jeff Powell
SVP Print, Sales & Marketing: David Gabriel

Editor in Chief: Axel Alonso
Chief Creative Officer: Joe Quesada
Publisher: Dan Buckley

DISNEY KINGDOMS: SEEKERS OF THE WEIRD. Contains material originally published in magazine form as DISNEY KINGDOMS: SEEKERS OF THE WEIRD #1-5. First printing 2014. ISBN# 978-0-7851-5452-5. Published by MARVEL WORLDWIDE, INC., a subsidiary of MARVEL ENTERTAINMENT, LLC. OFFICE OF PUBLICATION: 135 West 50th Street, New York, NY 10020. Elements based on Walt Disney's Museum of the Weird © Disney. **Printed in the U.S.A.** ALAN FINE, EVP - Office of the President, Marvel Worldwide, Inc. and EVP & CMO Marvel Characters B.V.; DAN BUCKLEY, Publisher & President - Print, Animation & Digital Divisions; JOE QUESADA, Chief Creative Officer; TOM BREVOORT, SVP of Publishing; DAVID BOGART, SVP of Operations & Procurement, Publishing; C.B. CEBULSKI, SVP of Creator & Content Development; DAVID GABRIEL, SVP Print, Sales & Marketing; JIM O'KEEFE, VP of Operations & Logistics; DAN CARR, Executive Director of Publishing Technology; SUSAN CRESPI, Editorial Operations Manager; ALEX MORALES, Publishing Operations Manager; STAN LEE, Chairman Emeritus. For information regarding advertising in Marvel Comics or on Marvel.com, please contact Niza Disla, Director of Marvel Partnerships, at ndisla@marvel.com. For Marvel subscription inquiries, please call 800-217-9158. **Manufactured between 5/30/2014 and 7/7/2014 by WORZALLA PUBLISHING CO., STEVENS POINT, WI, USA.**

10 9 8 7 6 5 4 3 2 1

SEEKERS OF THE WEIRD

Writer
BRANDON SEIFERT

Pencilers
KARL MOLINE & FILIPE ANDRADE (#3)

Inkers
RICK MAGYAR & FILIPE ANDRADE (#3)

Colorist
JEAN-FRANCOIS BEAULIEU

Letterer
VC'S JOE CARAMAGNA

Cover Art
MICHAEL DEL MUNDO

Walt Disney Imagineers
JIM CLARK, BRIAN CROSBY, TOM MORRIS & JOSH SHIPLEY

Assistant Editor
MARK BASSO

Editor
BILL ROSEMANN

MUSEUM OF THE WEIRD INSPIRED BY THE DESIGNS OF
ROLLY CRUMP

SPECIAL THANKS TO **DAVID GABRIEL,**
VANESSA HUNT, DENISE BROWN & MIKE JUSKO

INTRODUCTION

BY ROLLY CRUMP

I guess you could say comic books and action figures have always been a big part of my life. I began to draw at the age of three. Some of my earliest drawings were based on comic strip characters, cartoons, cowboys and even boxing matches featured in newsreels at the movie theater. I would draw from my imagination what I had seen on screen or in the newspaper. I still have a scrapbook my mom, who was my biggest supporter, kept of those early drawings.

As I got older the comic book hero's of the time, Superman, Batman, Red Rider, The Phantom, etc all played a part in my early development as an artist and cartoonist. I would trace the work of Hal Foster (Prince Valiant), Alex Raymond (Tarzan) and others, which helped me develop my own style.

My first real attempt at being a cartoonist was the assignment I had in high school. I developed a two page spread in pen and ink depicting various school characters and activities. It was printed on the inside cover of the school annual. After high school I went to work at a pottery but all of my after hours were spent drawing. I worked in pen, ink and watercolor and focused on pirates and hot rod cars.

At the time, if you were interested in becoming an artist you wanted to work at the Disney Studio. I was no different. As fate would have it, at a dinner my mom had I was introduced to a woman who had actually worked in animation at the studio. She gave me the name of someone to contact, which I did, and much to my surprise was asked to come in to personnel with my portfolio for an interview. Well, my so called "portfolio" consisted of all the art I had been doing since high school. That was it!

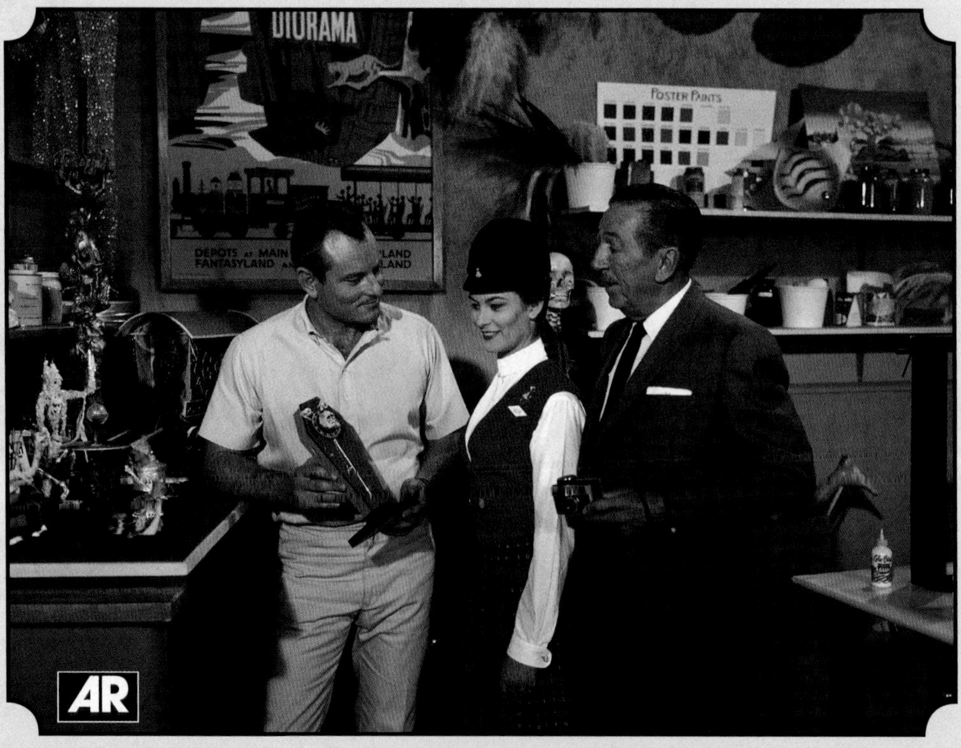
DIORAMA
FOSTER PAINTS

So, portfolio in hand, the interview over, I was told they would "get back to me" and incredibly enough they did. I was hired to work in animation as an "inbetweener" on Peter Pan. I had no idea what animation really was but I was thrilled to get the job. That was in 1952 and for the next seven years I received the best education and training from the other animators I was lucky enough to work with. They were all artists in their own right, each with their own unique style. I began to branch out and eventually developed my own style, which I think of as humorous poster art.

When I was asked to join WED (now Walt Disney Imagineering) as a show designer I was assigned to work on the development of the Haunted Mansion. I always felt the Mansion should be more than a "spook house". I believed it should be more imaginative and surrealistic than the typical "cat & the canary" haunted house. I began to draw sketches of some of the elements I felt should be in the Mansion. Many of these sketches were based on films I was inspired by such as Jean Cocteau's 1946 Beauty and the Beast and Fellini's Juliet of the Spirits. My idea was to fill the Haunted Mansion with strange creatures made up of various plant, animal and human parts that would become part of the architecture. The walls, columns, furniture, etc. would all come to life.

When it came time to present my ideas to Walt we actually showed him not only the sketches but models of the various creatures like the Candle Man and the Coffin Clock. We weren't sure at the time how these would actually be used in the Mansion. It was Walt that took the concept to the next level and gave it the name "Museum of the Weird". I believe if Walt had lived to see the Mansion completed, the Museum would have become an important part of the attraction.

A number of years ago the E-Ticket publication did a story about the Museum and the final paragraph read, "the Museum of the Weird, well, it exists only in memory and in the sketches by Rolly Crump from another time". Well, here we are fifty years later and the Museum is finally coming to life. It's not exactly the life that I had envisioned but I'm thrilled and delighted that it found life in the comics.

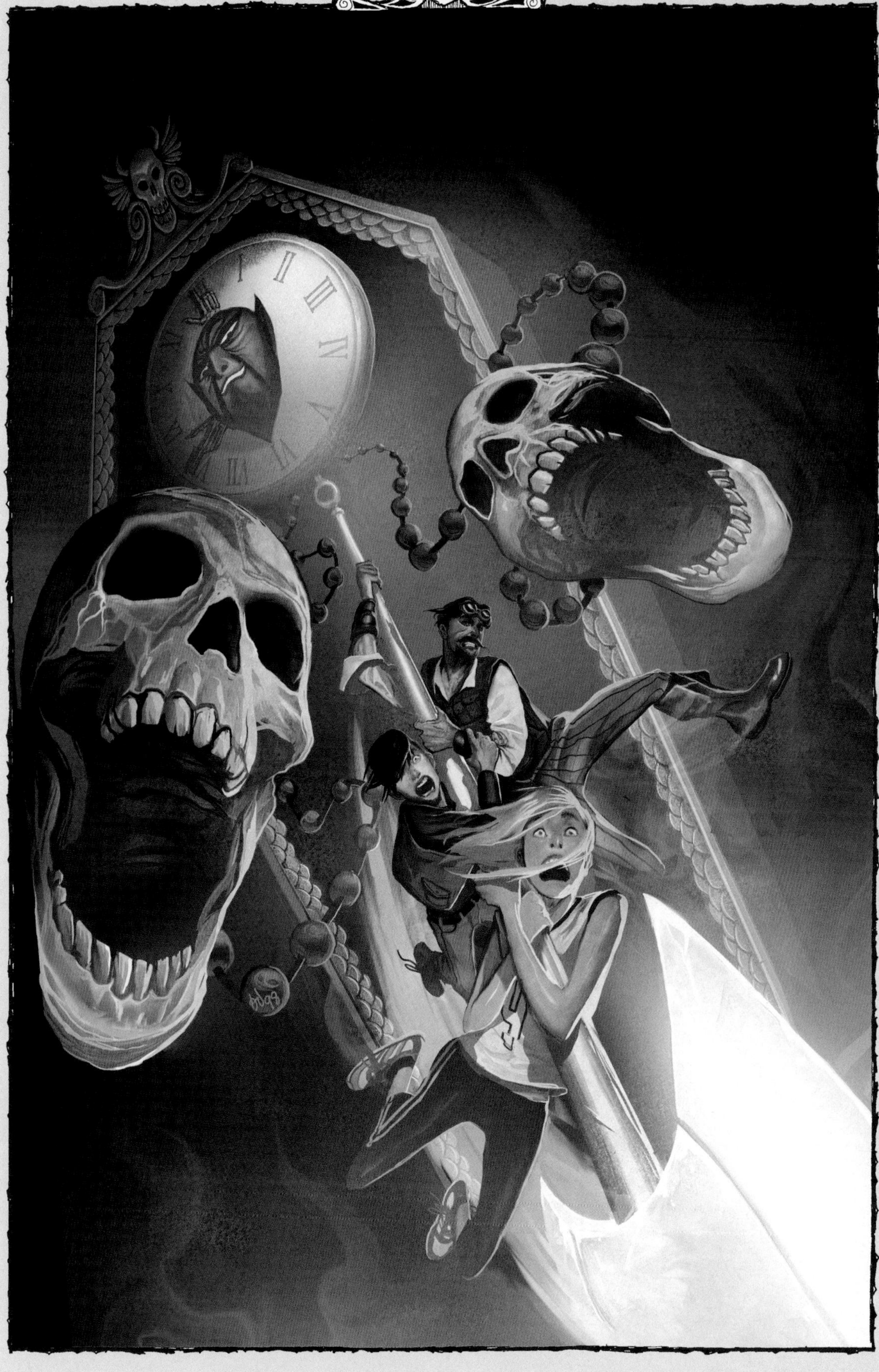

1

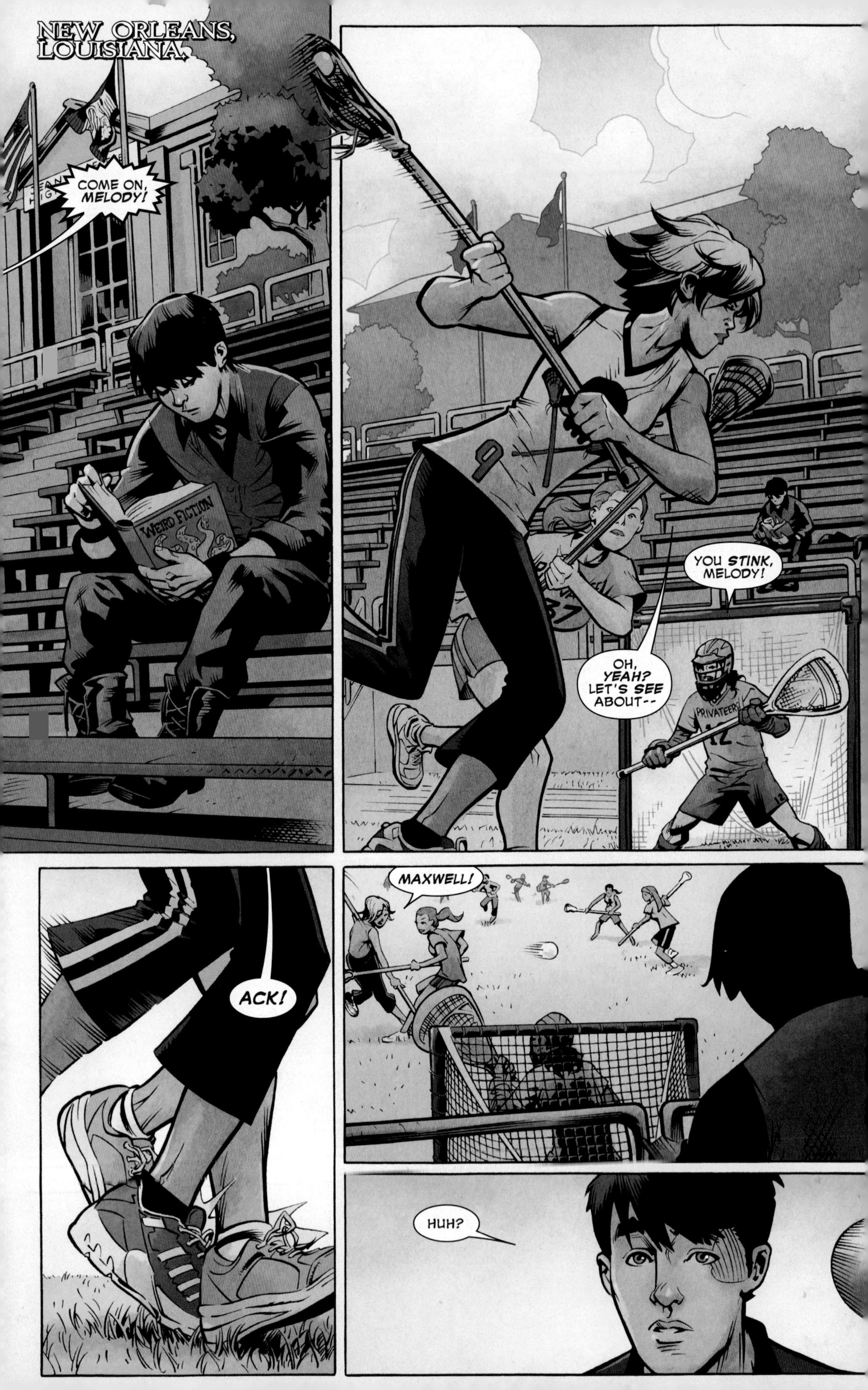
NEW ORLEANS, LOUISIANA.
COME ON, MELODY!
YOU STINK, MELODY!
OH, YEAH? LET'S SEE ABOUT--
PRIVATEERS
ACK!
MAXWELL!
HUH?

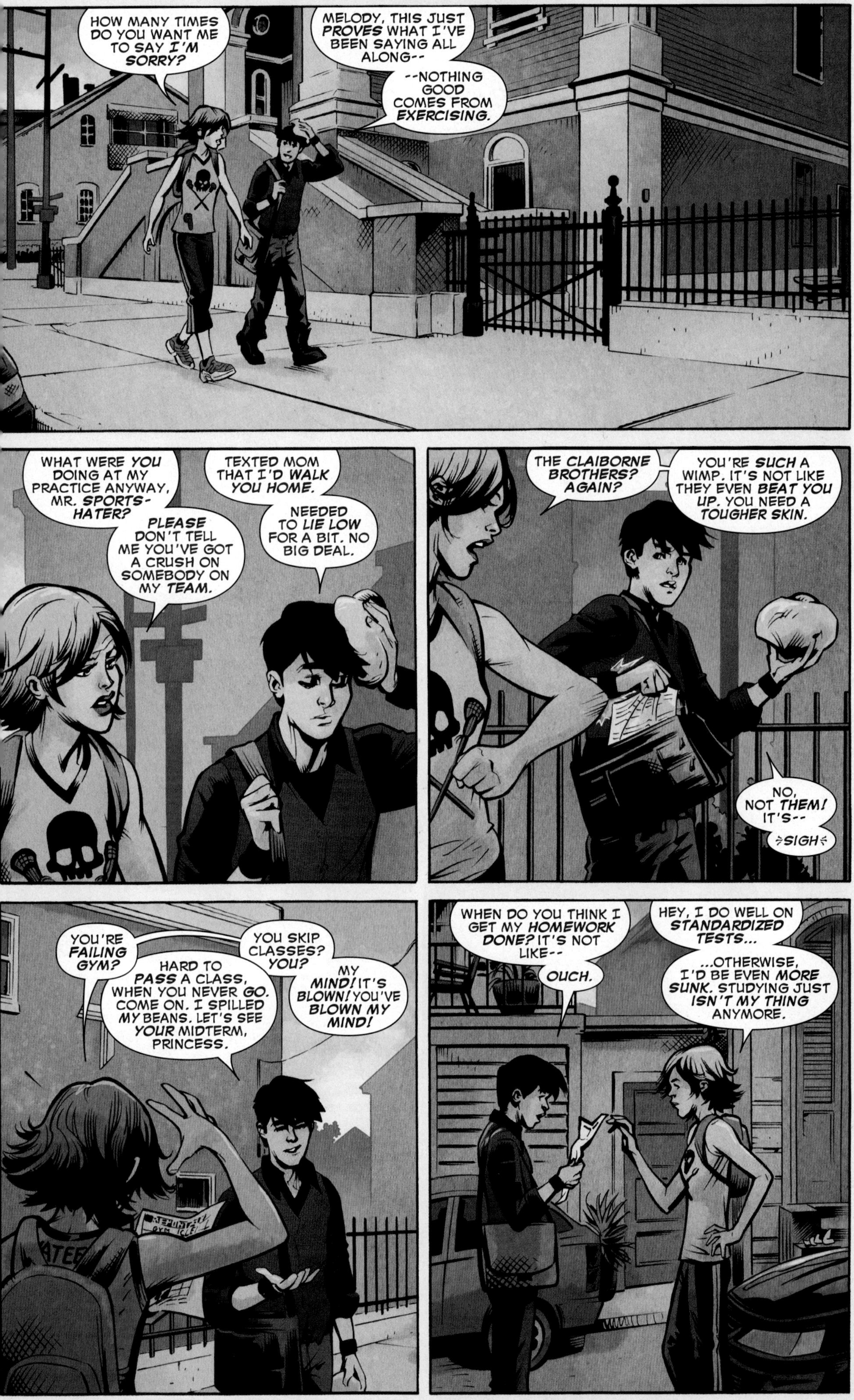
HOW MANY TIMES DO YOU WANT ME TO SAY I'M SORRY?
MELODY, THIS JUST PROVES WHAT I'VE BEEN SAYING ALL ALONG--
--NOTHING GOOD COMES FROM EXERCISING.
WHAT WERE YOU DOING AT MY PRACTICE ANYWAY, MR. SPORTS-HATER?
PLEASE DON'T TELL ME YOU'VE GOT A CRUSH ON SOMEBODY ON MY TEAM.
TEXTED MOM THAT I'D WALK YOU HOME.
NEEDED TO LIE LOW FOR A BIT. NO BIG DEAL.
THE CLAIBORNE BROTHERS? AGAIN?
YOU'RE SUCH A WIMP. IT'S NOT LIKE THEY EVEN BEAT YOU UP. YOU NEED A TOUGHER SKIN.
NO, NOT THEM! IT'S--
SIGH
YOU'RE FAILING GYM?
HARD TO PASS A CLASS, WHEN YOU NEVER GO. COME ON. I SPILLED MY BEANS. LET'S SEE YOUR MIDTERM, PRINCESS.
YOU SKIP CLASSES? YOU?
MY MIND! IT'S BLOWN! YOU'VE BLOWN MY MIND!
WHEN DO YOU THINK I GET MY HOMEWORK DONE? IT'S NOT LIKE--
OUCH.
HEY, I DO WELL ON STANDARDIZED TESTS...
...OTHERWISE, I'D BE EVEN MORE SUNK. STUDYING JUST ISN'T MY THING ANYMORE.

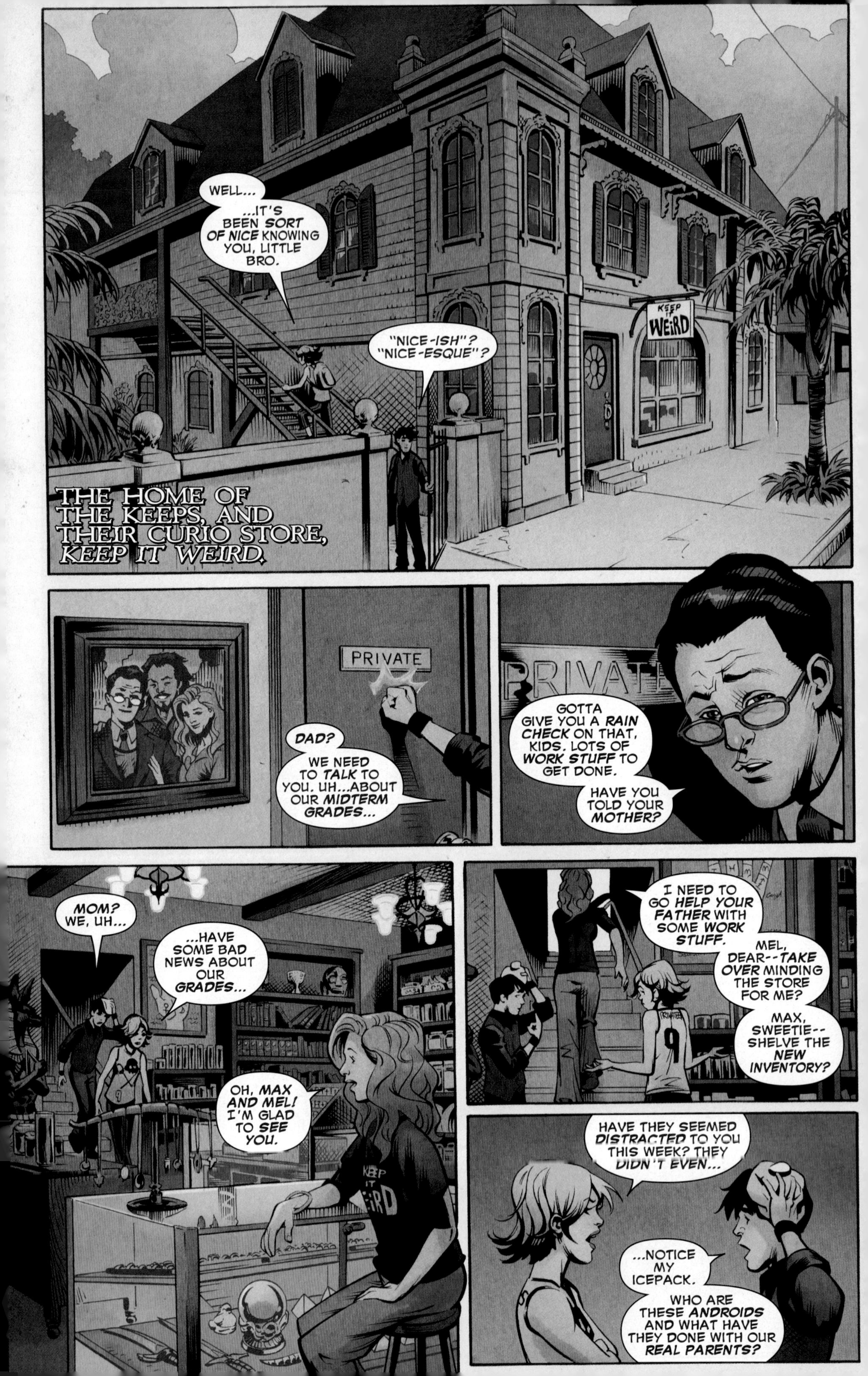
WELL...
...IT'S BEEN SORT OF NICE KNOWING YOU, LITTLE BRO.
"NICE-ISH"? "NICE-ESQUE"?
KEEP IT WEIRD
THE HOME OF THE KEEPS, AND THEIR CURIO STORE, KEEP IT WEIRD.
PRIVATE
DAD?
WE NEED TO TALK TO YOU. UH...ABOUT OUR MIDTERM GRADES...
PRIVATE
GOTTA GIVE YOU A RAIN CHECK ON THAT, KIDS. LOTS OF WORK STUFF TO GET DONE.
HAVE YOU TOLD YOUR MOTHER?
MOM? WE, UH...
...HAVE SOME BAD NEWS ABOUT OUR GRADES...
OH, MAX AND MEL! I'M GLAD TO SEE YOU.
KEEP IT WEIRD
I NEED TO GO HELP YOUR FATHER WITH SOME WORK STUFF.
MEL, DEAR--TAKE OVER MINDING THE STORE FOR ME?
MAX, SWEETIE--SHELVE THE NEW INVENTORY?
HAVE THEY SEEMED DISTRACTED TO YOU THIS WEEK? THEY DIDN'T EVEN...
...NOTICE MY ICEPACK.
WHO ARE THESE ANDROIDS AND WHAT HAVE THEY DONE WITH OUR REAL PARENTS?

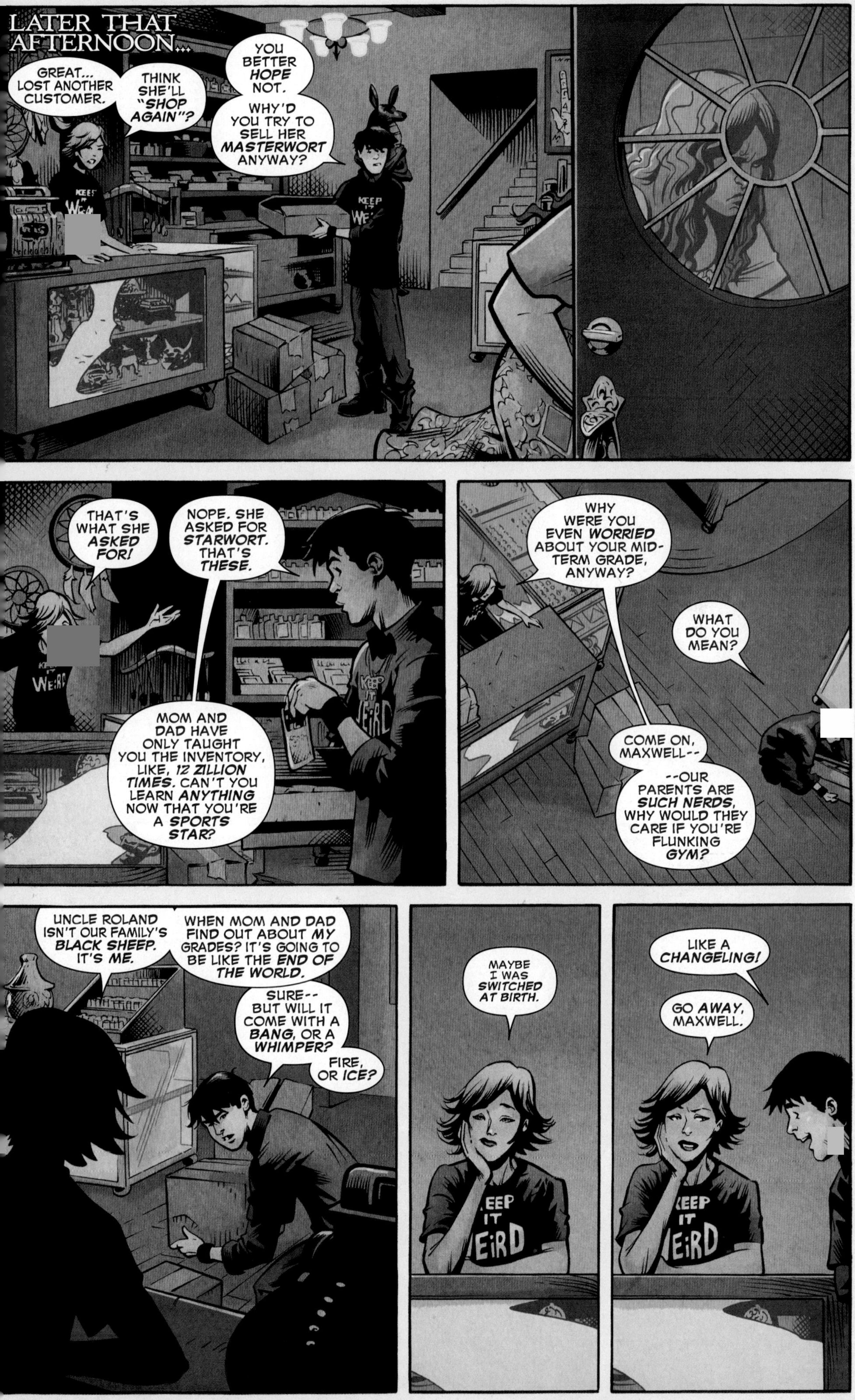
LATER THAT AFTERNOON...
GREAT... LOST ANOTHER CUSTOMER.
THINK SHE'LL "SHOP AGAIN"?
YOU BETTER HOPE NOT.
WHY'D YOU TRY TO SELL HER MASTERWORT ANYWAY?
THAT'S WHAT SHE ASKED FOR!
NOPE. SHE ASKED FOR STARWORT. THAT'S THESE.
MOM AND DAD HAVE ONLY TAUGHT YOU THE INVENTORY, LIKE, 12 ZILLION TIMES. CAN'T YOU LEARN ANYTHING NOW THAT YOU'RE A SPORTS STAR?
WHY WERE YOU EVEN WORRIED ABOUT YOUR MID-TERM GRADE, ANYWAY?
WHAT DO YOU MEAN?
COME ON, MAXWELL--
--OUR PARENTS ARE SUCH NERDS, WHY WOULD THEY CARE IF YOU'RE FLUNKING GYM?
UNCLE ROLAND ISN'T OUR FAMILY'S BLACK SHEEP. IT'S ME.
WHEN MOM AND DAD FIND OUT ABOUT MY GRADES? IT'S GOING TO BE LIKE THE END OF THE WORLD.
SURE-- BUT WILL IT COME WITH A BANG, OR A WHIMPER?
FIRE, OR ICE?
MAYBE I WAS SWITCHED AT BIRTH.
LIKE A CHANGELING!
GO AWAY, MAXWELL.

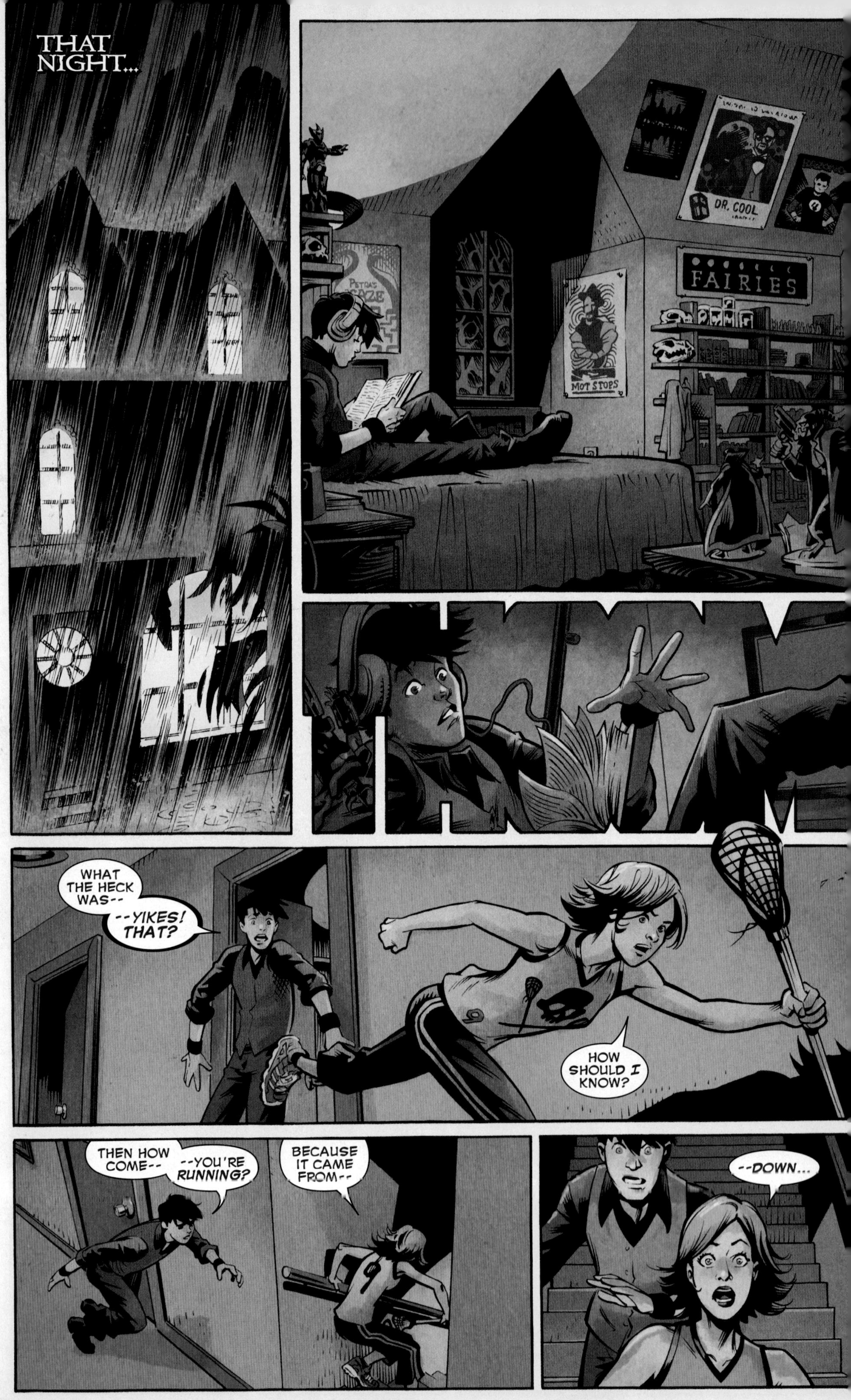
THAT NIGHT...
DR. COOL
FAIRIES
MOT STOPS
WHAT THE HECK WAS--
--YIKES! THAT?
HOW SHOULD I KNOW?
THEN HOW COME--
--YOU'RE RUNNING?
BECAUSE IT CAME FROM--
--DOWN...

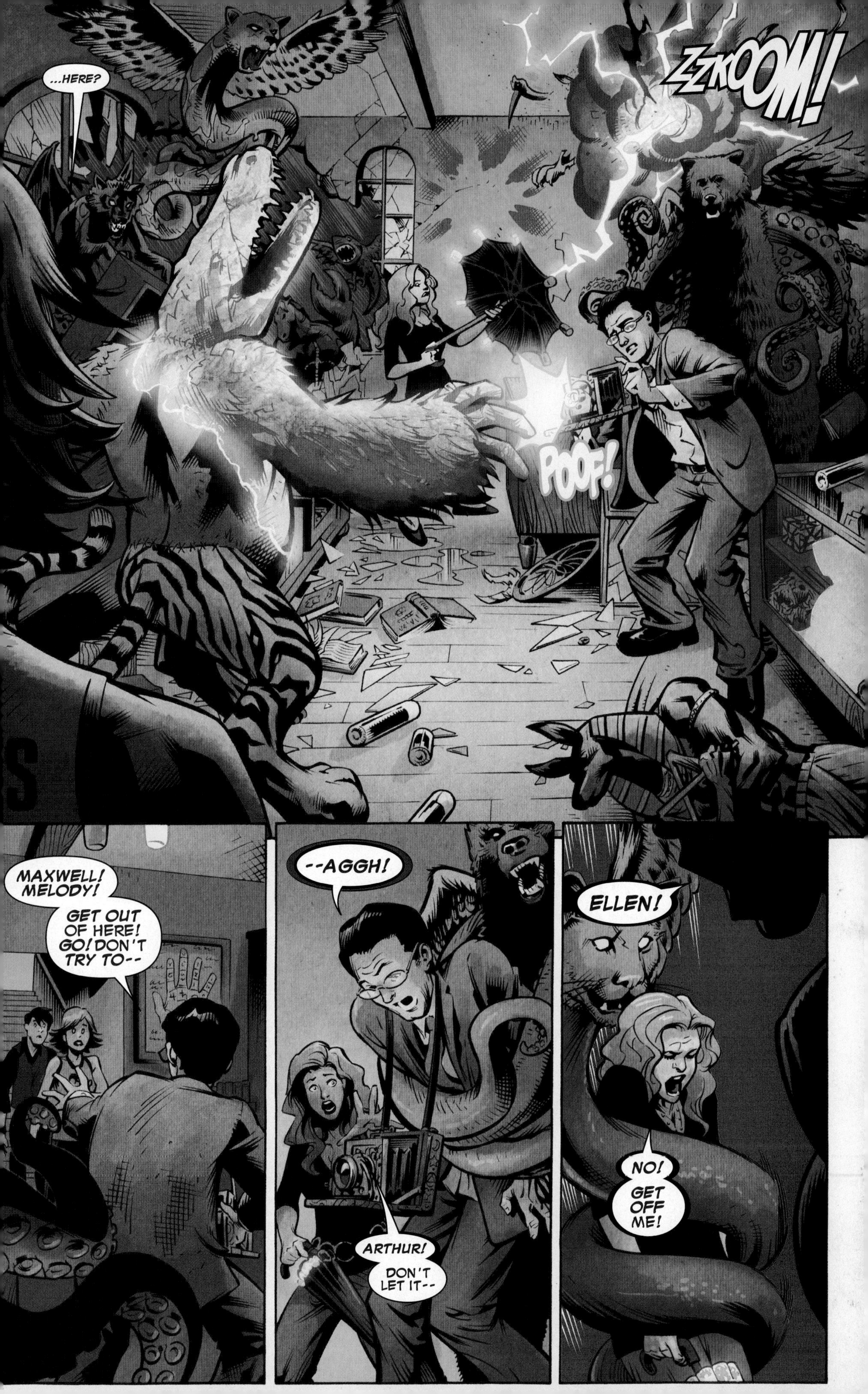
...HERE?
ZZKOOM!
POOF!
MAXWELL! MELODY!
GET OUT OF HERE! GO! DON'T TRY TO--
--AGGH!
ARTHUR!
DON'T LET IT--
ELLEN!
NO! GET OFF ME!

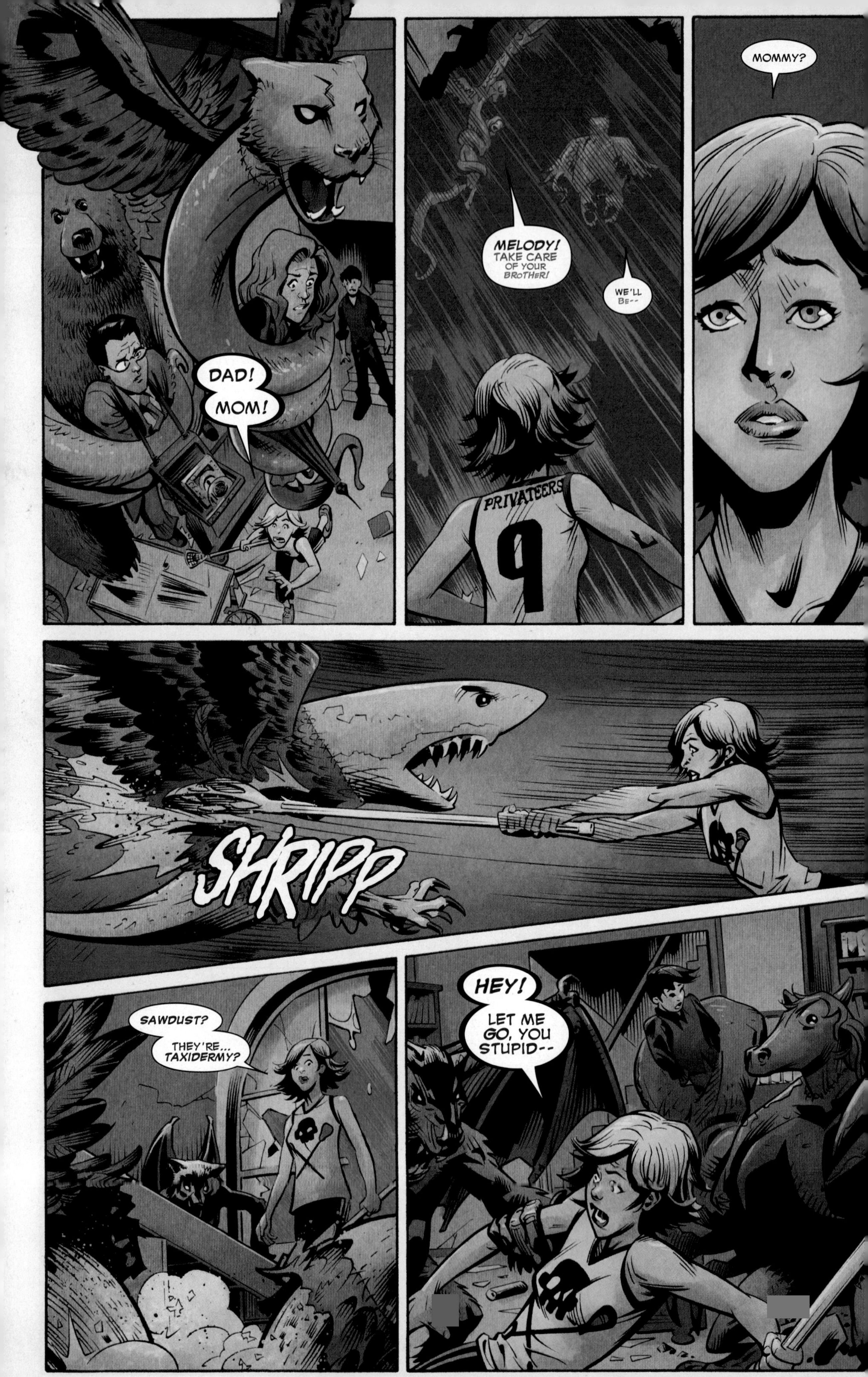
DAD!
MOM!
MELODY! TAKE CARE OF YOUR BROTHER!
WE'LL BE--
MOMMY?
SHRIPP
SAWDUST?
THEY'RE... TAXIDERMY?
HEY!
LET ME GO, YOU STUPID--

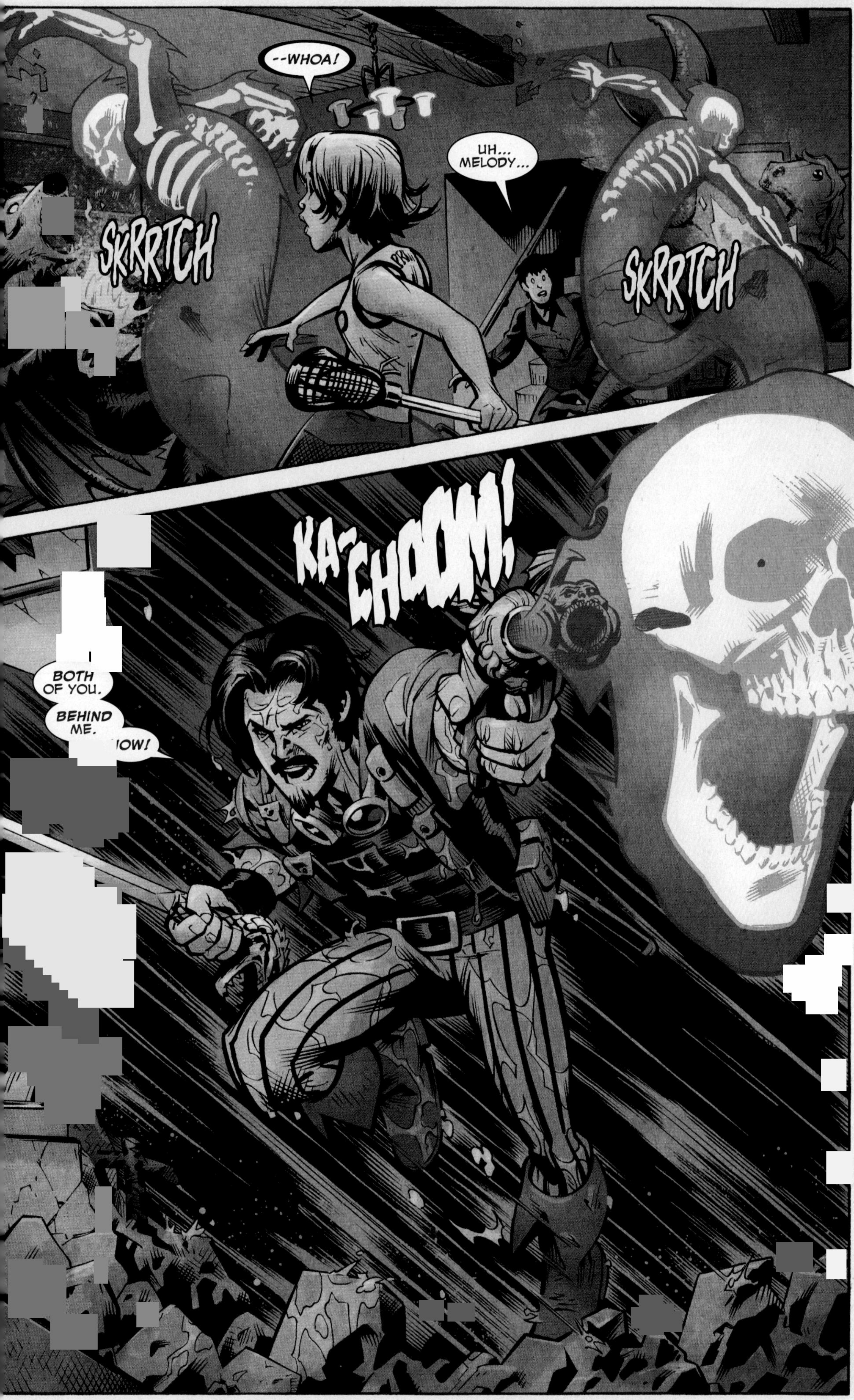
--WHOA!
UH... MELODY...
SKRRTCH
SKRRTCH
KA-CHOOM!
BOTH OF YOU.
BEHIND ME.

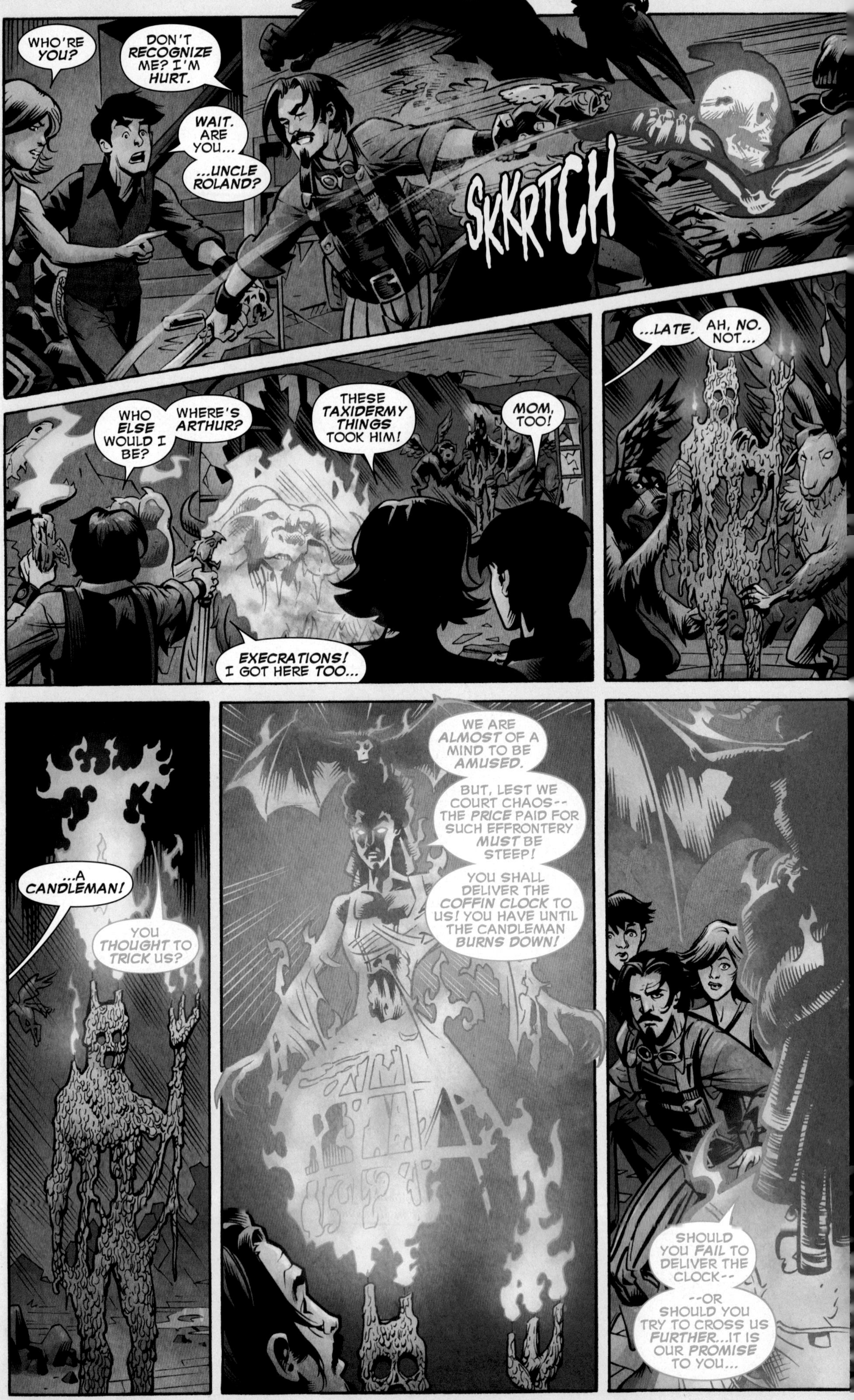
WHO'RE YOU?
DON'T RECOGNIZE ME? I'M HURT.
WAIT. ARE YOU...
...UNCLE ROLAND?
SKKRTCH
WHO ELSE WOULD I BE?
WHERE'S ARTHUR?
THESE TAXIDERMY THINGS TOOK HIM!
MOM, TOO!
EXECRATIONS! I GOT HERE TOO...
AH, NO. NOT...
...LATE.
...A CANDLEMAN!
YOU THOUGHT TO TRICK US?
WE ARE ALMOST OF A MIND TO BE AMUSED.
BUT, LEST WE COURT CHAOS-- THE PRICE PAID FOR SUCH EFFRONTERY MUST BE STEEP!
YOU SHALL DELIVER THE COFFIN CLOCK TO US! YOU HAVE UNTIL THE CANDLEMAN BURNS DOWN!
SHOULD YOU FAIL TO DELIVER THE CLOCK--
--OR SHOULD YOU TRY TO CROSS US FURTHER...IT IS OUR PROMISE TO YOU...

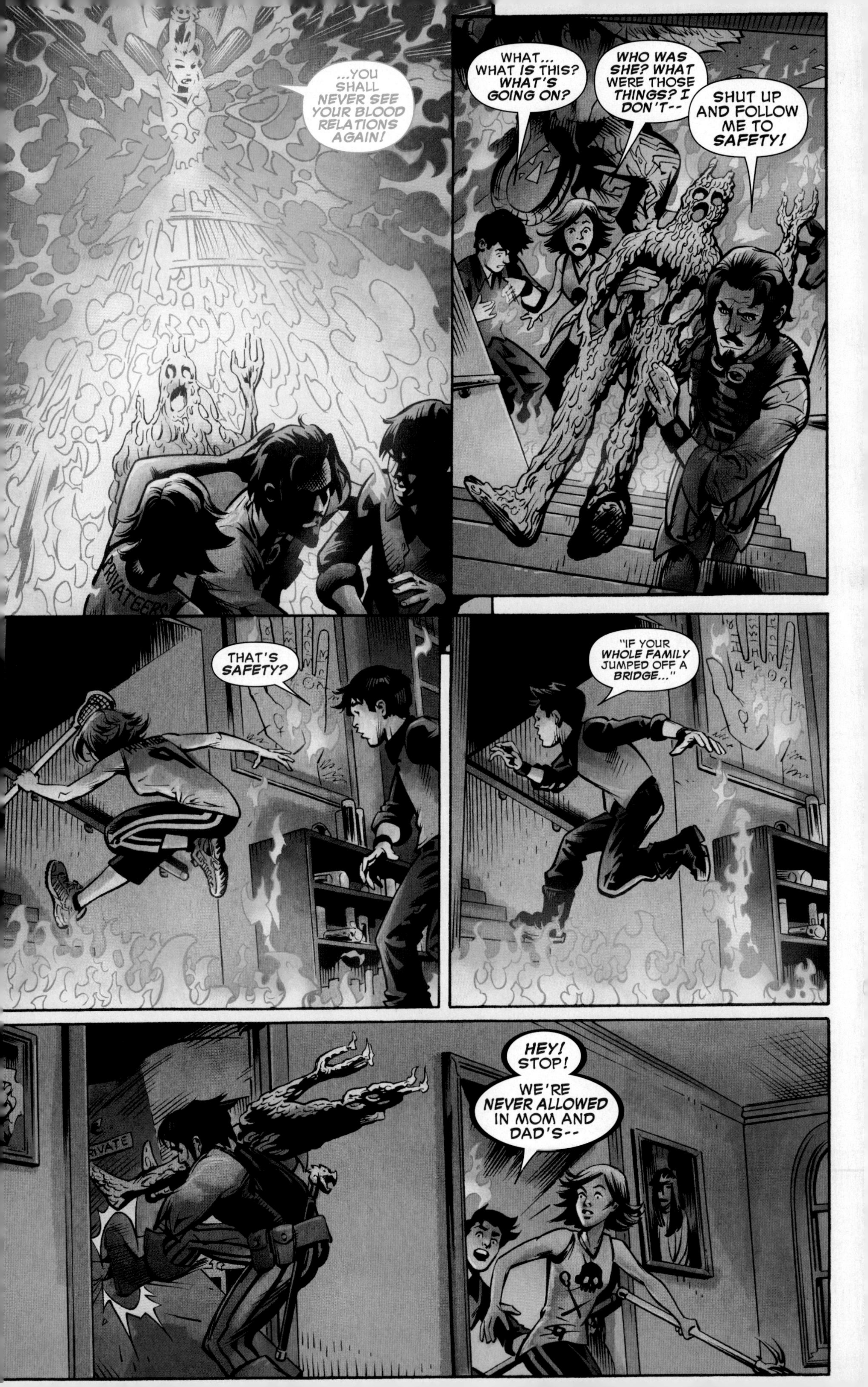
...YOU SHALL NEVER SEE YOUR BLOOD RELATIONS AGAIN!
WHAT... WHAT IS THIS? WHAT'S GOING ON?
WHO WAS SHE? WHAT WERE THOSE THINGS? I DON'T--
SHUT UP AND FOLLOW ME TO SAFETY!
PRIVATEERS
THAT'S SAFETY?
"IF YOUR WHOLE FAMILY JUMPED OFF A BRIDGE..."
PRIVATE
HEY! STOP!
WE'RE NEVER ALLOWED IN MOM AND DAD'S--

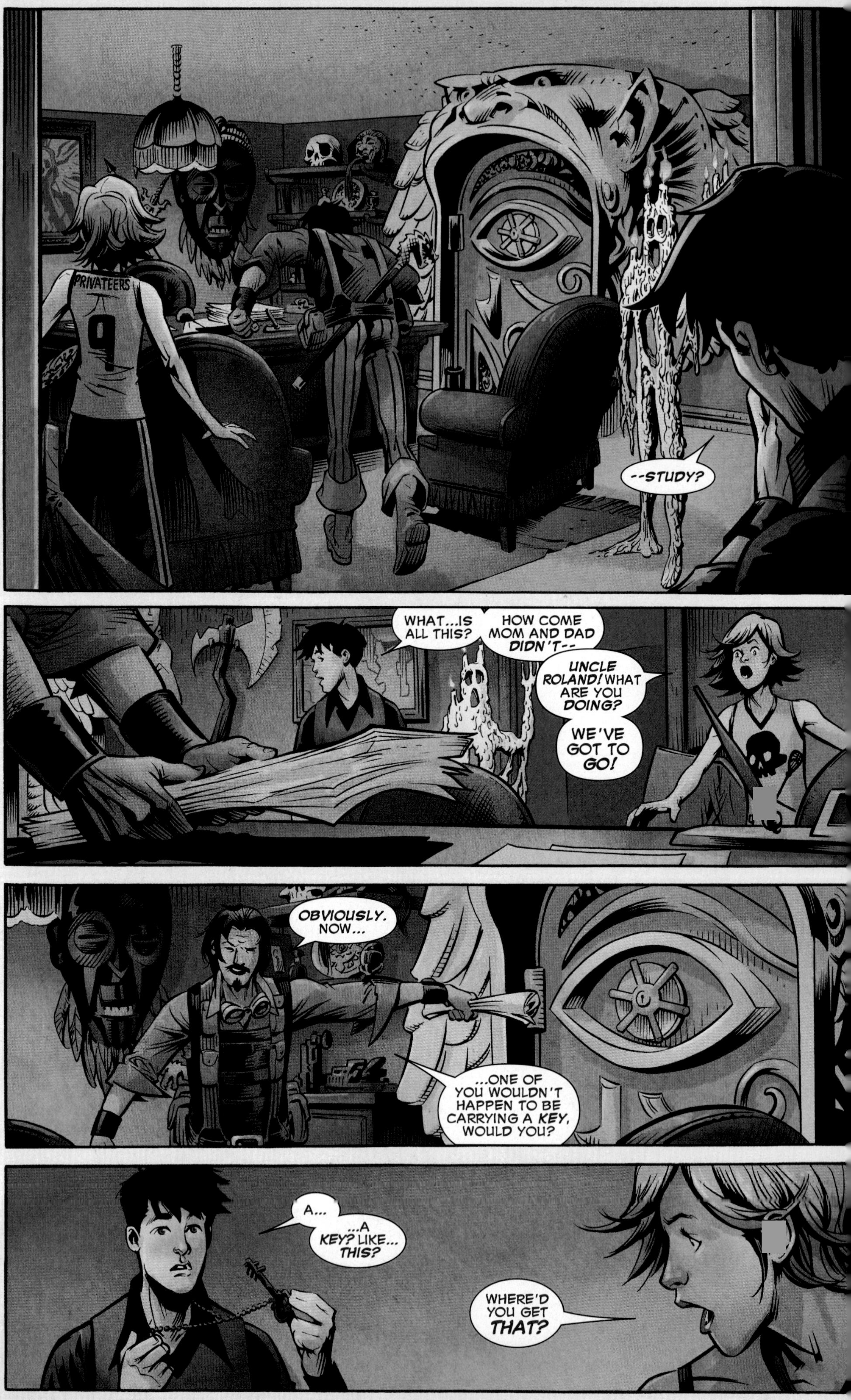
--STUDY?
WHAT...IS ALL THIS?
HOW COME MOM AND DAD DIDN'T--
UNCLE ROLAND! WHAT ARE YOU DOING?
WE'VE GOT TO GO!
OBVIOUSLY. NOW...
...ONE OF YOU WOULDN'T HAPPEN TO BE CARRYING A KEY, WOULD YOU?
A...
...A KEY? LIKE... THIS?
WHERE'D YOU GET THAT?

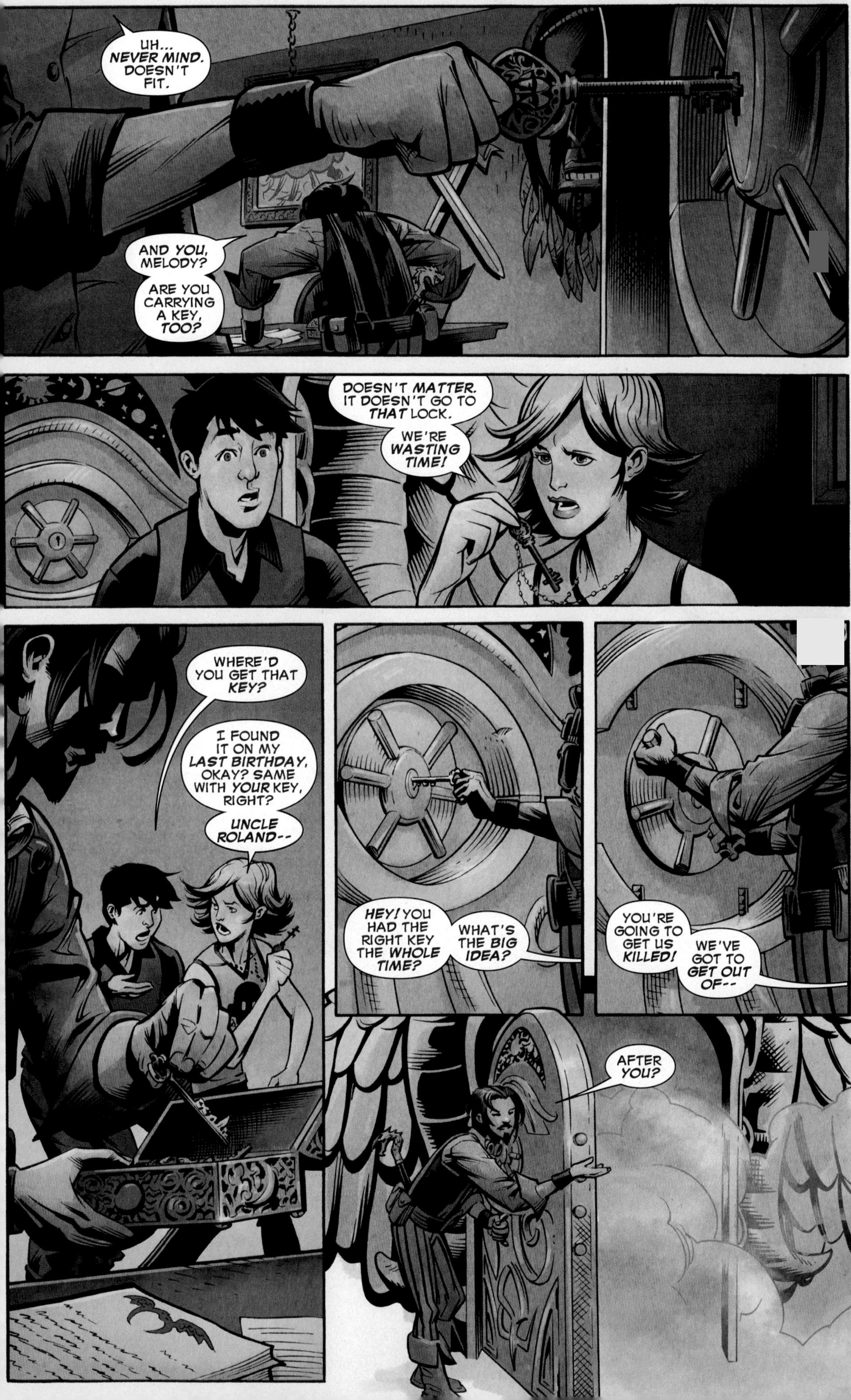
UH... NEVER MIND. DOESN'T FIT.
AND YOU, MELODY?
ARE YOU CARRYING A KEY, TOO?
DOESN'T MATTER. IT DOESN'T GO TO THAT LOCK.
WE'RE WASTING TIME!
WHERE'D YOU GET THAT KEY?
I FOUND IT ON MY LAST BIRTHDAY, OKAY? SAME WITH YOUR KEY, RIGHT?
UNCLE ROLAND--
HEY! YOU HAD THE RIGHT KEY THE WHOLE TIME?
WHAT'S THE BIG IDEA?
YOU'RE GOING TO GET US KILLED!
WE'VE GOT TO GET OUT OF--
AFTER YOU?

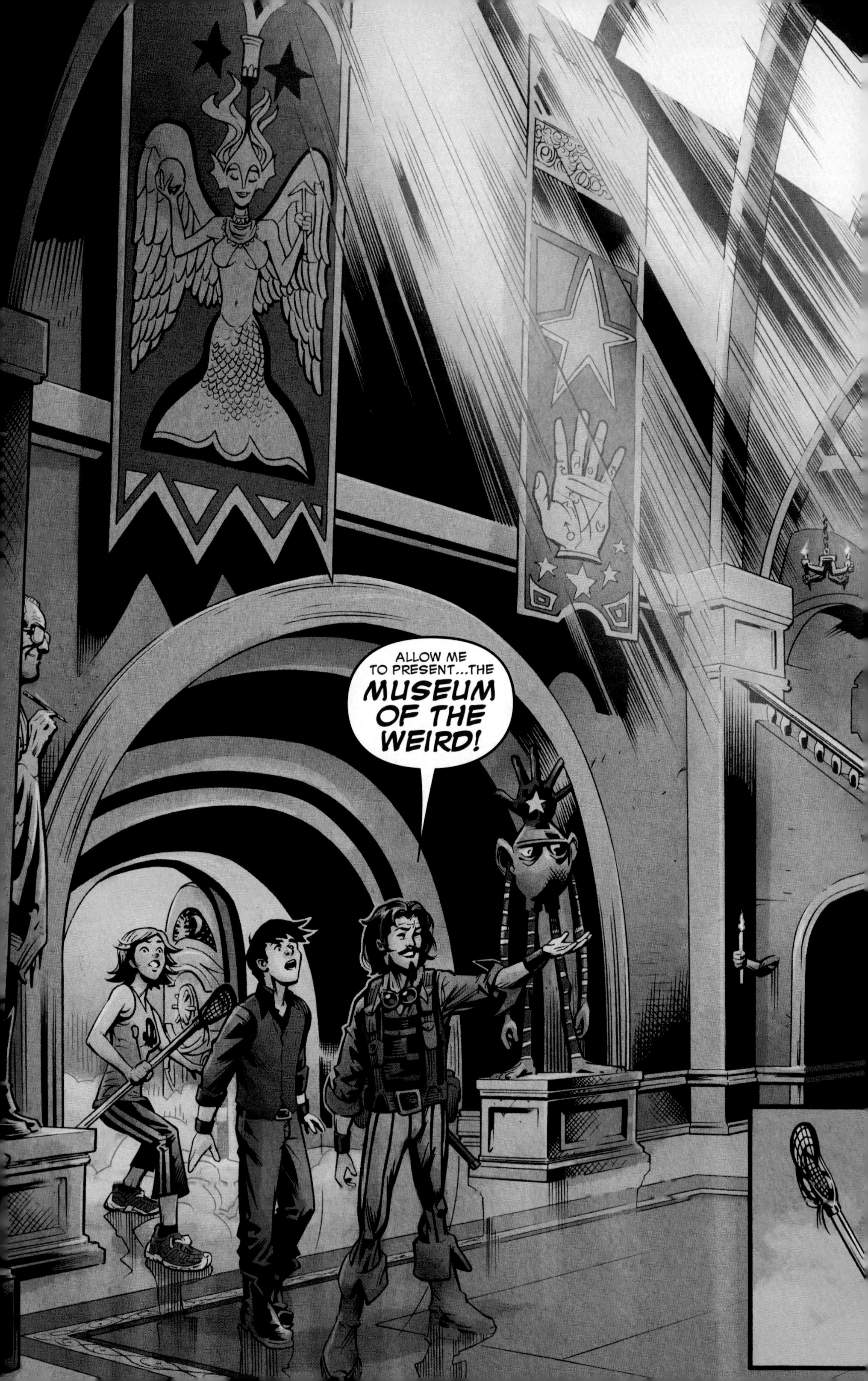
ALLOW ME TO PRESENT...THE MUSEUM OF THE WEIRD!

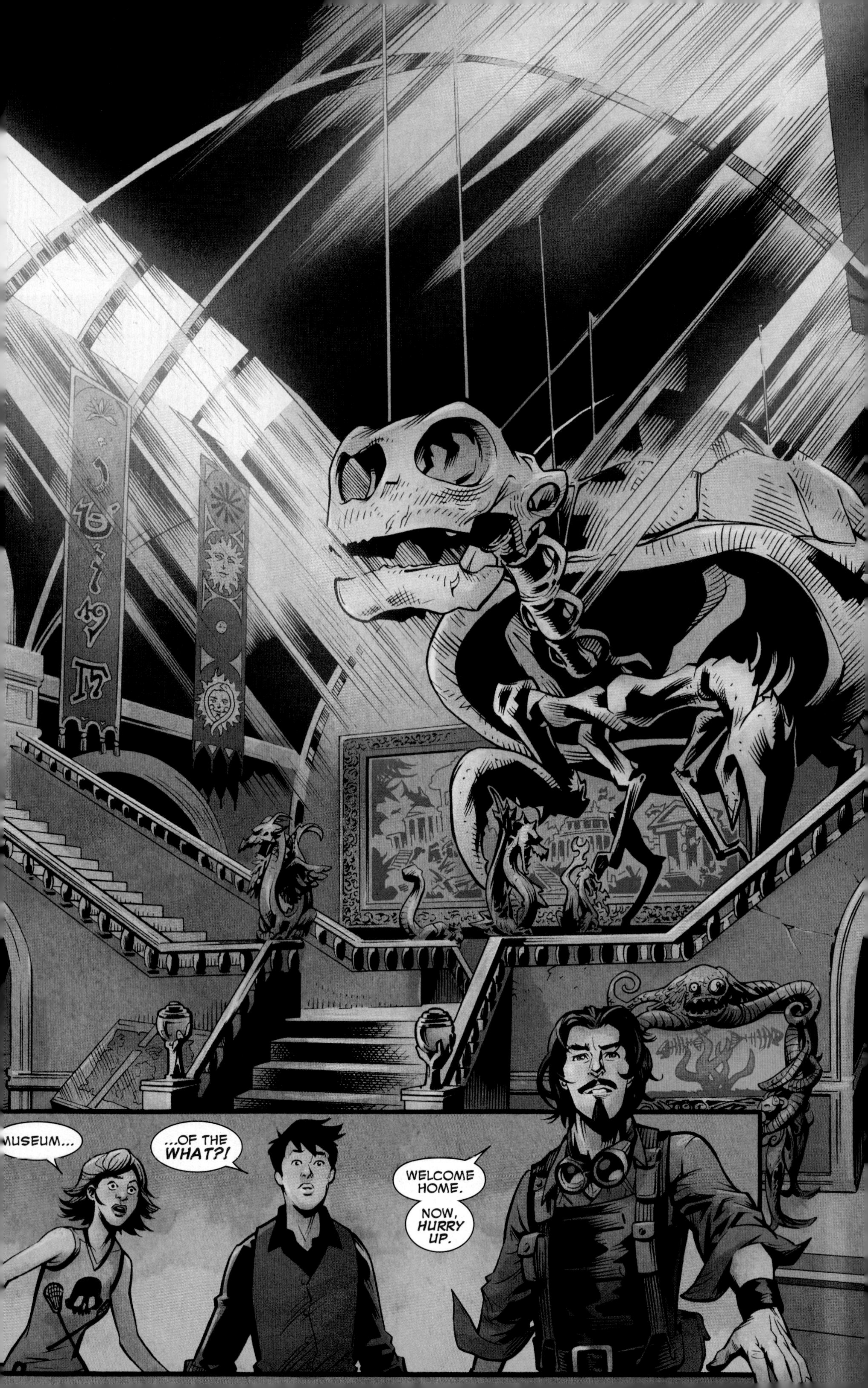
MUSEUM...
...OF THE WHAT?!
WELCOME HOME.
NOW, HURRY UP.

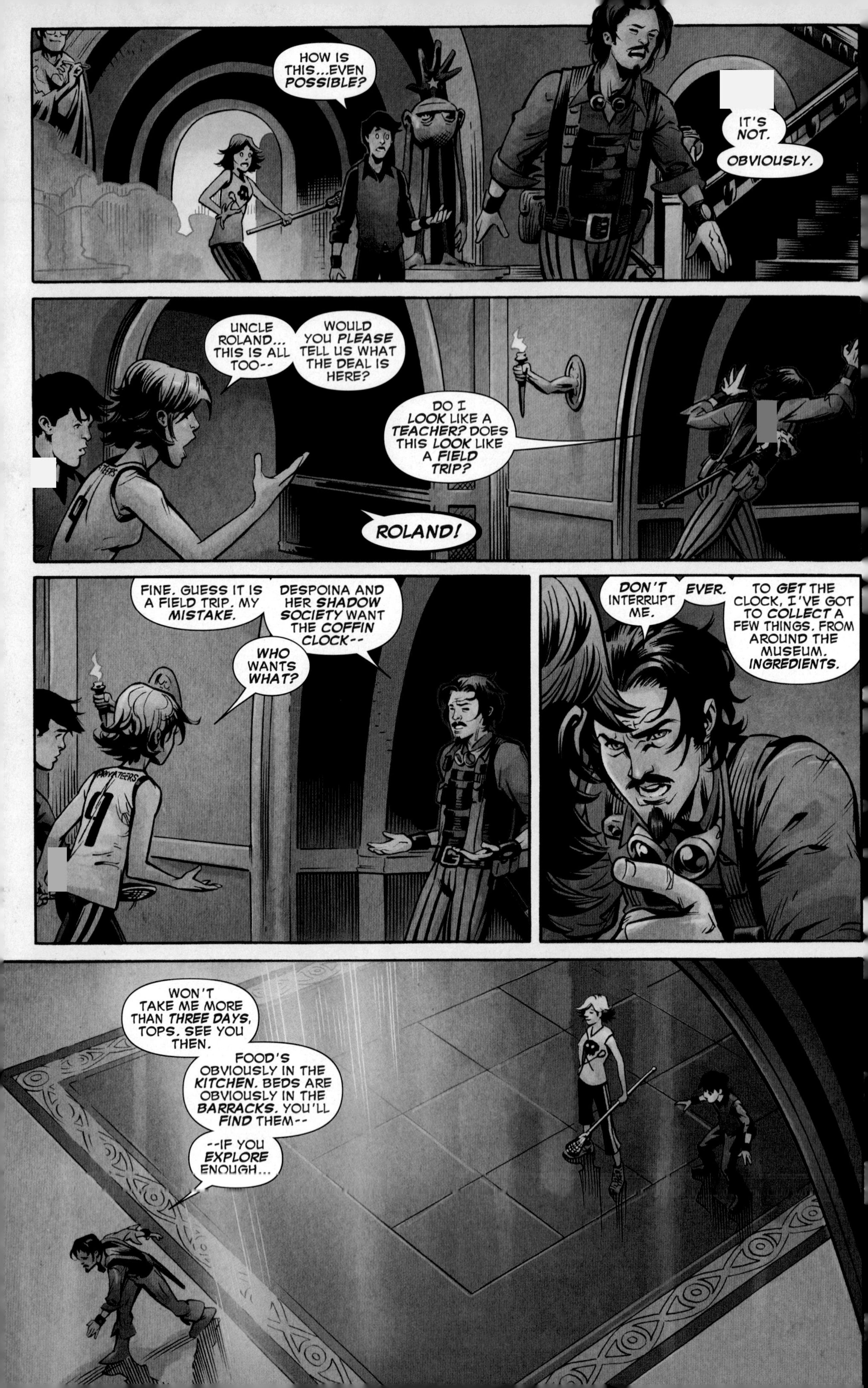
HOW IS THIS...EVEN POSSIBLE?
IT'S NOT.
OBVIOUSLY.
UNCLE ROLAND... THIS IS ALL TOO--
WOULD YOU PLEASE TELL US WHAT THE DEAL IS HERE?
DO I LOOK LIKE A TEACHER? DOES THIS LOOK LIKE A FIELD TRIP?
ROLAND!
FINE. GUESS IT IS A FIELD TRIP. MY MISTAKE.
DESPOINA AND HER SHADOW SOCIETY WANT THE COFFIN CLOCK--
WHO WANTS WHAT?
DON'T INTERRUPT ME.
EVER.
TO GET THE CLOCK, I'VE GOT TO COLLECT A FEW THINGS. FROM AROUND THE MUSEUM. INGREDIENTS.
WON'T TAKE ME MORE THAN THREE DAYS, TOPS. SEE YOU THEN.
FOOD'S OBVIOUSLY IN THE KITCHEN. BEDS ARE OBVIOUSLY IN THE BARRACKS. YOU'LL FIND THEM--
--IF YOU EXPLORE ENOUGH...

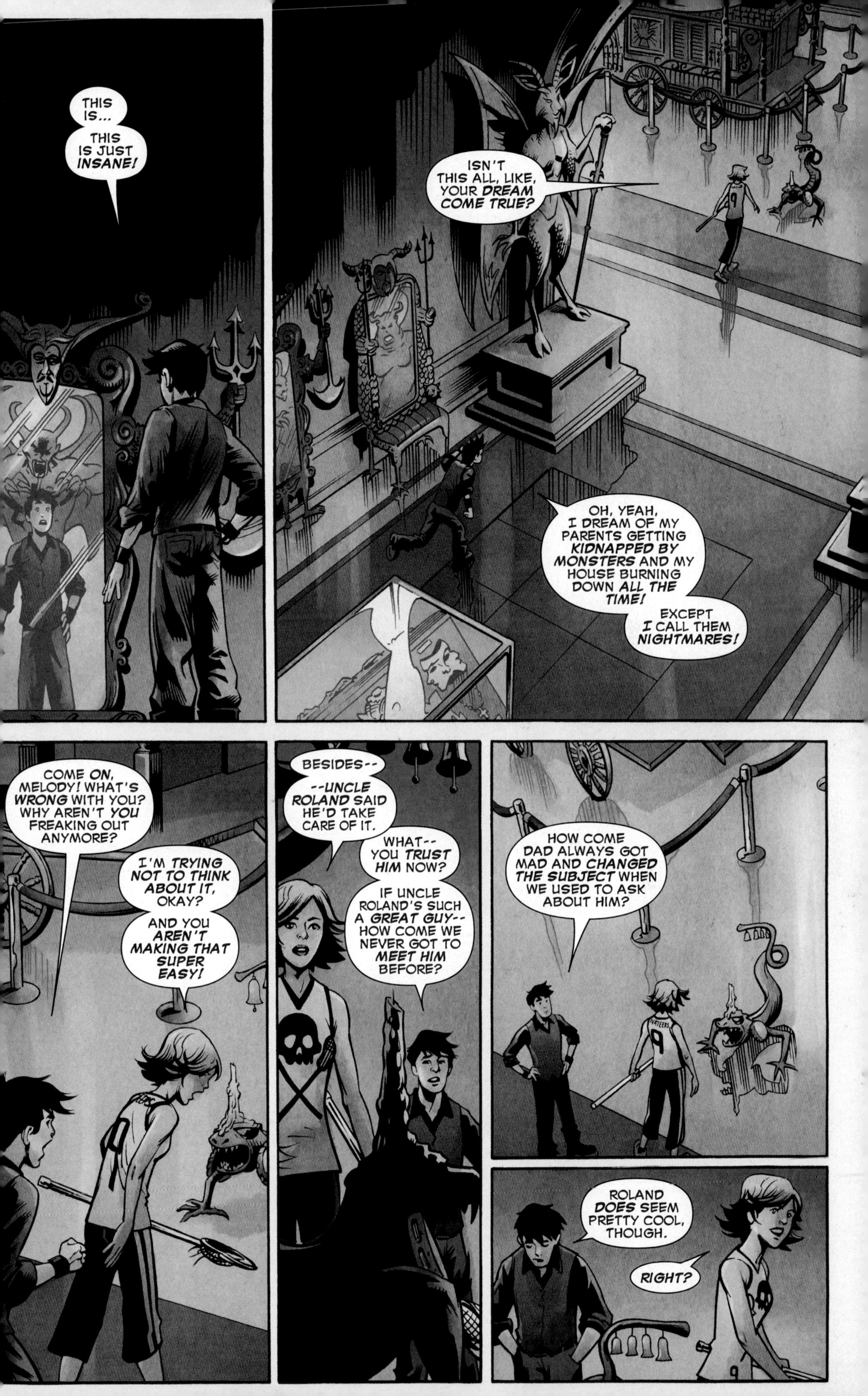

THIS IS...
THIS IS JUST INSANE!
ISN'T THIS ALL, LIKE, YOUR DREAM COME TRUE?
OH, YEAH, I DREAM OF MY PARENTS GETTING KIDNAPPED BY MONSTERS AND MY HOUSE BURNING DOWN ALL THE TIME!
EXCEPT I CALL THEM NIGHTMARES!
COME ON, MELODY! WHAT'S WRONG WITH YOU? WHY AREN'T YOU FREAKING OUT ANYMORE?
I'M TRYING NOT TO THINK ABOUT IT, OKAY?
AND YOU AREN'T MAKING THAT SUPER EASY!
BESIDES--
--UNCLE ROLAND SAID HE'D TAKE CARE OF IT.
WHAT-- YOU TRUST HIM NOW?
IF UNCLE ROLAND'S SUCH A GREAT GUY-- HOW COME WE NEVER GOT TO MEET HIM BEFORE?
HOW COME DAD ALWAYS GOT MAD AND CHANGED THE SUBJECT WHEN WE USED TO ASK ABOUT HIM?
ROLAND DOES SEEM PRETTY COOL, THOUGH.
RIGHT?

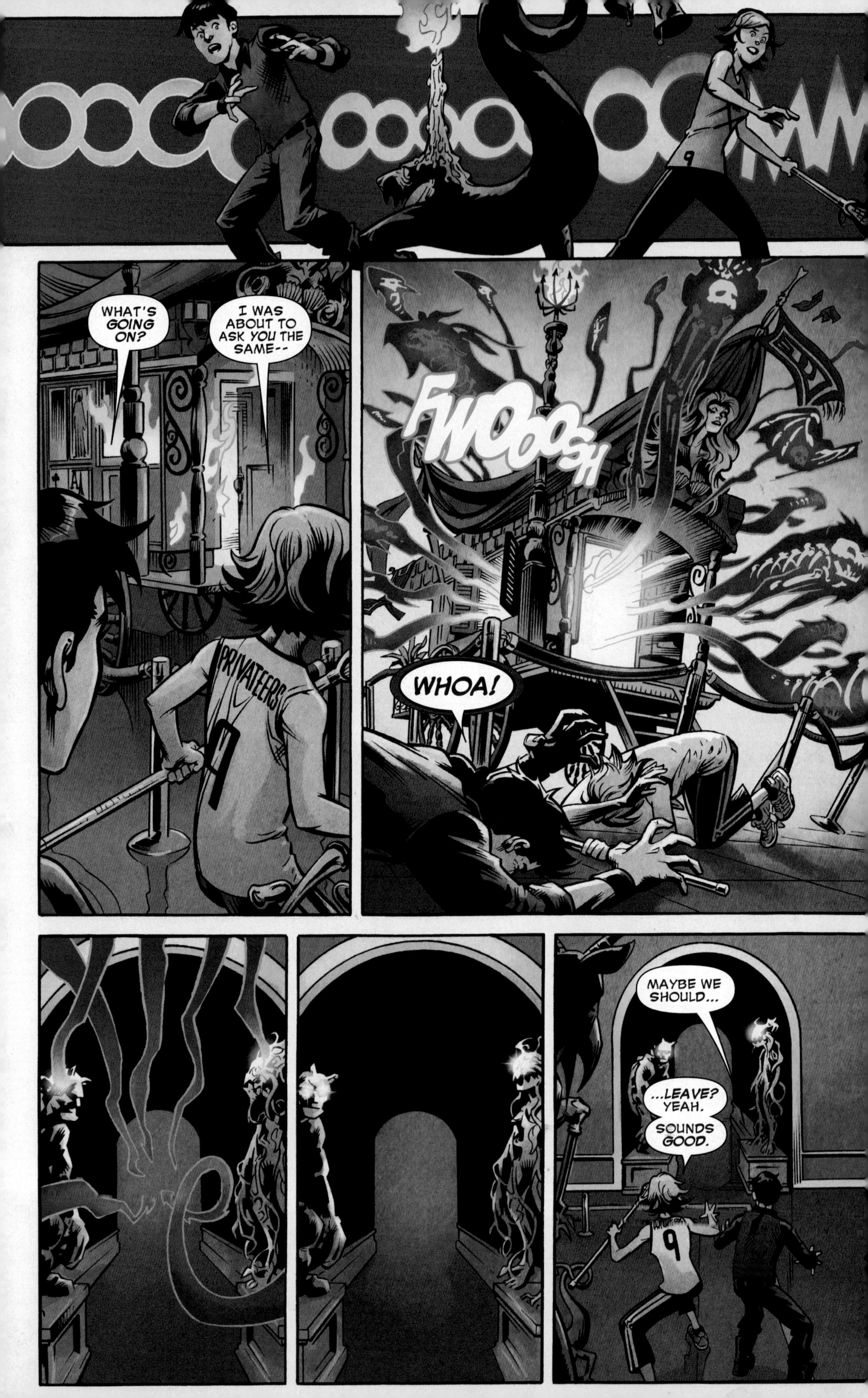
OOOOOOOOOOOOOOWW
WHAT'S GOING ON?
I WAS ABOUT TO ASK YOU THE SAME--
FWOOOSH
WHOA!
MAYBE WE SHOULD...
...LEAVE? YEAH.
SOUNDS GOOD.

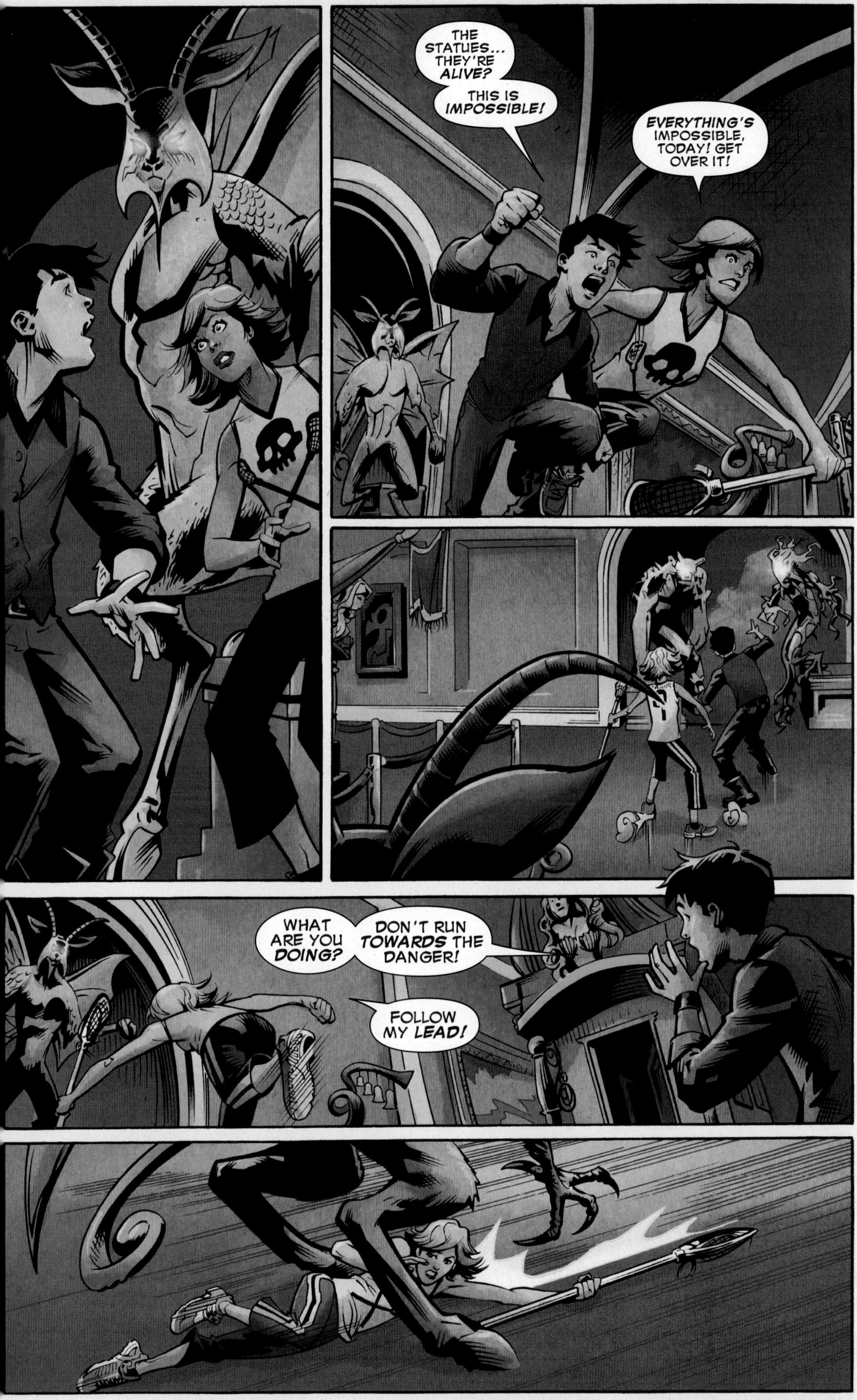
THE STATUES... THEY'RE *ALIVE?*
THIS IS *IMPOSSIBLE!*
EVERYTHING'S IMPOSSIBLE, TODAY! GET OVER IT!
WHAT ARE YOU *DOING?*
DON'T RUN *TOWARDS* THE DANGER!
FOLLOW MY *LEAD!*

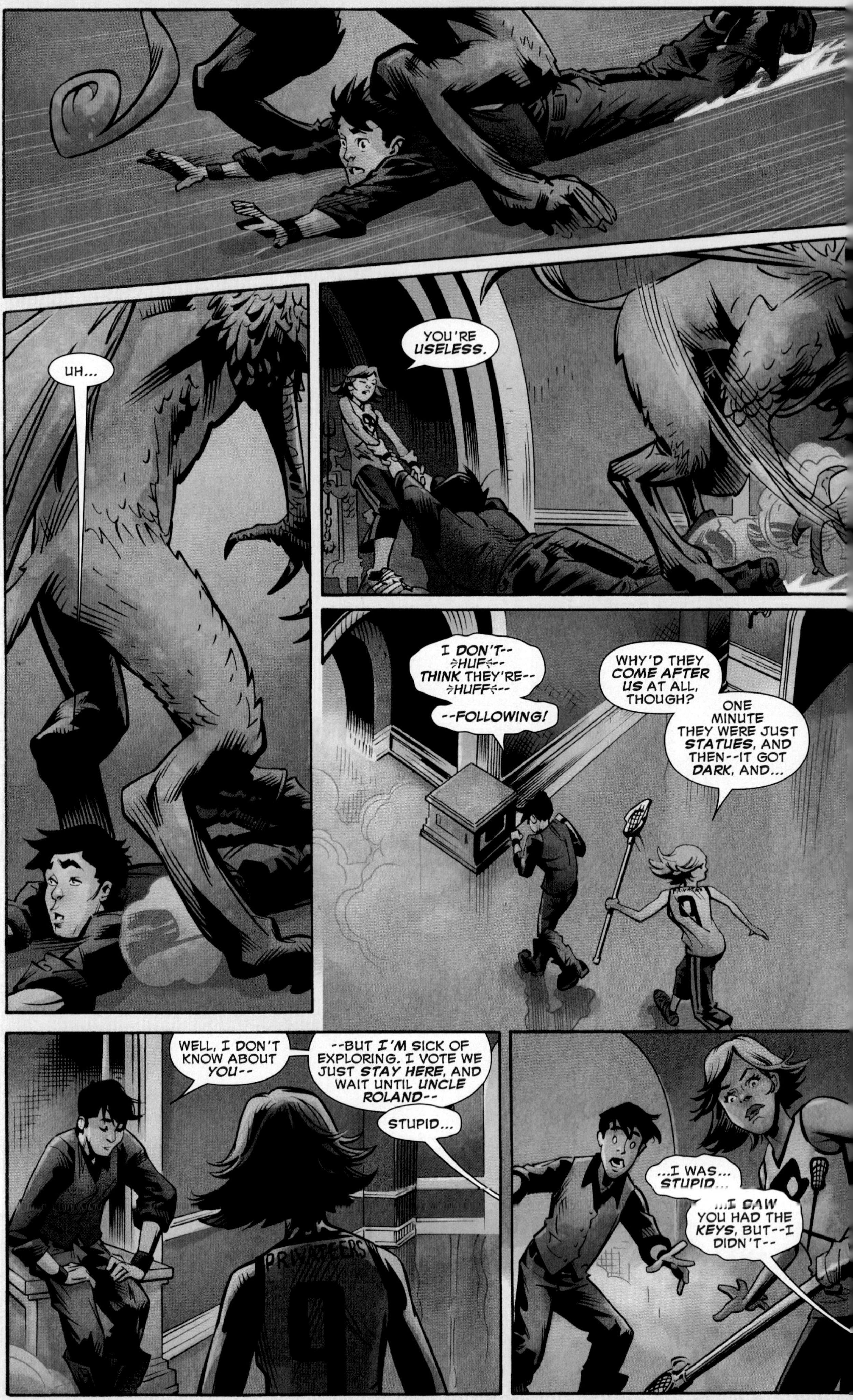
UH...
YOU'RE USELESS.
I DON'T-- ≈HUF≈-- THINK THEY'RE-- ≈HUFF≈--
--FOLLOWING!
WHY'D THEY COME AFTER US AT ALL, THOUGH?
ONE MINUTE THEY WERE JUST STATUES, AND THEN--IT GOT DARK, AND...
WELL, I DON'T KNOW ABOUT YOU--
--BUT I'M SICK OF EXPLORING. I VOTE WE JUST STAY HERE, AND WAIT UNTIL UNCLE ROLAND--
STUPID...
...I WAS... STUPID...
...I SAW YOU HAD THE KEYS, BUT--I DIDN'T--

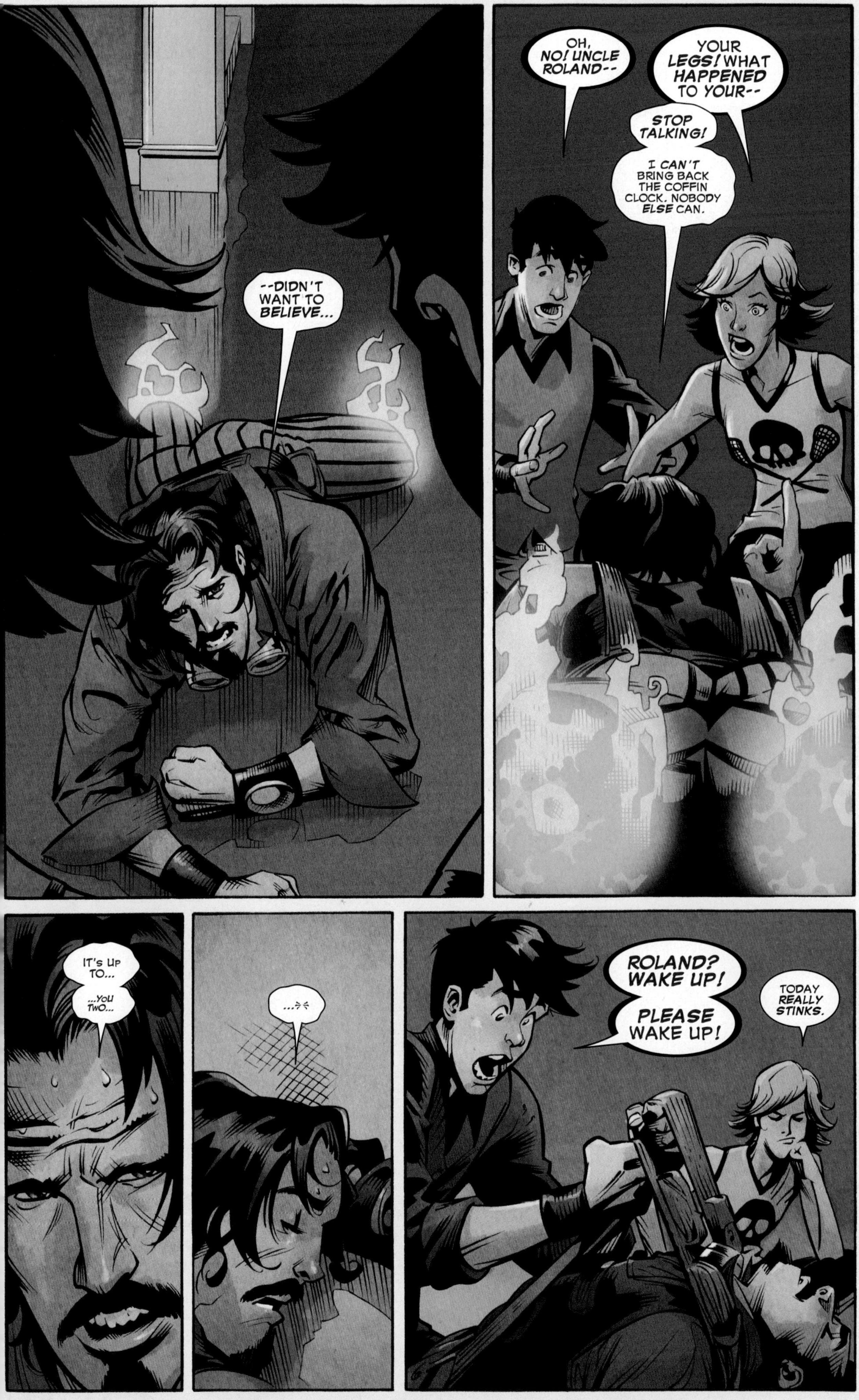
--DIDN'T WANT TO BELIEVE...
OH, NO! UNCLE ROLAND--
YOUR LEGS! WHAT HAPPENED TO YOUR--
STOP TALKING!
I CAN'T BRING BACK THE COFFIN CLOCK. NOBODY ELSE CAN.
IT'S UP TO...
...YOU TWO...
ROLAND? WAKE UP!
PLEASE WAKE UP!
TODAY REALLY STINKS.

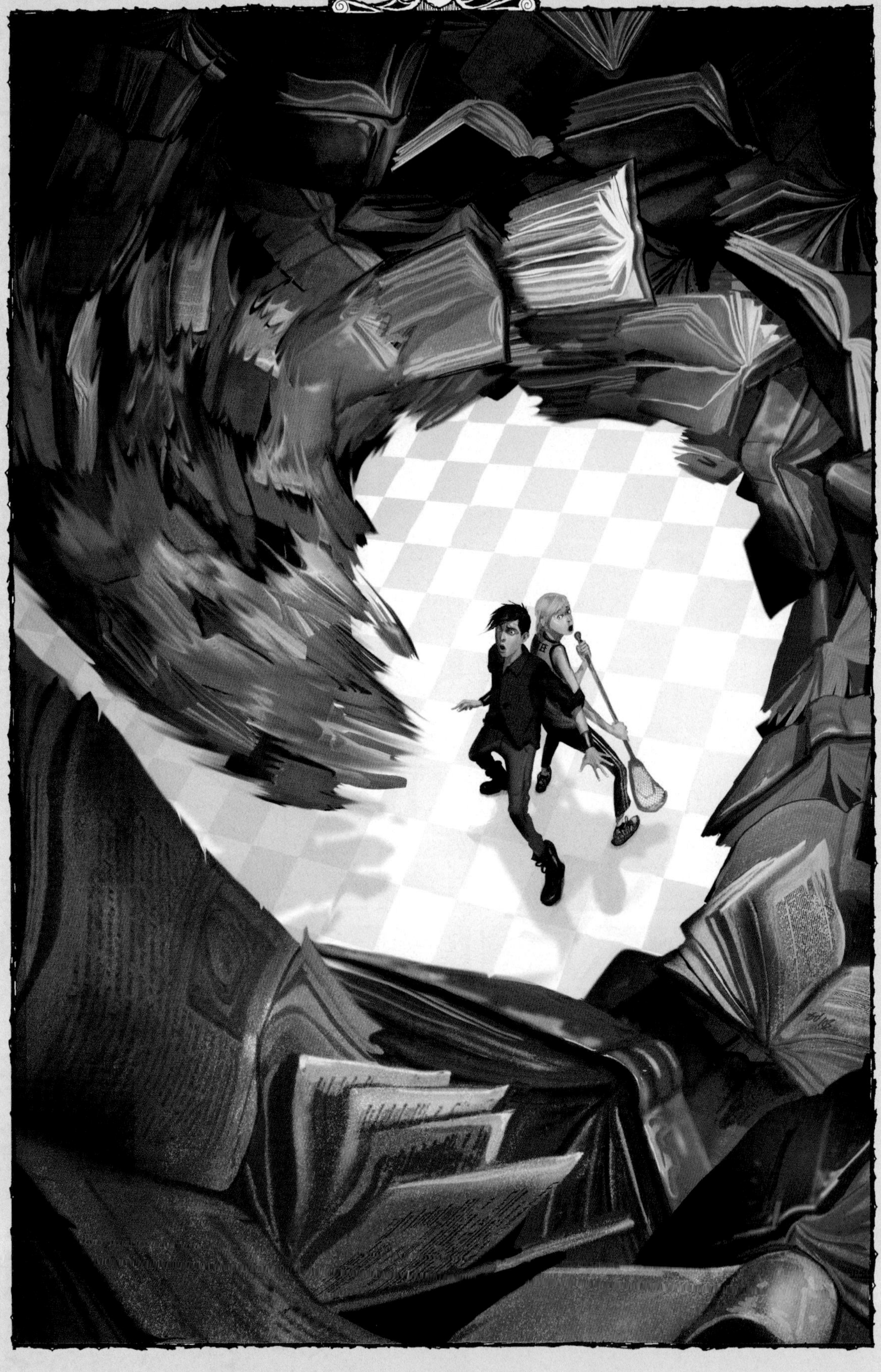

2

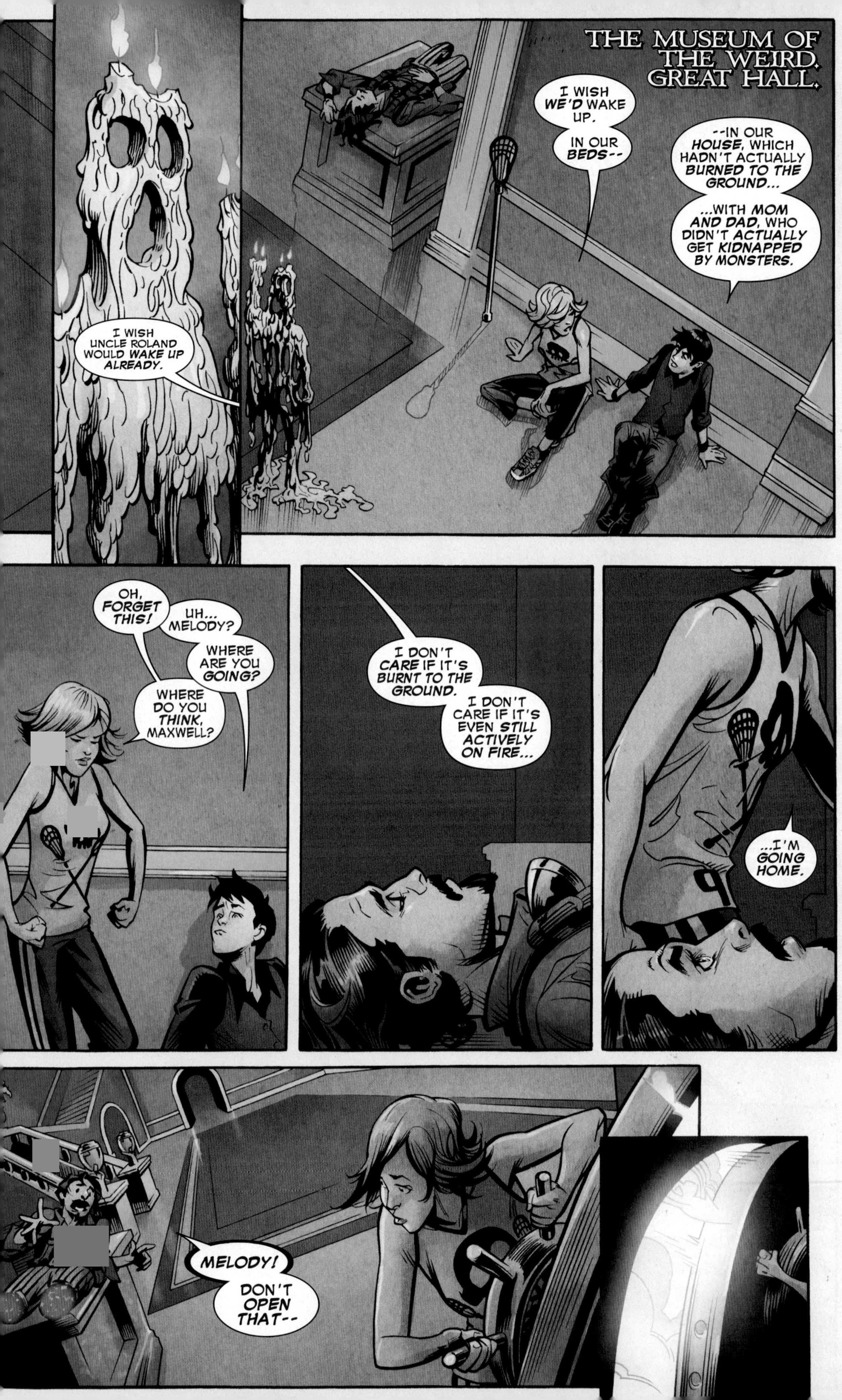
THE MUSEUM OF THE WEIRD. GREAT HALL.
I WISH UNCLE ROLAND WOULD WAKE UP ALREADY.
I WISH WE'D WAKE UP.
IN OUR BEDS--
--IN OUR HOUSE, WHICH HADN'T ACTUALLY BURNED TO THE GROUND...
...WITH MOM AND DAD, WHO DIDN'T ACTUALLY GET KIDNAPPED BY MONSTERS.
OH, FORGET THIS!
UH... MELODY?
WHERE ARE YOU GOING?
WHERE DO YOU THINK, MAXWELL?
I DON'T CARE IF IT'S BURNT TO THE GROUND.
I DON'T CARE IF IT'S EVEN STILL ACTIVELY ON FIRE...
...I'M GOING HOME.
MELODY!
DON'T OPEN THAT--

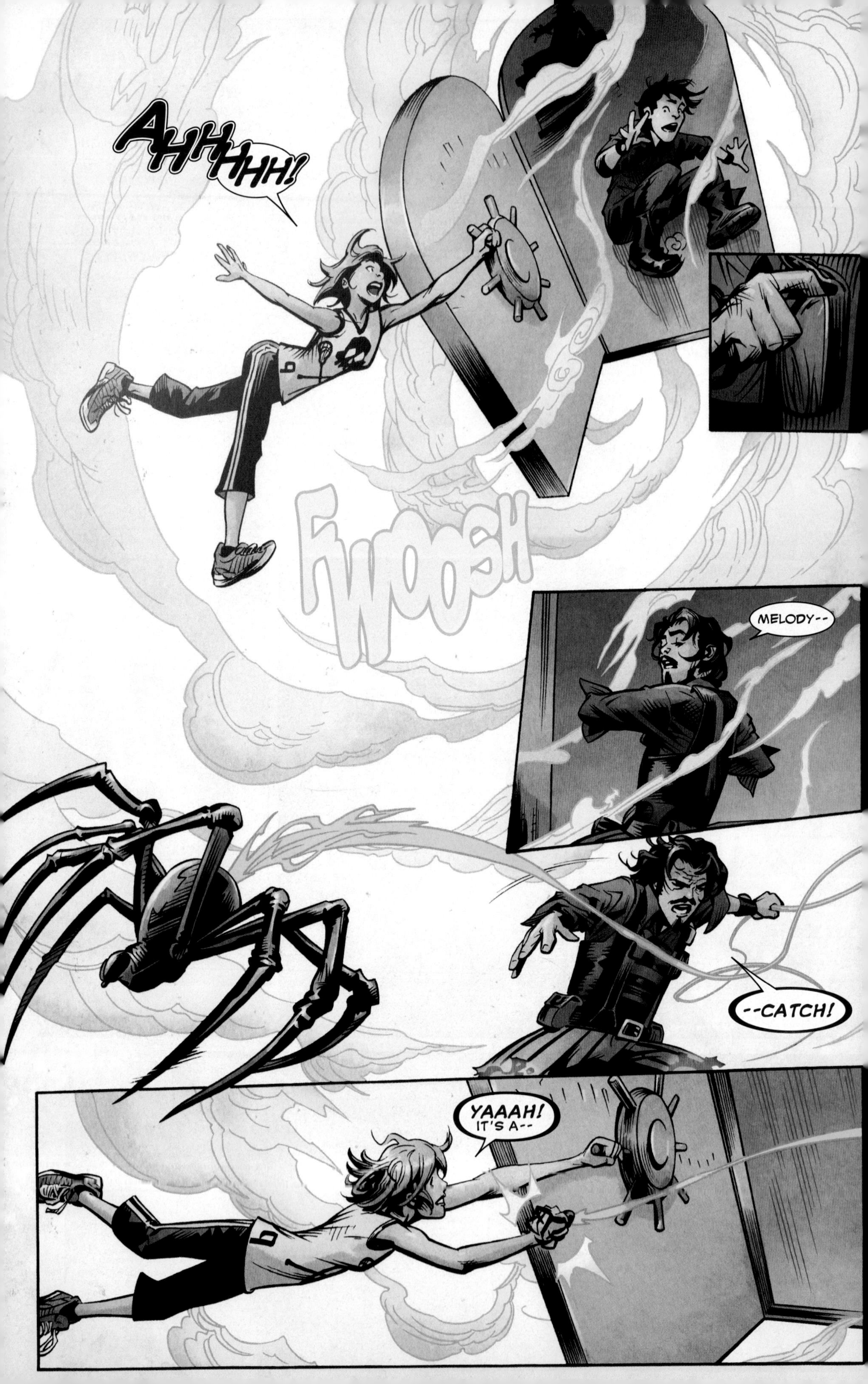
AHHHHH!
FWOOSH
MELODY--
--CATCH!
YAAAH! IT'S A--

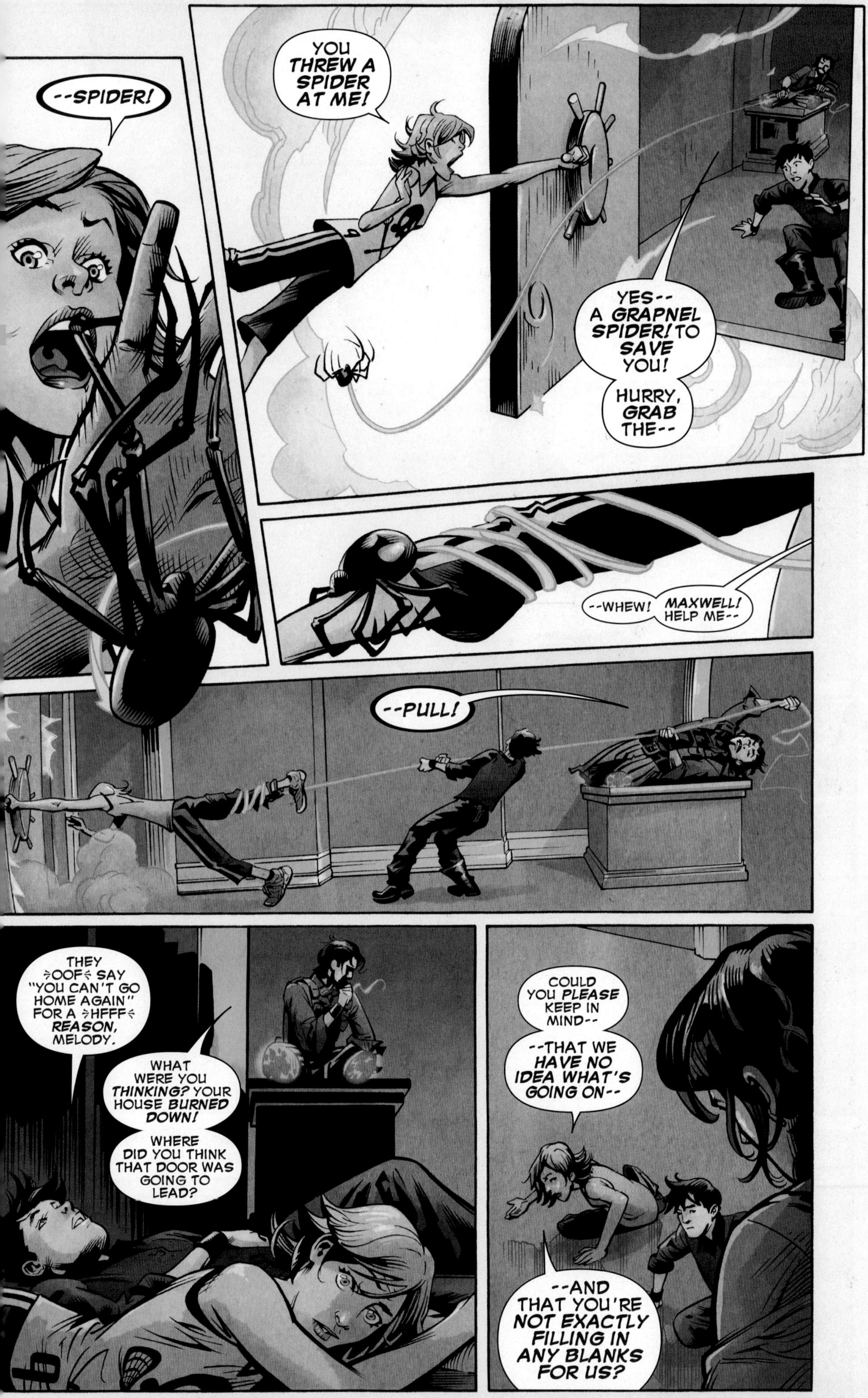
--SPIDER!
YOU THREW A SPIDER AT ME!
YES-- A GRAPNEL SPIDER! TO SAVE YOU!
HURRY, GRAB THE--
--WHEW!
MAXWELL! HELP ME--
--PULL!
THEY ⇒OOF⇐ SAY "YOU CAN'T GO HOME AGAIN" FOR A ⇒HFFF⇐ REASON, MELODY.
WHAT WERE YOU THINKING? YOUR HOUSE BURNED DOWN!
WHERE DID YOU THINK THAT DOOR WAS GOING TO LEAD?
COULD YOU PLEASE KEEP IN MIND--
--THAT WE HAVE NO IDEA WHAT'S GOING ON--
--AND THAT YOU'RE NOT EXACTLY FILLING IN ANY BLANKS FOR US?

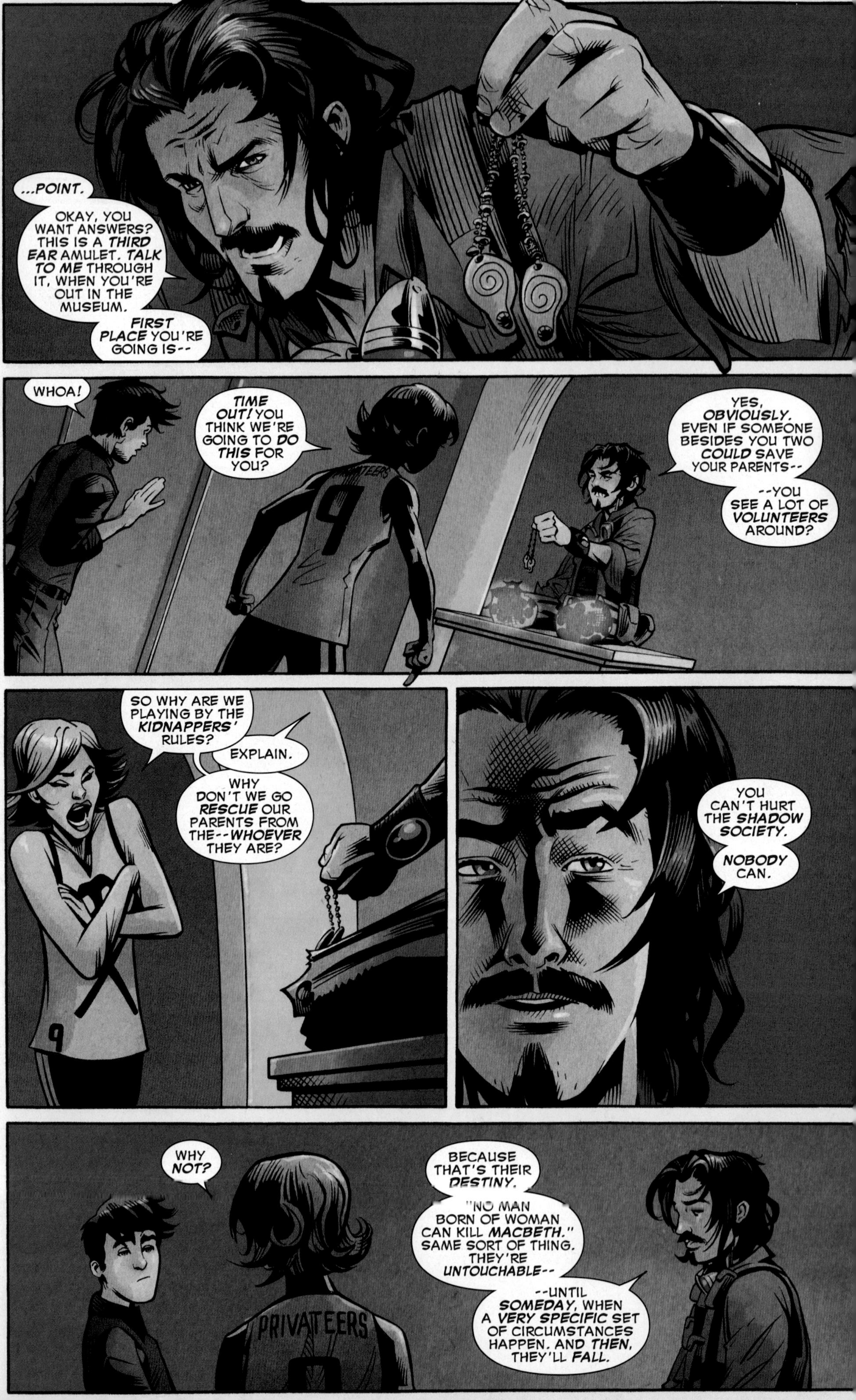
...POINT.
OKAY, YOU WANT ANSWERS? THIS IS A THIRD EAR AMULET. TALK TO ME THROUGH IT, WHEN YOU'RE OUT IN THE MUSEUM.
FIRST PLACE YOU'RE GOING IS--
WHOA!
TIME OUT! YOU THINK WE'RE GOING TO DO THIS FOR YOU?
YES, OBVIOUSLY. EVEN IF SOMEONE BESIDES YOU TWO COULD SAVE YOUR PARENTS--
--YOU SEE A LOT OF VOLUNTEERS AROUND?
SO WHY ARE WE PLAYING BY THE KIDNAPPERS' RULES?
EXPLAIN.
WHY DON'T WE GO RESCUE OUR PARENTS FROM THE--WHOEVER THEY ARE?
YOU CAN'T HURT THE SHADOW SOCIETY.
NOBODY CAN.
WHY NOT?
BECAUSE THAT'S THEIR DESTINY.
"NO MAN BORN OF WOMAN CAN KILL MACBETH." SAME SORT OF THING. THEY'RE UNTOUCHABLE--
--UNTIL SOMEDAY, WHEN A VERY SPECIFIC SET OF CIRCUMSTANCES HAPPEN. AND THEN, THEY'LL FALL.

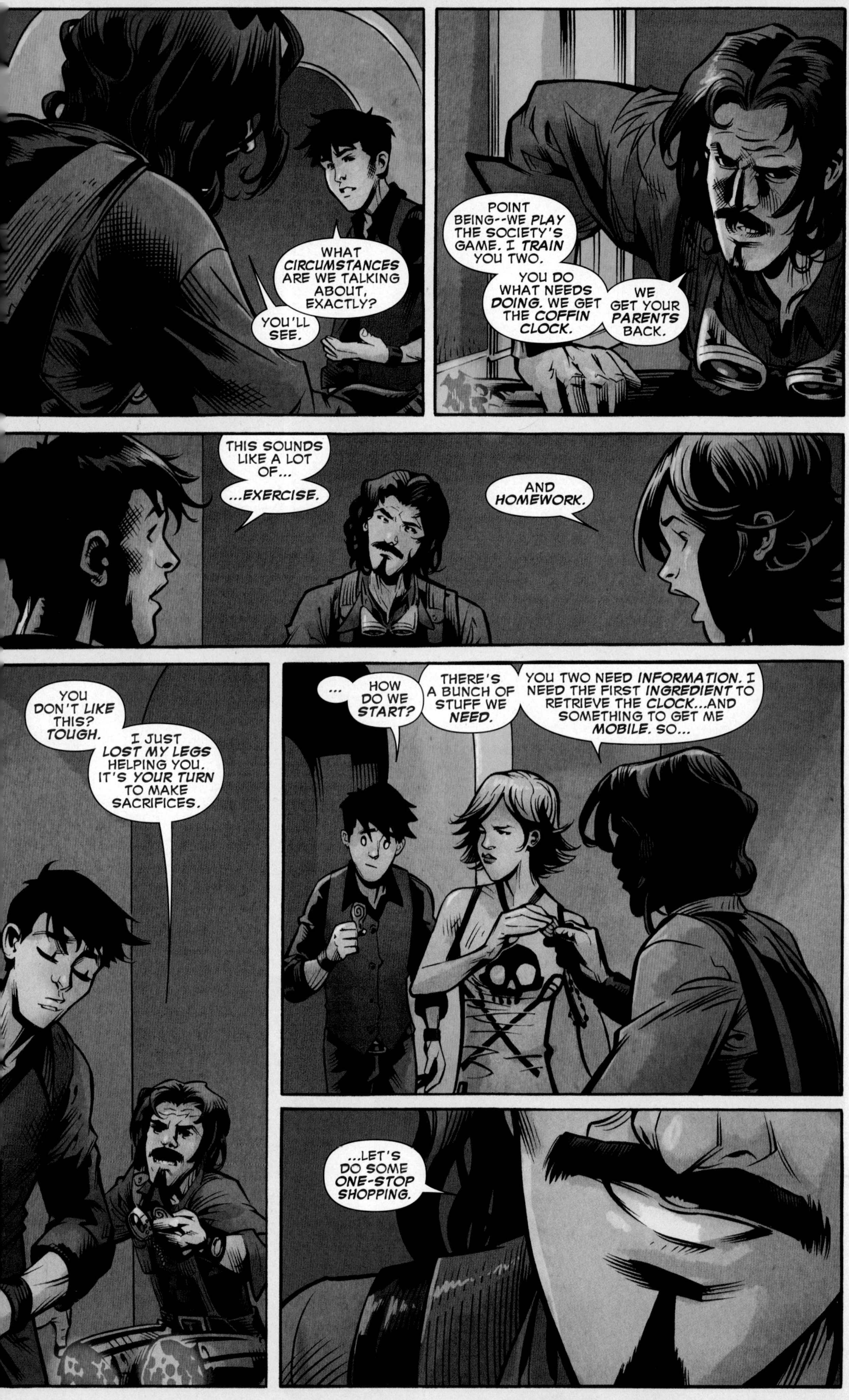
WHAT CIRCUMSTANCES ARE WE TALKING ABOUT, EXACTLY?
YOU'LL SEE.
POINT BEING--WE PLAY THE SOCIETY'S GAME. I TRAIN YOU TWO.
YOU DO WHAT NEEDS DOING. WE GET THE COFFIN CLOCK.
WE GET YOUR PARENTS BACK.
THIS SOUNDS LIKE A LOT OF...
...EXERCISE.
AND HOMEWORK.
YOU DON'T LIKE THIS? TOUGH.
I JUST LOST MY LEGS HELPING YOU. IT'S YOUR TURN TO MAKE SACRIFICES.
...
HOW DO WE START?
THERE'S A BUNCH OF STUFF WE NEED.
YOU TWO NEED INFORMATION. I NEED THE FIRST INGREDIENT TO RETRIEVE THE CLOCK...AND SOMETHING TO GET ME MOBILE. SO...
...LET'S DO SOME ONE-STOP SHOPPING.

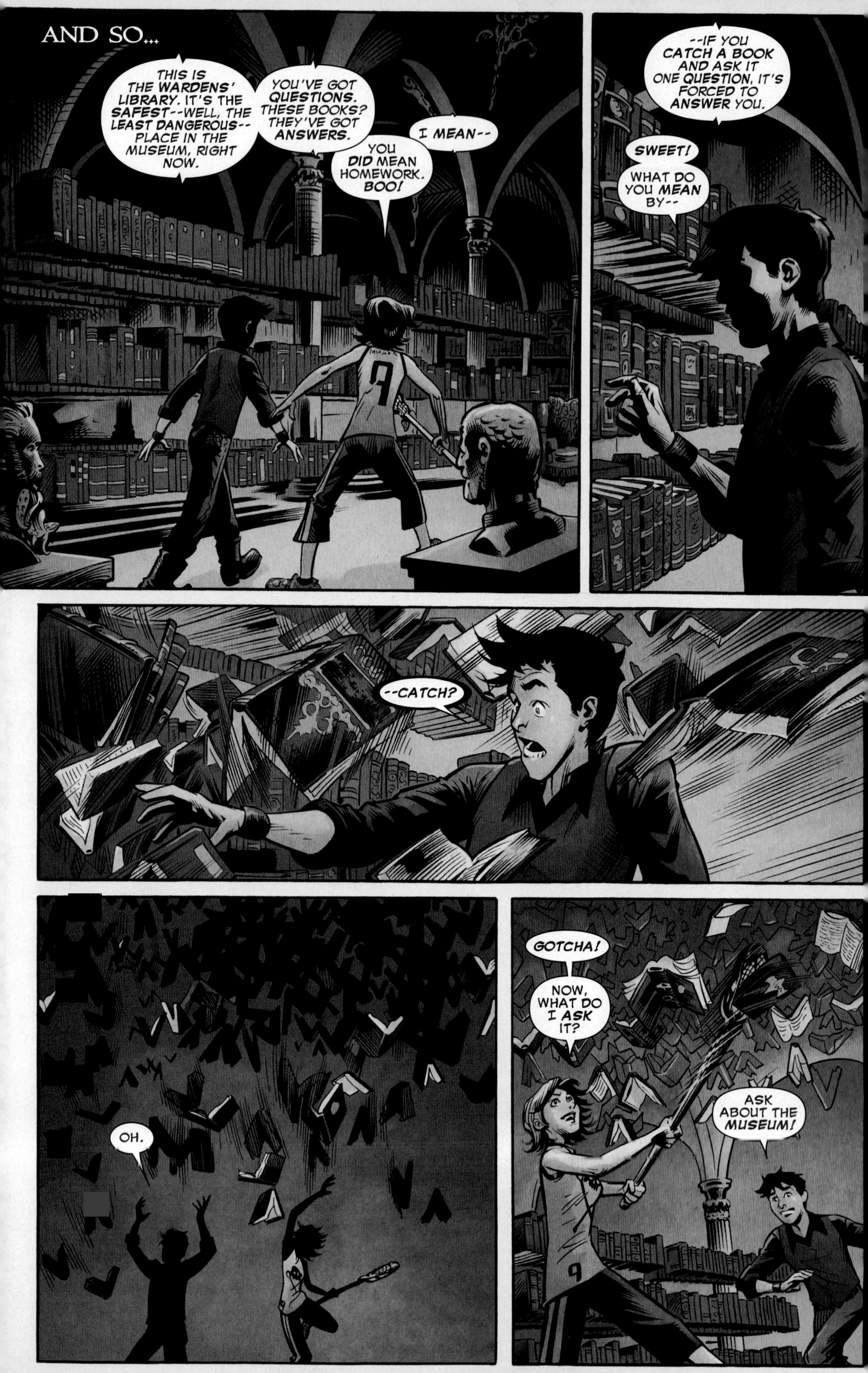
AND SO...
THIS IS THE WARDENS' LIBRARY. IT'S THE SAFEST--WELL, THE LEAST DANGEROUS--PLACE IN THE MUSEUM, RIGHT NOW.
YOU'VE GOT QUESTIONS. THESE BOOKS? THEY'VE GOT ANSWERS.
I MEAN--
YOU DID MEAN HOMEWORK. BOO!
--IF YOU CATCH A BOOK AND ASK IT ONE QUESTION, IT'S FORCED TO ANSWER YOU.
SWEET!
WHAT DO YOU MEAN BY--
--CATCH?
OH.
GOTCHA!
NOW, WHAT DO I ASK IT?
ASK ABOUT THE MUSEUM!

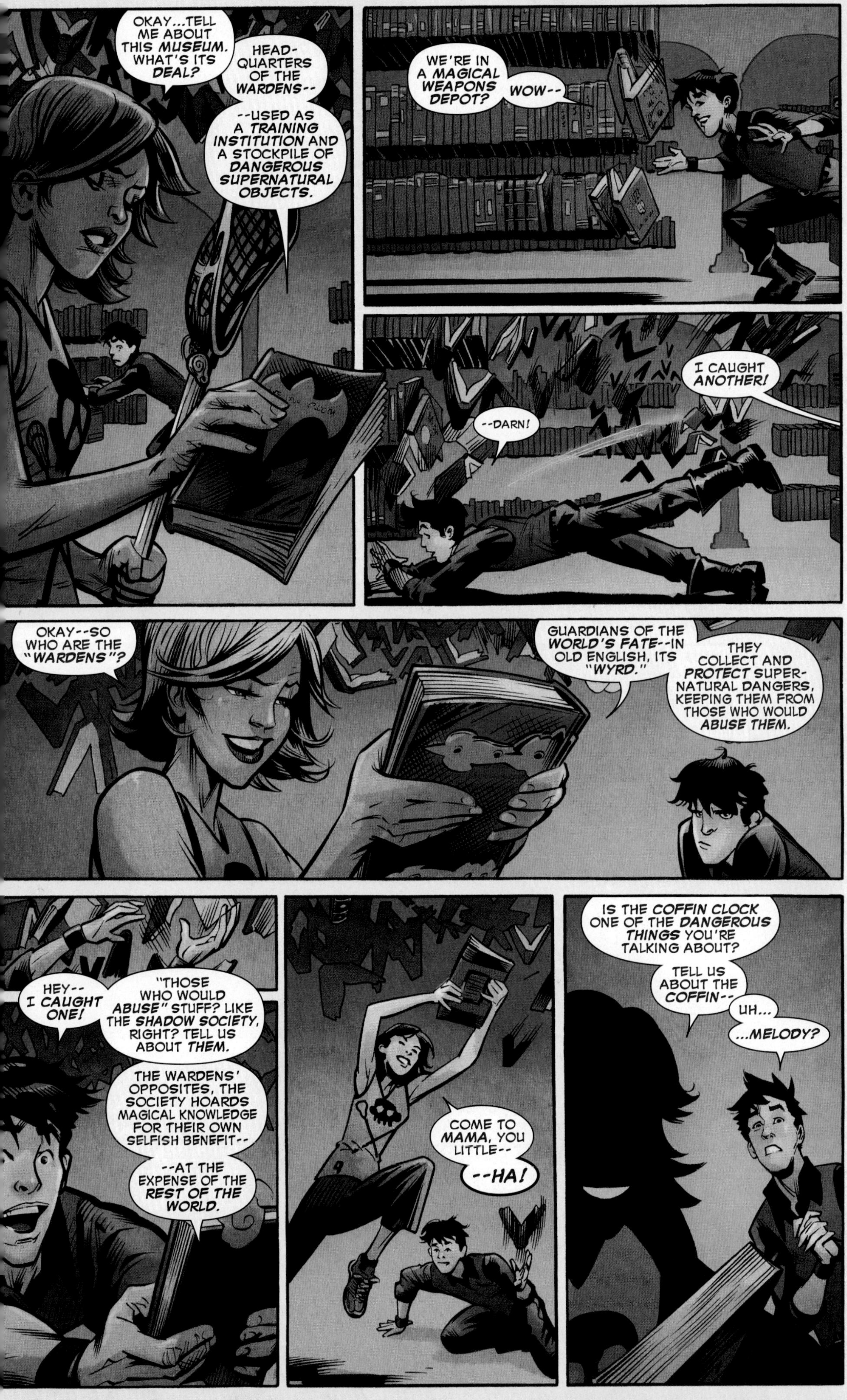
OKAY...TELL ME ABOUT THIS MUSEUM. WHAT'S ITS DEAL?
HEAD-QUARTERS OF THE WARDENS--
--USED AS A TRAINING INSTITUTION AND A STOCKPILE OF DANGEROUS SUPERNATURAL OBJECTS.
WE'RE IN A MAGICAL WEAPONS DEPOT?
WOW--
I CAUGHT ANOTHER!
--DARN!
OKAY--SO WHO ARE THE "WARDENS"?
GUARDIANS OF THE WORLD'S FATE--IN OLD ENGLISH, ITS "WYRD."
THEY COLLECT AND PROTECT SUPER-NATURAL DANGERS, KEEPING THEM FROM THOSE WHO WOULD ABUSE THEM.
HEY-- I CAUGHT ONE!
"THOSE WHO WOULD ABUSE" STUFF? LIKE THE SHADOW SOCIETY, RIGHT? TELL US ABOUT THEM.
THE WARDENS' OPPOSITES, THE SOCIETY HOARDS MAGICAL KNOWLEDGE FOR THEIR OWN SELFISH BENEFIT--
--AT THE EXPENSE OF THE REST OF THE WORLD.
COME TO MAMA, YOU LITTLE--
--HA!
IS THE COFFIN CLOCK ONE OF THE DANGEROUS THINGS YOU'RE TALKING ABOUT?
TELL US ABOUT THE COFFIN--
UH...
...MELODY?

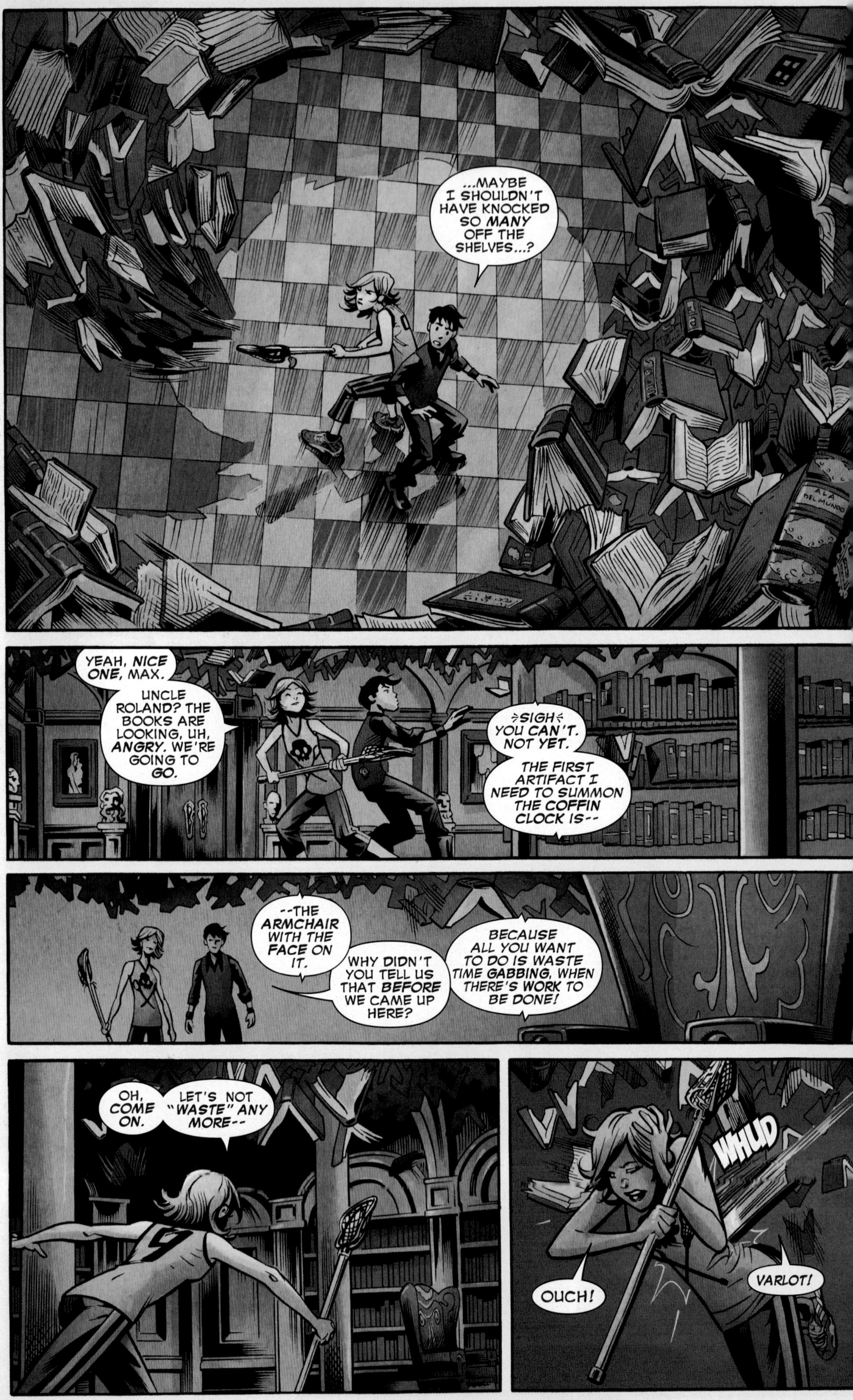
...MAYBE I SHOULDN'T HAVE KNOCKED SO MANY OFF THE SHELVES...?
YEAH, NICE ONE, MAX.
UNCLE ROLAND? THE BOOKS ARE LOOKING, UH, ANGRY. WE'RE GOING TO GO.
SIGH YOU CAN'T. NOT YET.
THE FIRST ARTIFACT I NEED TO SUMMON THE COFFIN CLOCK IS--
--THE ARMCHAIR WITH THE FACE ON IT.
WHY DIDN'T YOU TELL US THAT BEFORE WE CAME UP HERE?
BECAUSE ALL YOU WANT TO DO IS WASTE TIME GABBING, WHEN THERE'S WORK TO BE DONE!
OH, COME ON.
LET'S NOT "WASTE" ANY MORE--
WHUD
OUCH!
VARLOT!

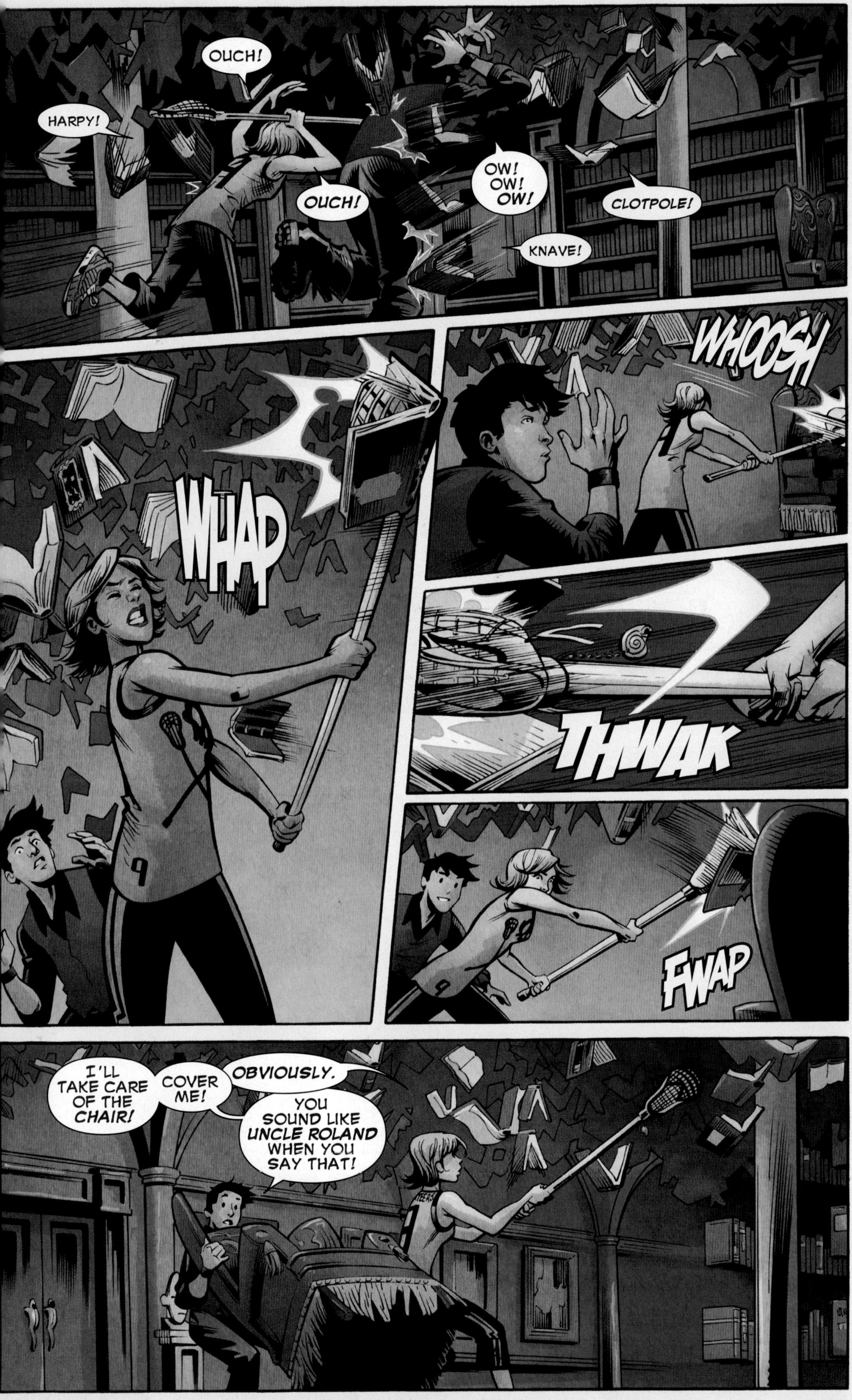

OUCH!
HARPY!
OUCH!
OW! OW! OW!
CLOTPOLE!
KNAVE!
WHAP
WHOOSH
THWAK
FWAP
I'LL TAKE CARE OF THE CHAIR!
COVER ME!
OBVIOUSLY.
YOU SOUND LIKE UNCLE ROLAND WHEN YOU SAY THAT!

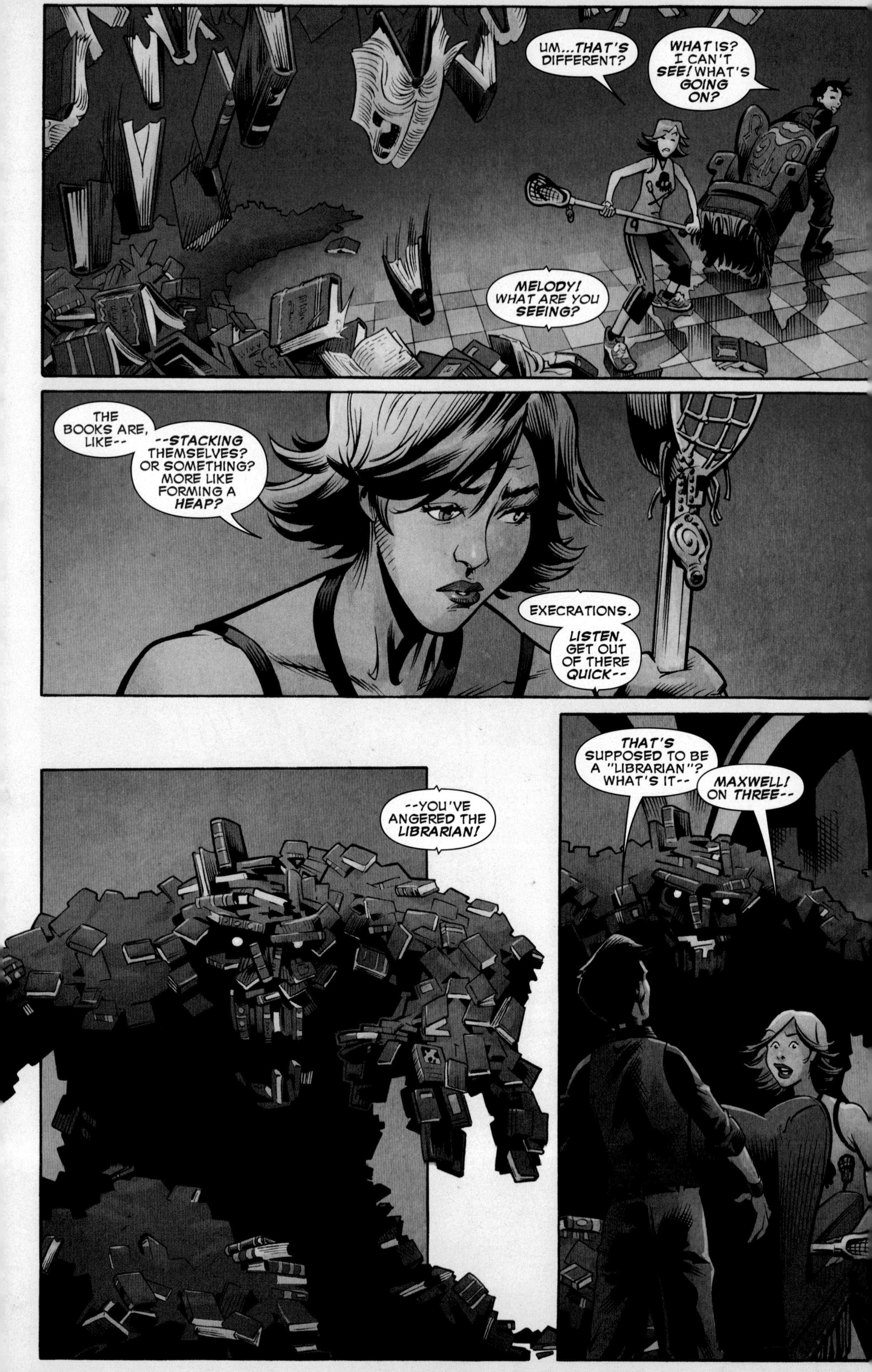
UM...THAT'S DIFFERENT?
WHAT IS? I CAN'T SEE! WHAT'S GOING ON?
MELODY! WHAT ARE YOU SEEING?
THE BOOKS ARE, LIKE--
--STACKING THEMSELVES? OR SOMETHING? MORE LIKE FORMING A HEAP?
EXECRATIONS.
LISTEN. GET OUT OF THERE QUICK--
--YOU'VE ANGERED THE LIBRARIAN!
THAT'S SUPPOSED TO BE A "LIBRARIAN"? WHAT'S IT--
MAXWELL! ON THREE--

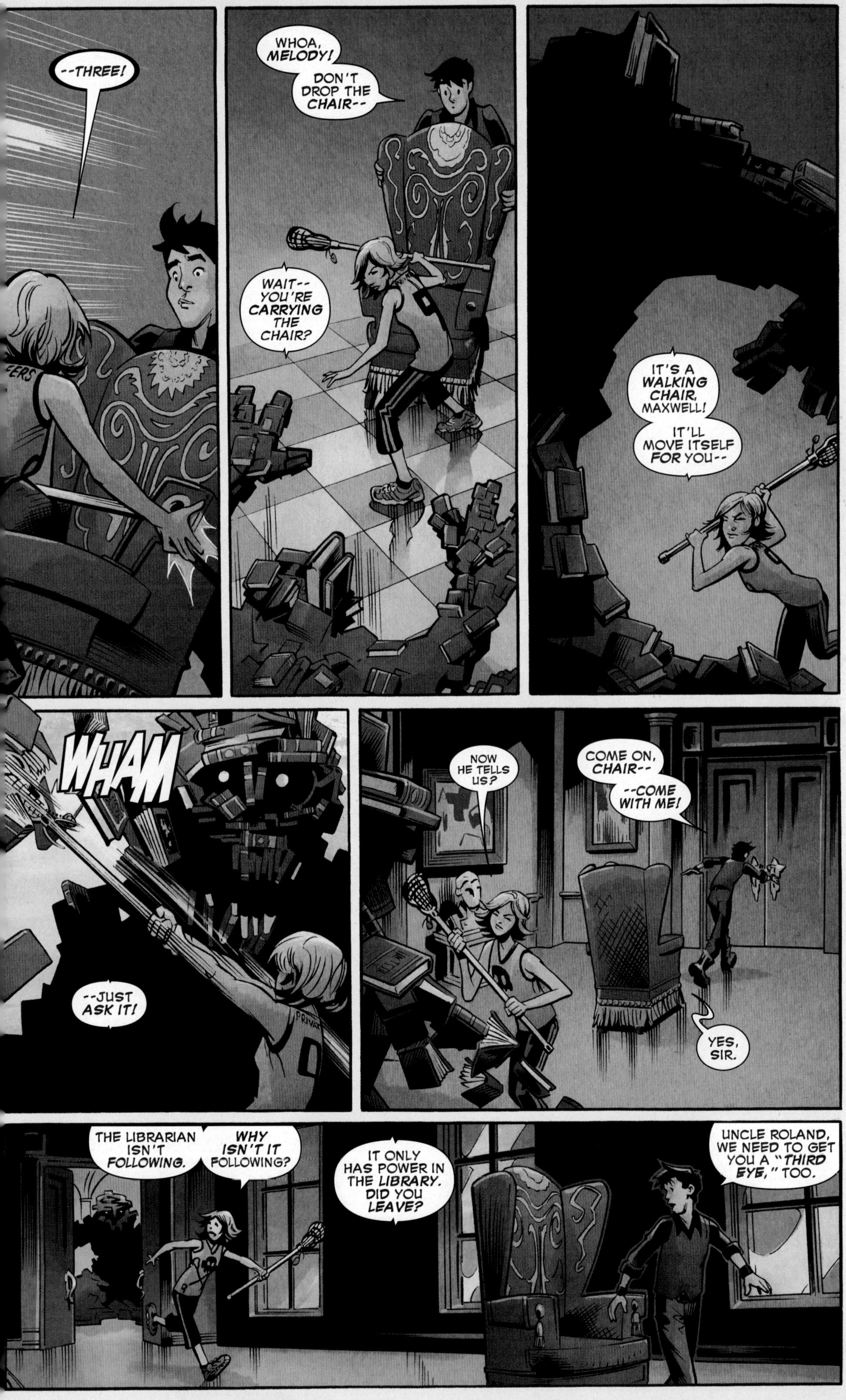
--THREE!
EERS
WHOA, MELODY!
DON'T DROP THE CHAIR--
WAIT-- YOU'RE CARRYING THE CHAIR?
IT'S A WALKING CHAIR, MAXWELL!
IT'LL MOVE ITSELF FOR YOU--
WHAM
--JUST ASK IT!
PRIVA
NOW HE TELLS US?
COME ON, CHAIR--
--COME WITH ME!
YES, SIR.
THE LIBRARIAN ISN'T FOLLOWING.
WHY ISN'T IT FOLLOWING?
IT ONLY HAS POWER IN THE LIBRARY. DID YOU LEAVE?
UNCLE ROLAND, WE NEED TO GET YOU A "THIRD EYE," TOO.

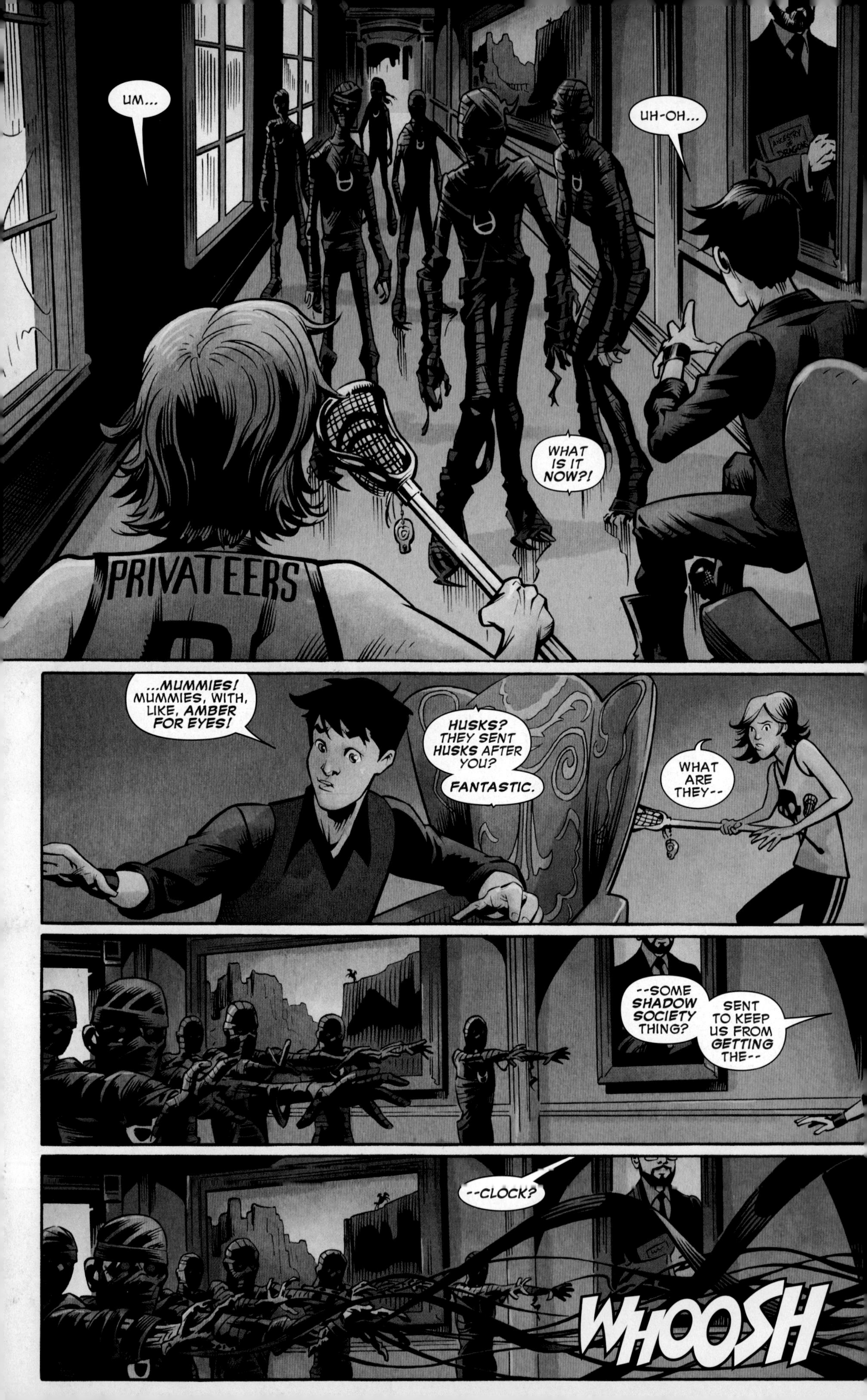
UM...
UH-OH...
ANCESTRY OF DRAGONS
WHAT IS IT NOW?!
PRIVATEERS
...MUMMIES! MUMMIES, WITH, LIKE, AMBER FOR EYES!
HUSKS? THEY SENT HUSKS AFTER YOU?
FANTASTIC.
WHAT ARE THEY--
--SOME SHADOW SOCIETY THING?
SENT TO KEEP US FROM GETTING THE--
--CLOCK?
WHOOSH

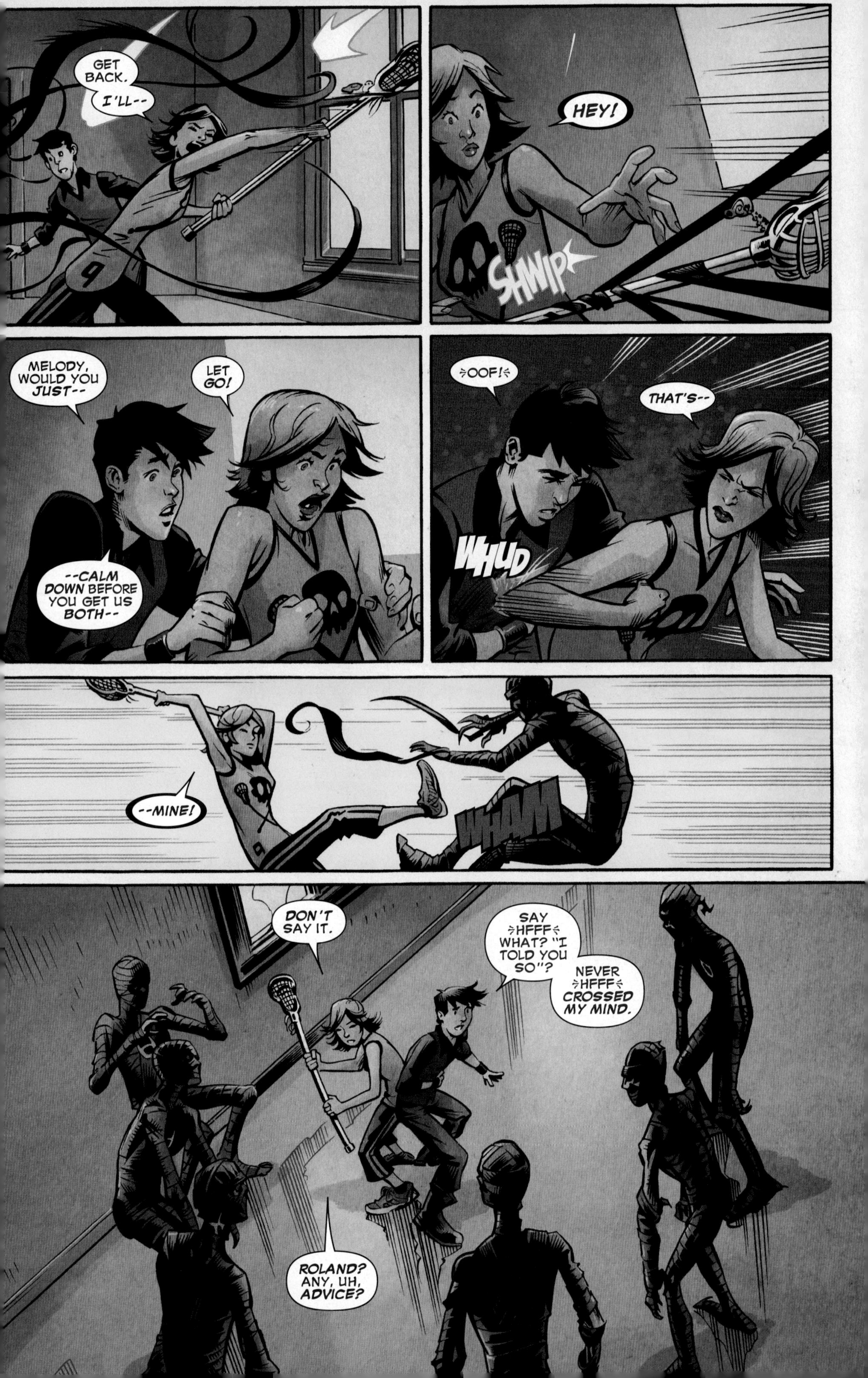
GET BACK. I'LL--
HEY!
SHWIP
MELODY, WOULD YOU JUST--
LET GO!
--CALM DOWN BEFORE YOU GET US BOTH--
OOF!
THAT'S--
WHUD
--MINE!
WHAM
DON'T SAY IT.
SAY HFFF WHAT? "I TOLD YOU SO"?
NEVER HFFF CROSSED MY MIND.
ROLAND? ANY, UH, ADVICE?

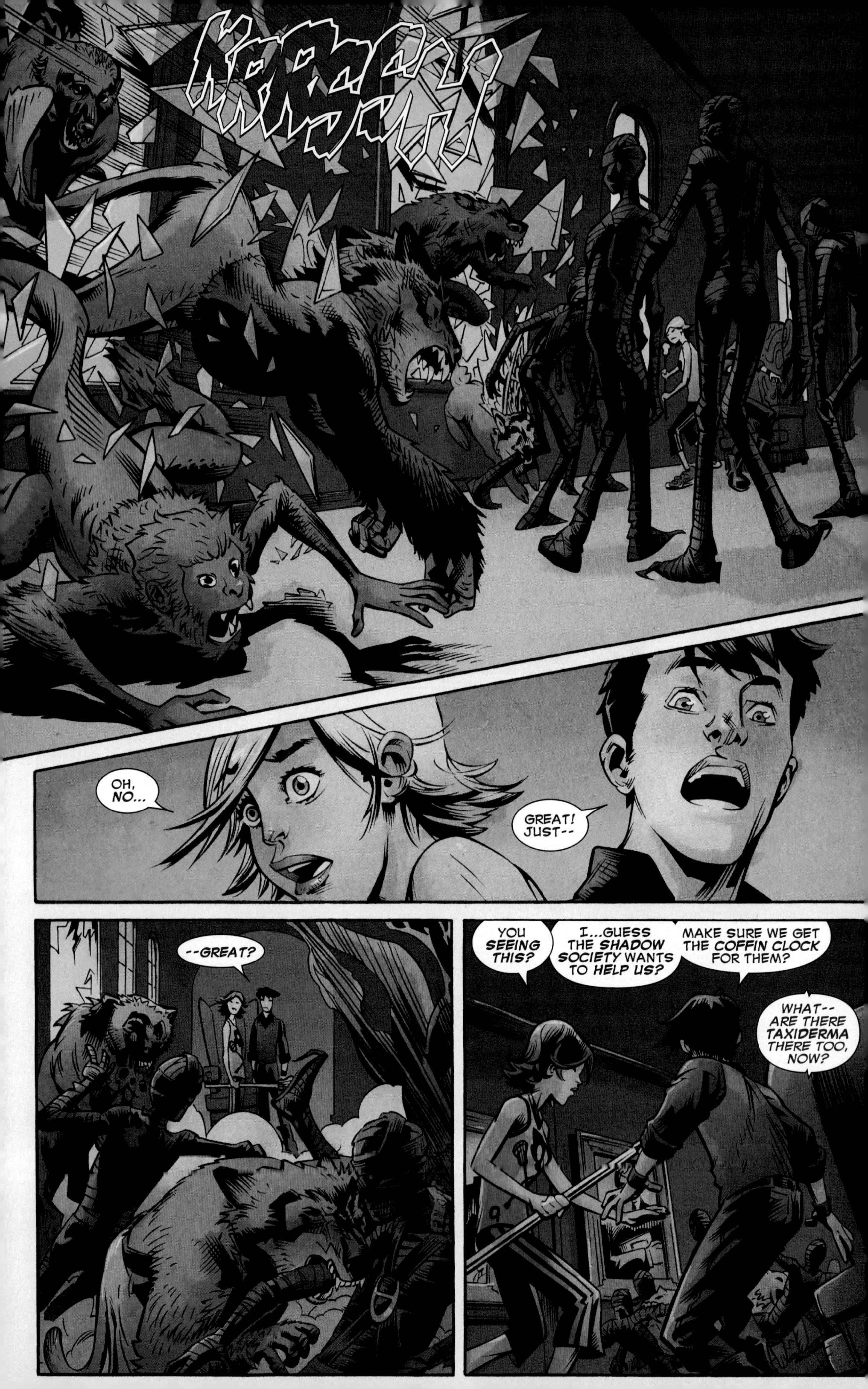
OH, NO...
GREAT! JUST--
--GREAT?
YOU SEEING THIS?
I...GUESS THE SHADOW SOCIETY WANTS TO HELP US?
MAKE SURE WE GET THE COFFIN CLOCK FOR THEM?
WHAT-- ARE THERE TAXIDERMA THERE TOO, NOW?

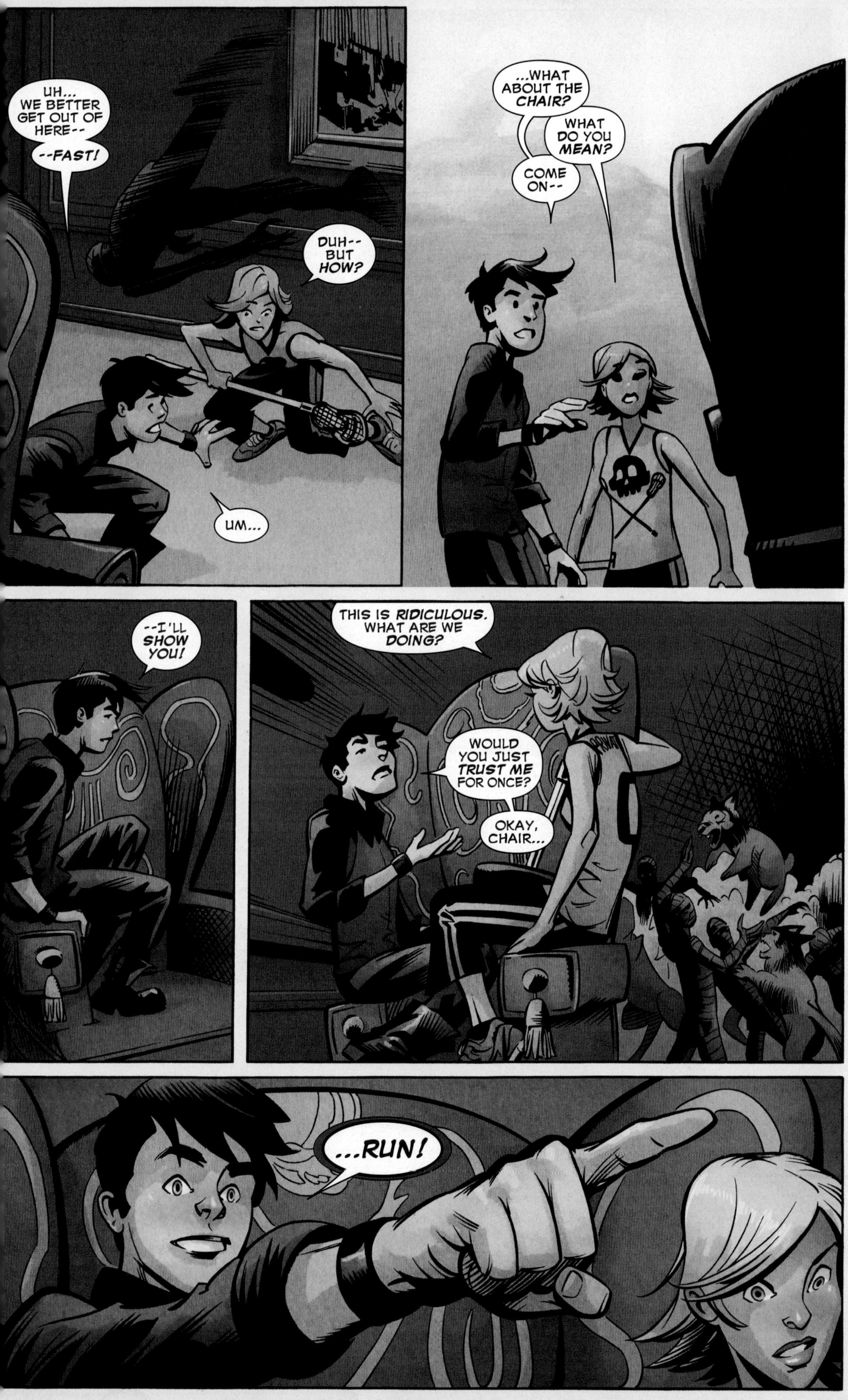
UH... WE BETTER GET OUT OF HERE--
--FAST!
DUH-- BUT HOW?
UM...
...WHAT ABOUT THE CHAIR?
WHAT DO YOU MEAN?
COME ON--
--I'LL SHOW YOU!
THIS IS RIDICULOUS. WHAT ARE WE DOING?
WOULD YOU JUST TRUST ME FOR ONCE?
OKAY, CHAIR...
...RUN!

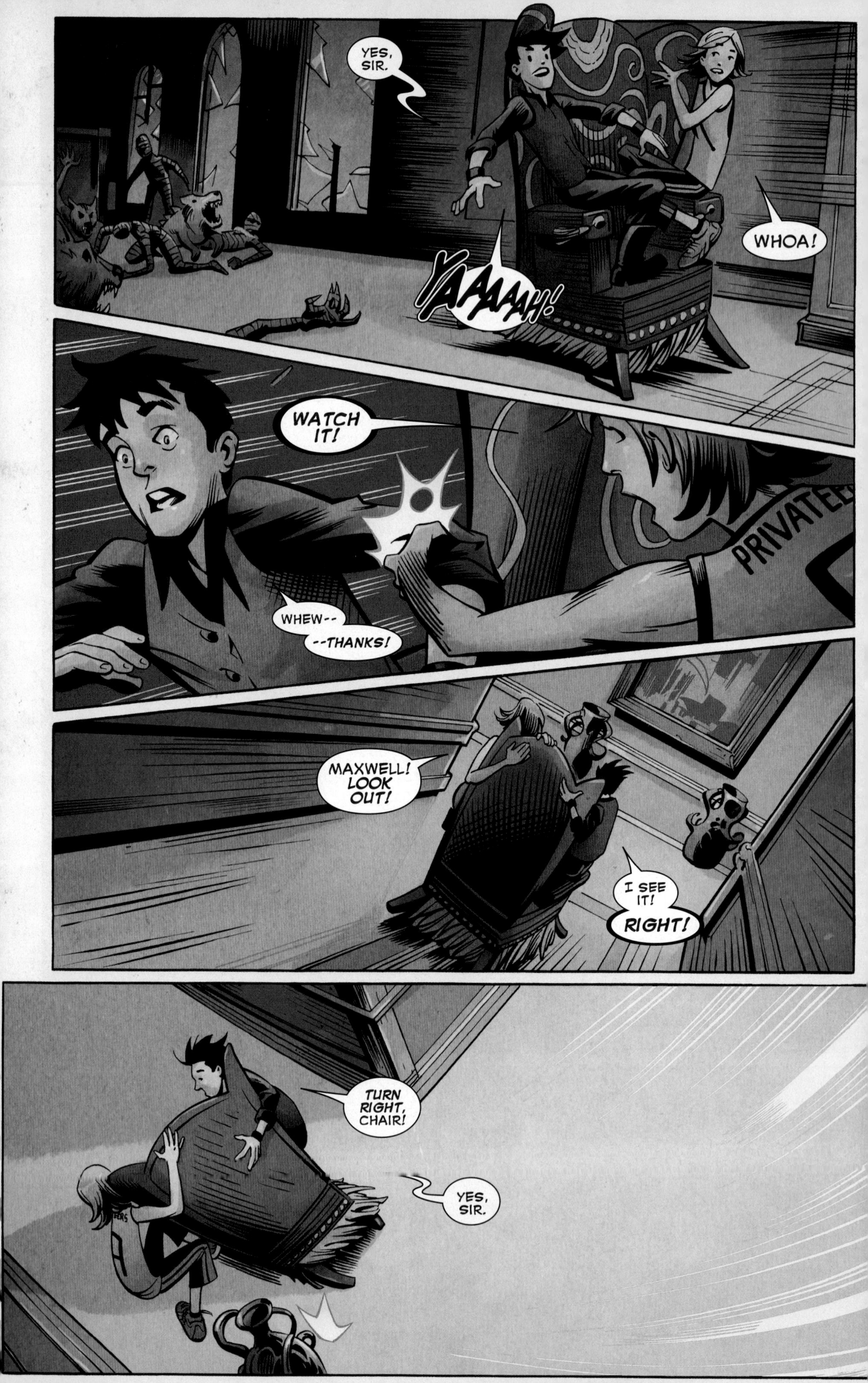
YES, SIR.
WHOA!
YAAAAAH!
WATCH IT!
PRIVATEE
WHEW--
--THANKS!
MAXWELL! LOOK OUT!
I SEE IT!
RIGHT!
TURN RIGHT, CHAIR!
YES, SIR.

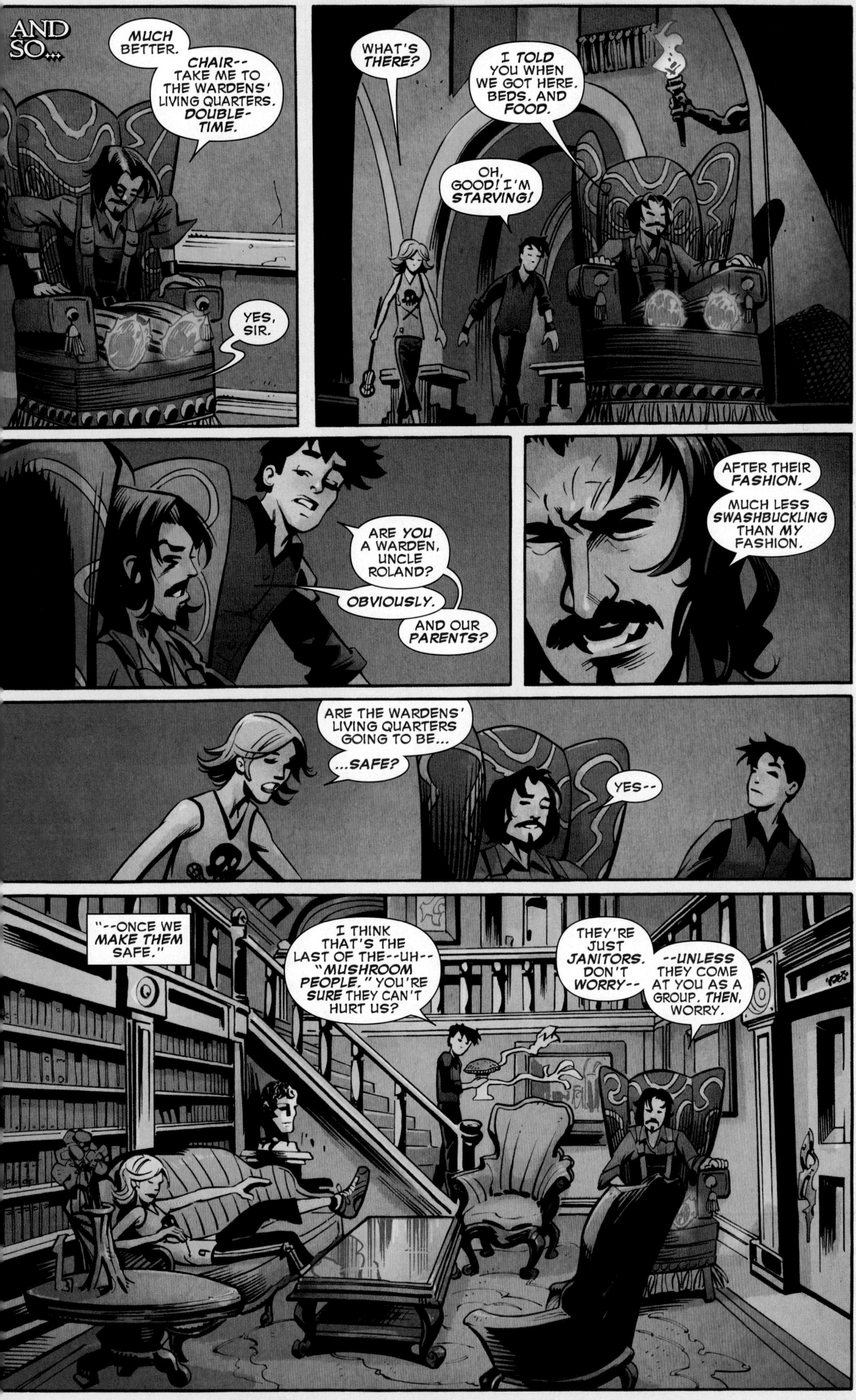
AND SO...
MUCH BETTER.
CHAIR-- TAKE ME TO THE WARDENS' LIVING QUARTERS. DOUBLE-TIME.
YES, SIR.
WHAT'S THERE?
I TOLD YOU WHEN WE GOT HERE. BEDS. AND FOOD.
OH, GOOD! I'M STARVING!
ARE YOU A WARDEN, UNCLE ROLAND?
OBVIOUSLY.
AND OUR PARENTS?
AFTER THEIR FASHION.
MUCH LESS SWASHBUCKLING THAN MY FASHION.
ARE THE WARDENS' LIVING QUARTERS GOING TO BE...
...SAFE?
YES--
"--ONCE WE MAKE THEM SAFE."
I THINK THAT'S THE LAST OF THE--UH-- "MUSHROOM PEOPLE." YOU'RE SURE THEY CAN'T HURT US?
THEY'RE JUST JANITORS. DON'T WORRY--
--UNLESS THEY COME AT YOU AS A GROUP. THEN, WORRY.

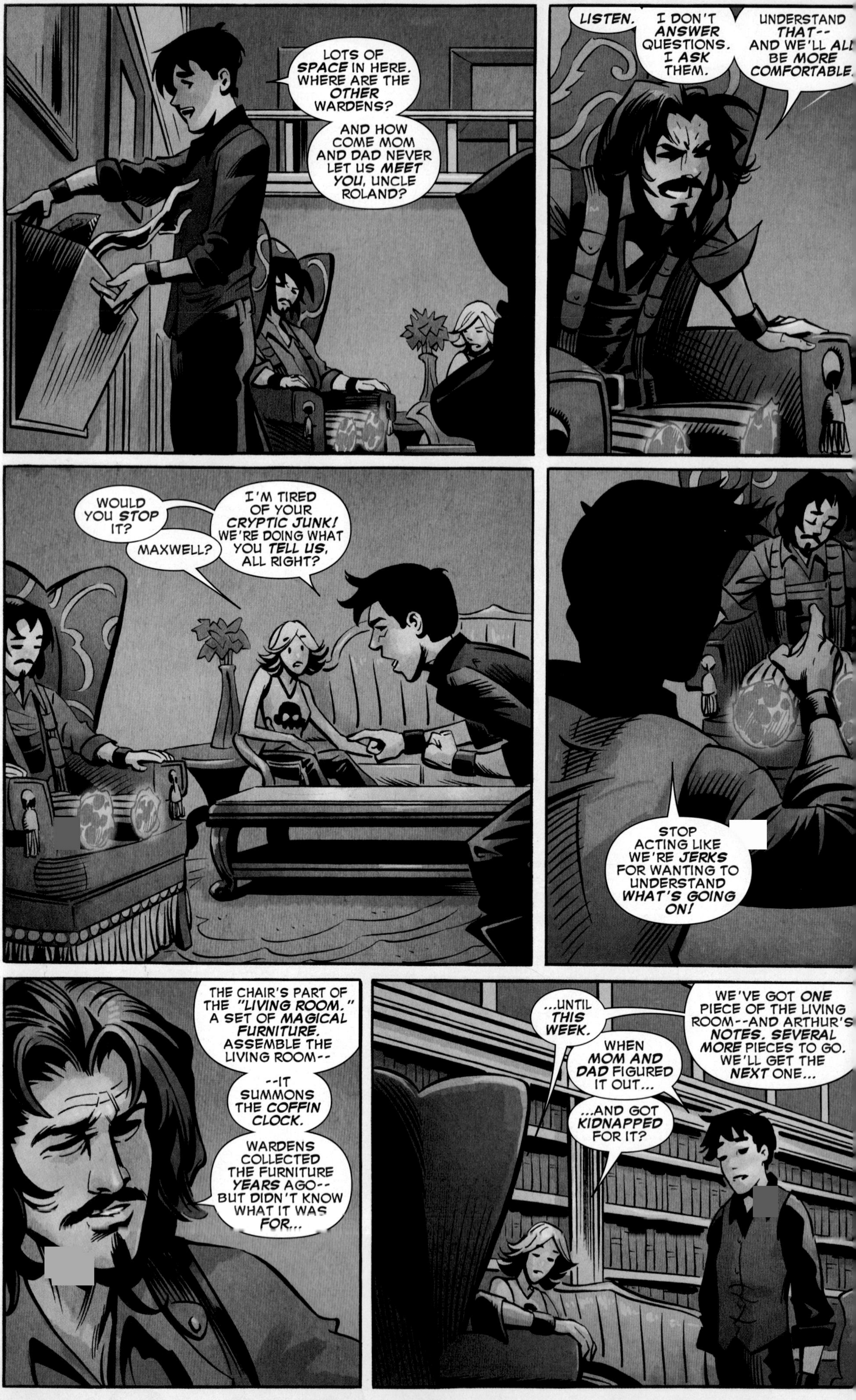
LOTS OF SPACE IN HERE. WHERE ARE THE OTHER WARDENS?
AND HOW COME MOM AND DAD NEVER LET US MEET YOU, UNCLE ROLAND?
LISTEN.
I DON'T ANSWER QUESTIONS. I ASK THEM.
UNDERSTAND THAT-- AND WE'LL ALL BE MORE COMFORTABLE.
WOULD YOU STOP IT?
MAXWELL?
I'M TIRED OF YOUR CRYPTIC JUNK! WE'RE DOING WHAT YOU TELL US, ALL RIGHT?
STOP ACTING LIKE WE'RE JERKS FOR WANTING TO UNDERSTAND WHAT'S GOING ON!
THE CHAIR'S PART OF THE "LIVING ROOM." A SET OF MAGICAL FURNITURE. ASSEMBLE THE LIVING ROOM--
--IT SUMMONS THE COFFIN CLOCK.
WARDENS COLLECTED THE FURNITURE YEARS AGO-- BUT DIDN'T KNOW WHAT IT WAS FOR...
...UNTIL THIS WEEK.
WHEN MOM AND DAD FIGURED IT OUT...
...AND GOT KIDNAPPED FOR IT?
WE'VE GOT ONE PIECE OF THE LIVING ROOM--AND ARTHUR'S NOTES. SEVERAL MORE PIECES TO GO. WE'LL GET THE NEXT ONE...

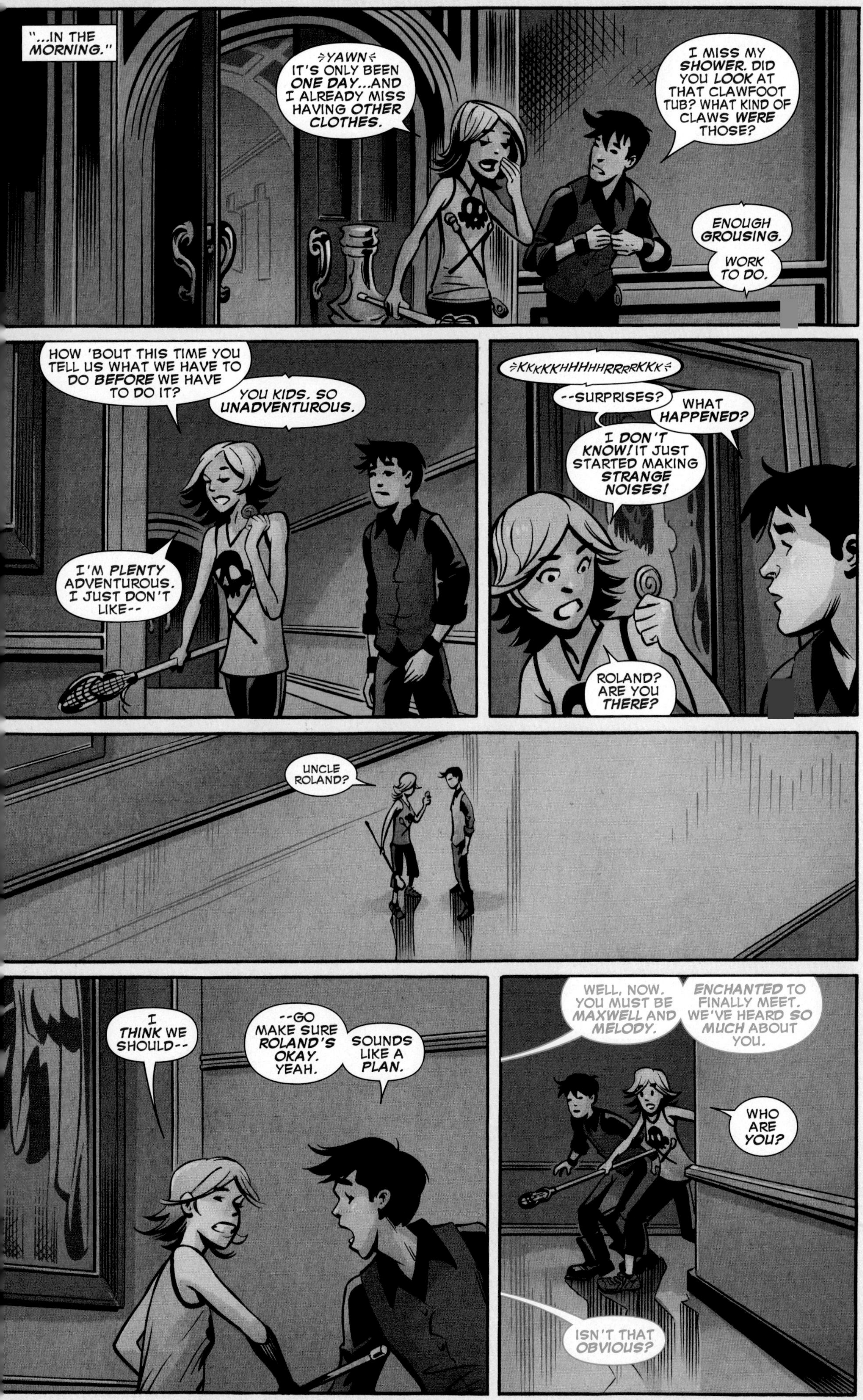
"...IN THE MORNING."
≠YAWN≠ IT'S ONLY BEEN ONE DAY...AND I ALREADY MISS HAVING OTHER CLOTHES.
I MISS MY SHOWER. DID YOU LOOK AT THAT CLAWFOOT TUB? WHAT KIND OF CLAWS WERE THOSE?
ENOUGH GROUSING.
WORK TO DO.
HOW 'BOUT THIS TIME YOU TELL US WHAT WE HAVE TO DO BEFORE WE HAVE TO DO IT?
YOU KIDS. SO UNADVENTUROUS.
I'M PLENTY ADVENTUROUS. I JUST DON'T LIKE--
KKKKKHHHHHRRRRKKK
--SURPRISES?
WHAT HAPPENED?
I DON'T KNOW! IT JUST STARTED MAKING STRANGE NOISES!
ROLAND? ARE YOU THERE?
UNCLE ROLAND?
I THINK WE SHOULD--
--GO MAKE SURE ROLAND'S OKAY. YEAH.
SOUNDS LIKE A PLAN.
WELL, NOW. YOU MUST BE MAXWELL AND MELODY.
ENCHANTED TO FINALLY MEET. WE'VE HEARD SO MUCH ABOUT YOU.
WHO ARE YOU?
ISN'T THAT OBVIOUS?

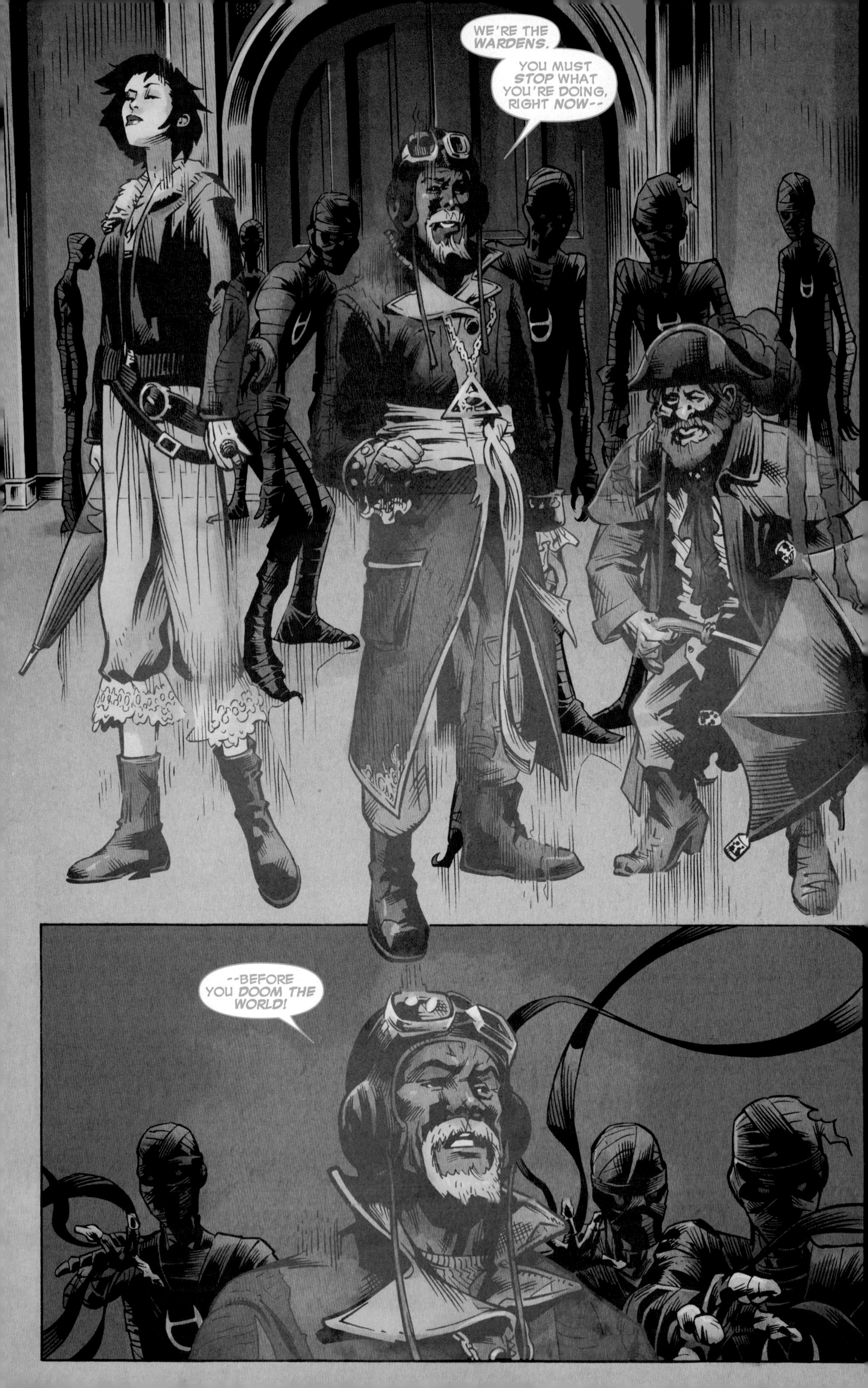
WE'RE THE WARDENS.
YOU MUST STOP WHAT YOU'RE DOING, RIGHT NOW--
--BEFORE YOU DOOM THE WORLD!

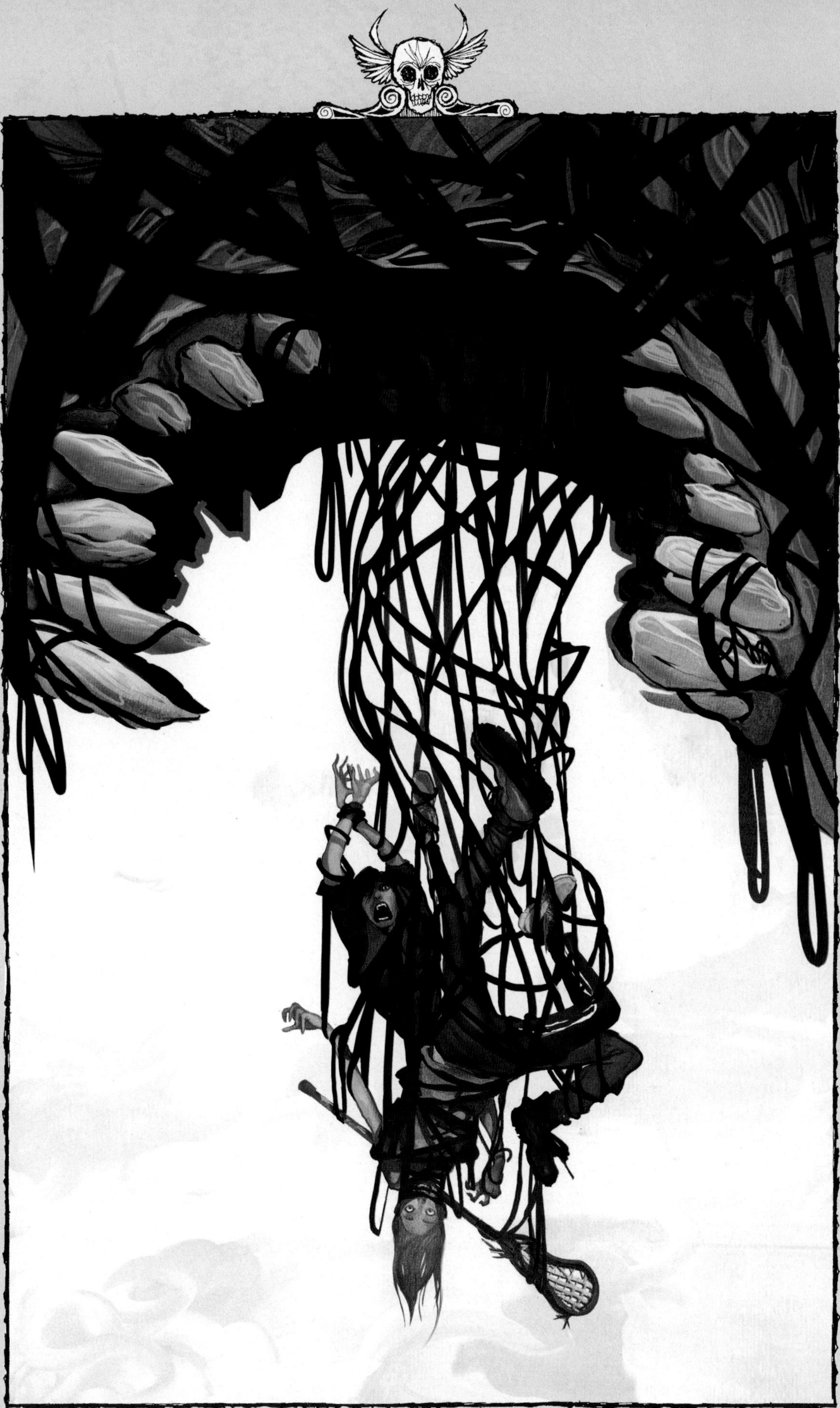

3

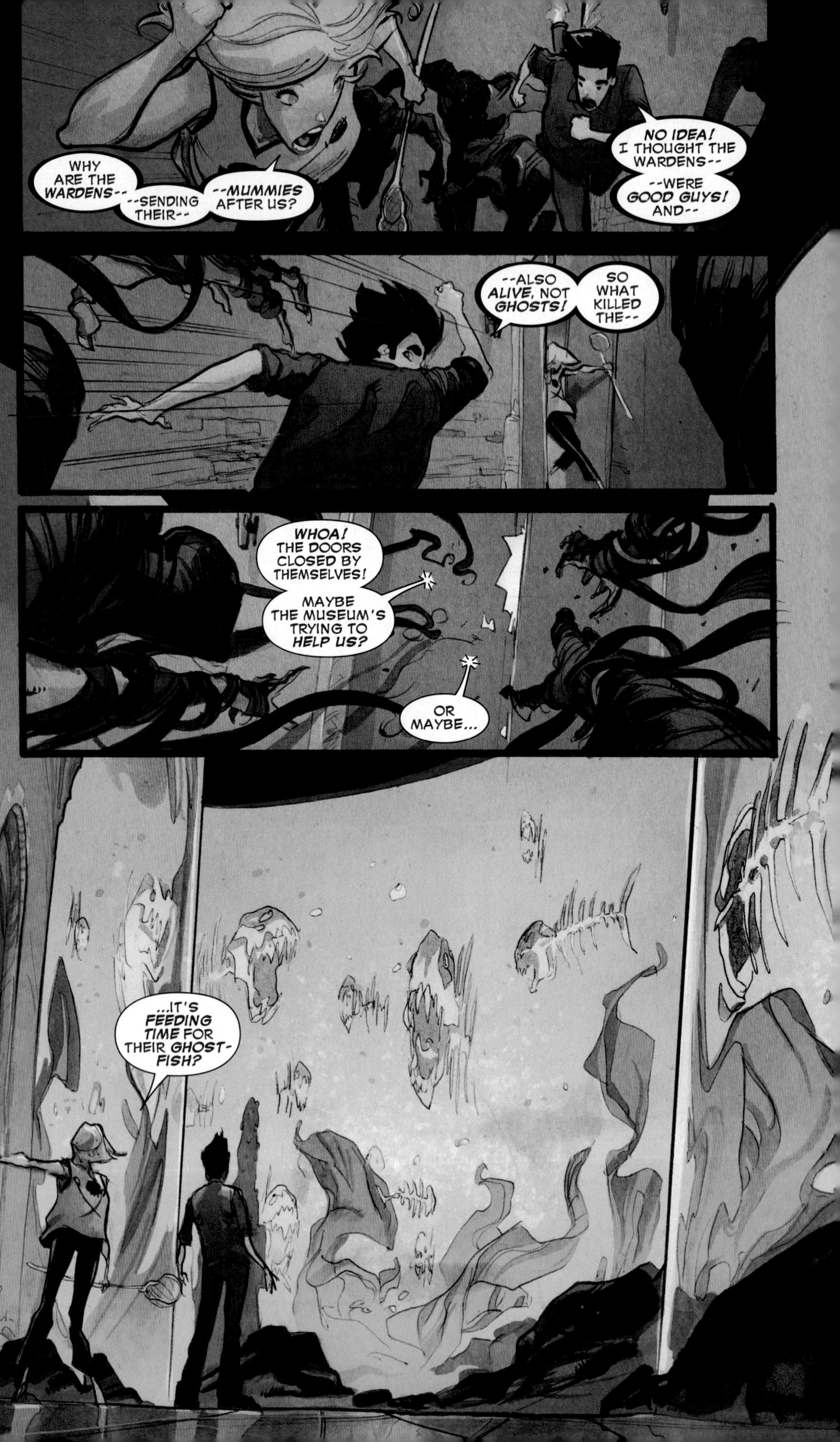
WHY ARE THE WARDENS--
--SENDING THEIR--
--MUMMIES AFTER US?
NO IDEA! I THOUGHT THE WARDENS--
--WERE GOOD GUYS! AND--
--ALSO ALIVE, NOT GHOSTS!
SO WHAT KILLED THE--
WHOA! THE DOORS CLOSED BY THEMSELVES!
MAYBE THE MUSEUM'S TRYING TO HELP US?
OR MAYBE...
...IT'S FEEDING TIME FOR THEIR GHOST-FISH?

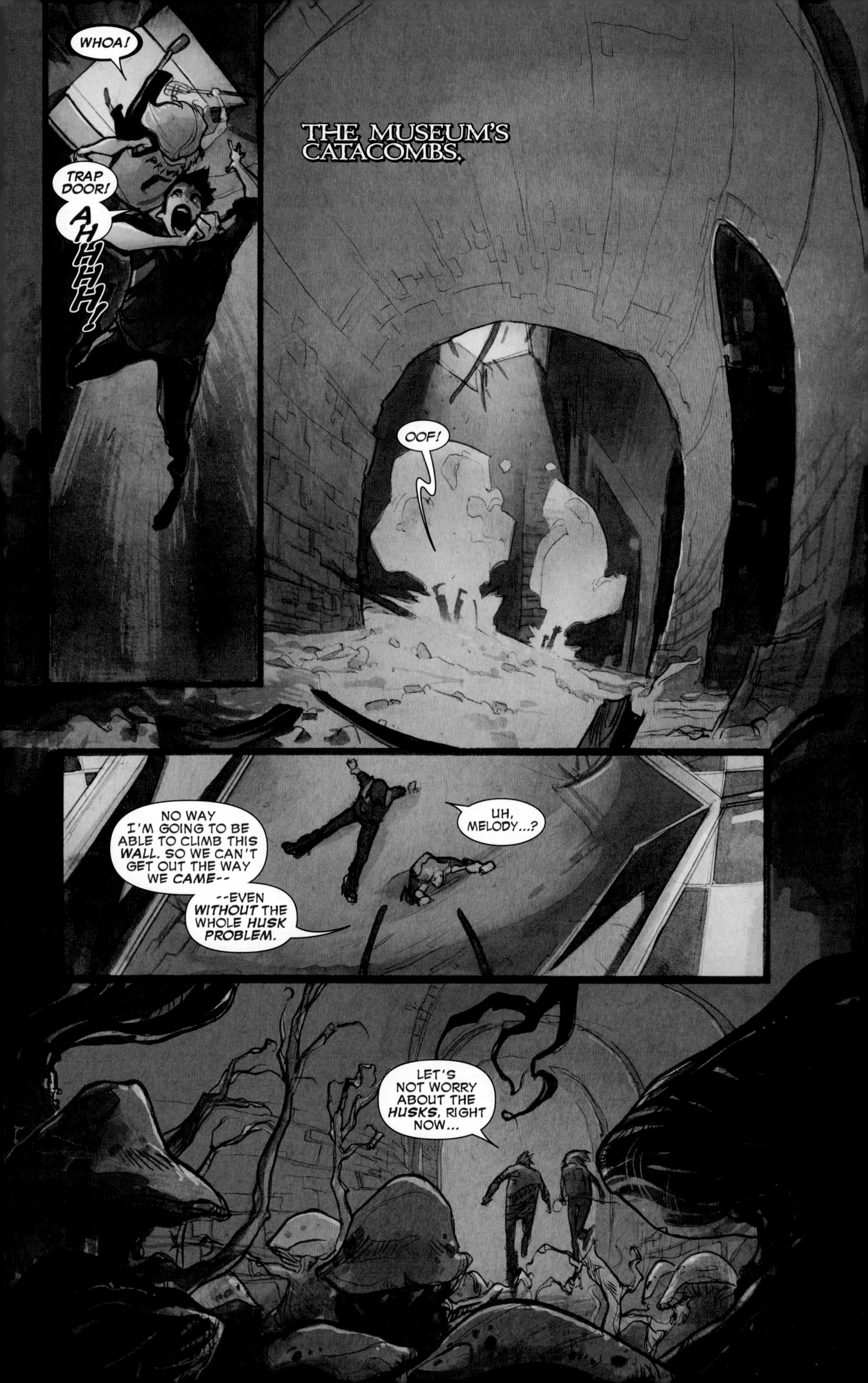
WHOA!
TRAP DOOR!
AHHHHH!
THE MUSEUM'S CATACOMBS.
OOF!
NO WAY I'M GOING TO BE ABLE TO CLIMB THIS WALL. SO WE CAN'T GET OUT THE WAY WE CAME--
UH, MELODY...?
--EVEN WITHOUT THE WHOLE HUSK PROBLEM.
LET'S NOT WORRY ABOUT THE HUSKS, RIGHT NOW...

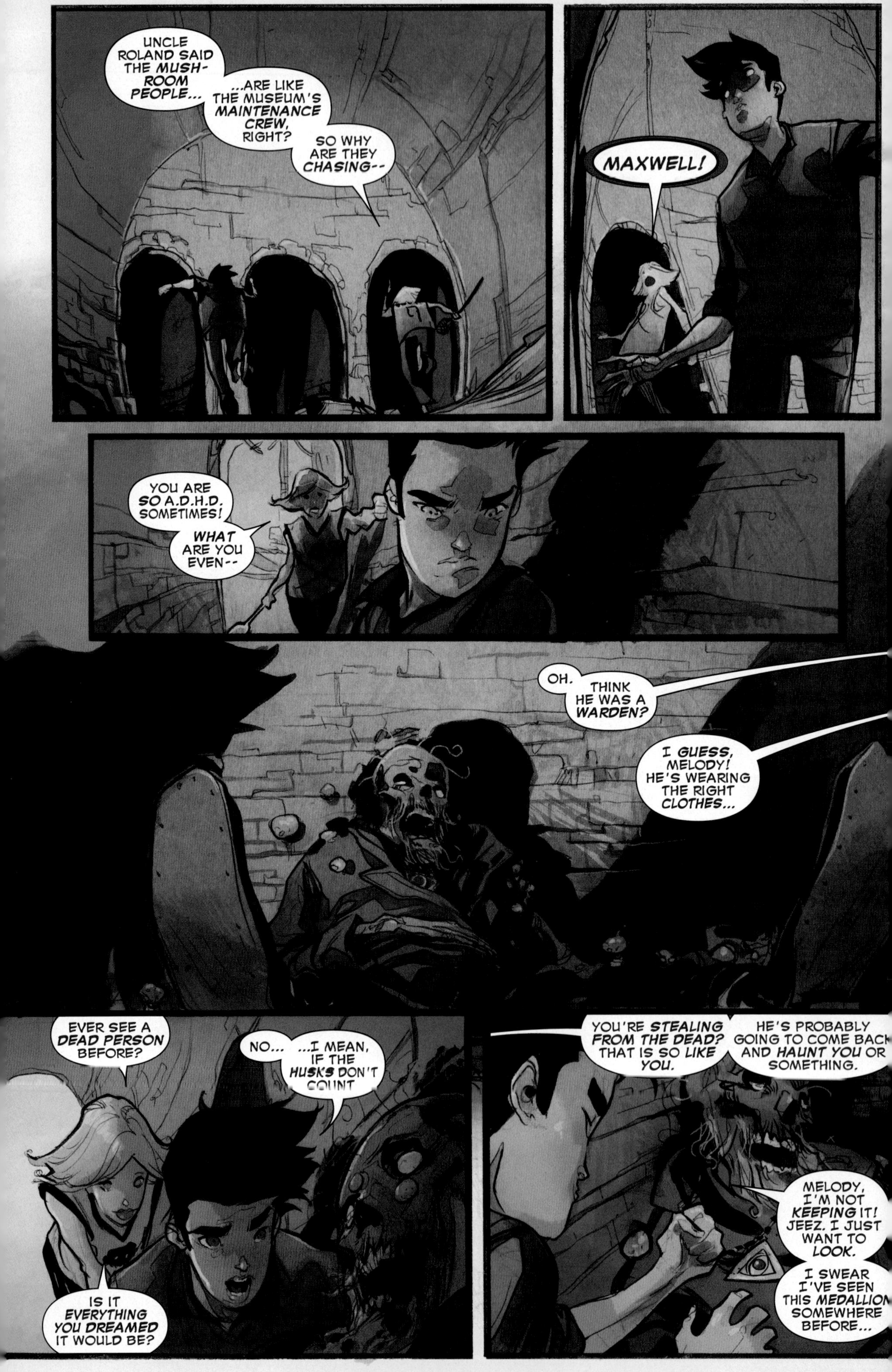
UNCLE ROLAND SAID THE MUSH-ROOM PEOPLE...
...ARE LIKE THE MUSEUM'S MAINTENANCE CREW, RIGHT?
SO WHY ARE THEY CHASING--
MAXWELL!
YOU ARE SO A.D.H.D. SOMETIMES!
WHAT ARE YOU EVEN--
OH.
THINK HE WAS A WARDEN?
I GUESS, MELODY! HE'S WEARING THE RIGHT CLOTHES...
EVER SEE A DEAD PERSON BEFORE?
NO...
...I MEAN, IF THE HUSKS DON'T COUNT
IS IT EVERYTHING YOU DREAMED IT WOULD BE?
YOU'RE STEALING FROM THE DEAD? THAT IS SO LIKE YOU.
HE'S PROBABLY GOING TO COME BACK AND HAUNT YOU OR SOMETHING.
MELODY, I'M NOT KEEPING IT! JEEZ. I JUST WANT TO LOOK.
I SWEAR I'VE SEEN THIS MEDALLION SOMEWHERE BEFORE...

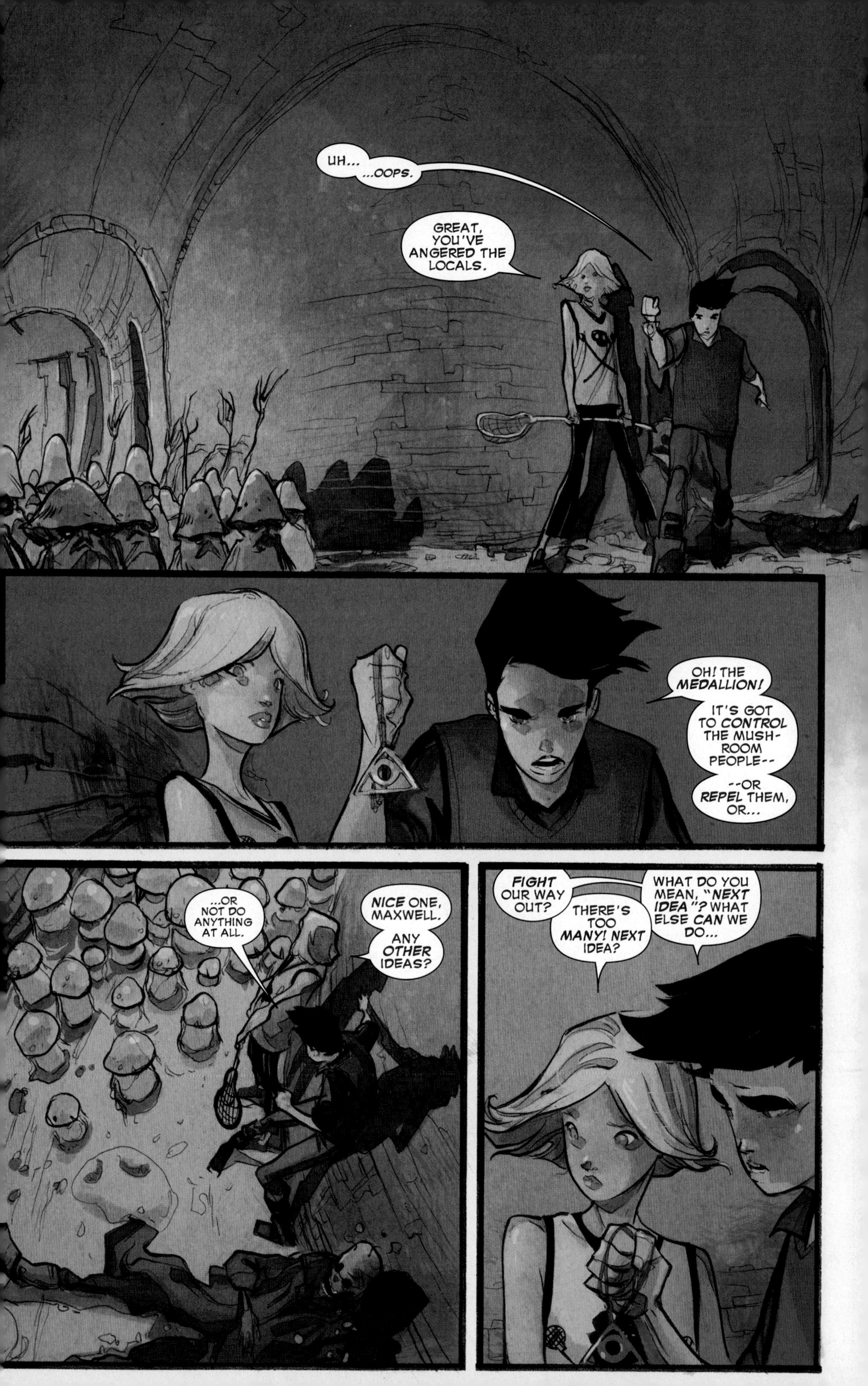
UH... ...OOPS.
GREAT, YOU'VE ANGERED THE LOCALS.
OH! THE MEDALLION!
IT'S GOT TO CONTROL THE MUSH-ROOM PEOPLE--
--OR REPEL THEM, OR...
...OR NOT DO ANYTHING AT ALL.
NICE ONE, MAXWELL.
ANY OTHER IDEAS?
FIGHT OUR WAY OUT?
THERE'S TOO MANY! NEXT IDEA?
WHAT DO YOU MEAN, "NEXT IDEA"? WHAT ELSE CAN WE DO...

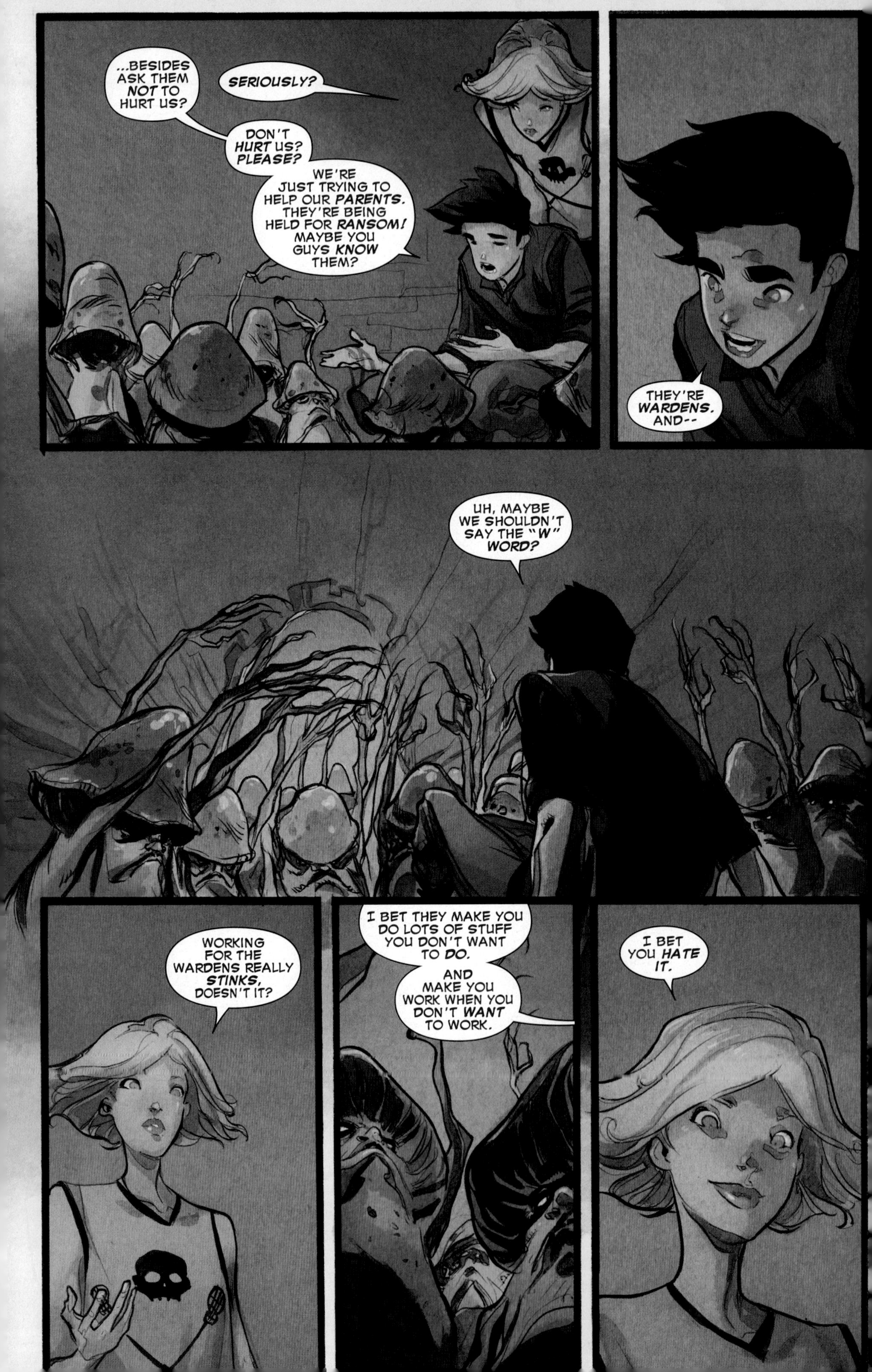
...BESIDES ASK THEM NOT TO HURT US?
SERIOUSLY?
DON'T HURT US? PLEASE?
WE'RE JUST TRYING TO HELP OUR PARENTS. THEY'RE BEING HELD FOR RANSOM! MAYBE YOU GUYS KNOW THEM?
THEY'RE WARDENS. AND--
UH, MAYBE WE SHOULDN'T SAY THE "W" WORD?
WORKING FOR THE WARDENS REALLY STINKS, DOESN'T IT?
I BET THEY MAKE YOU DO LOTS OF STUFF YOU DON'T WANT TO DO.
AND MAKE YOU WORK WHEN YOU DON'T WANT TO WORK.
I BET YOU HATE IT.

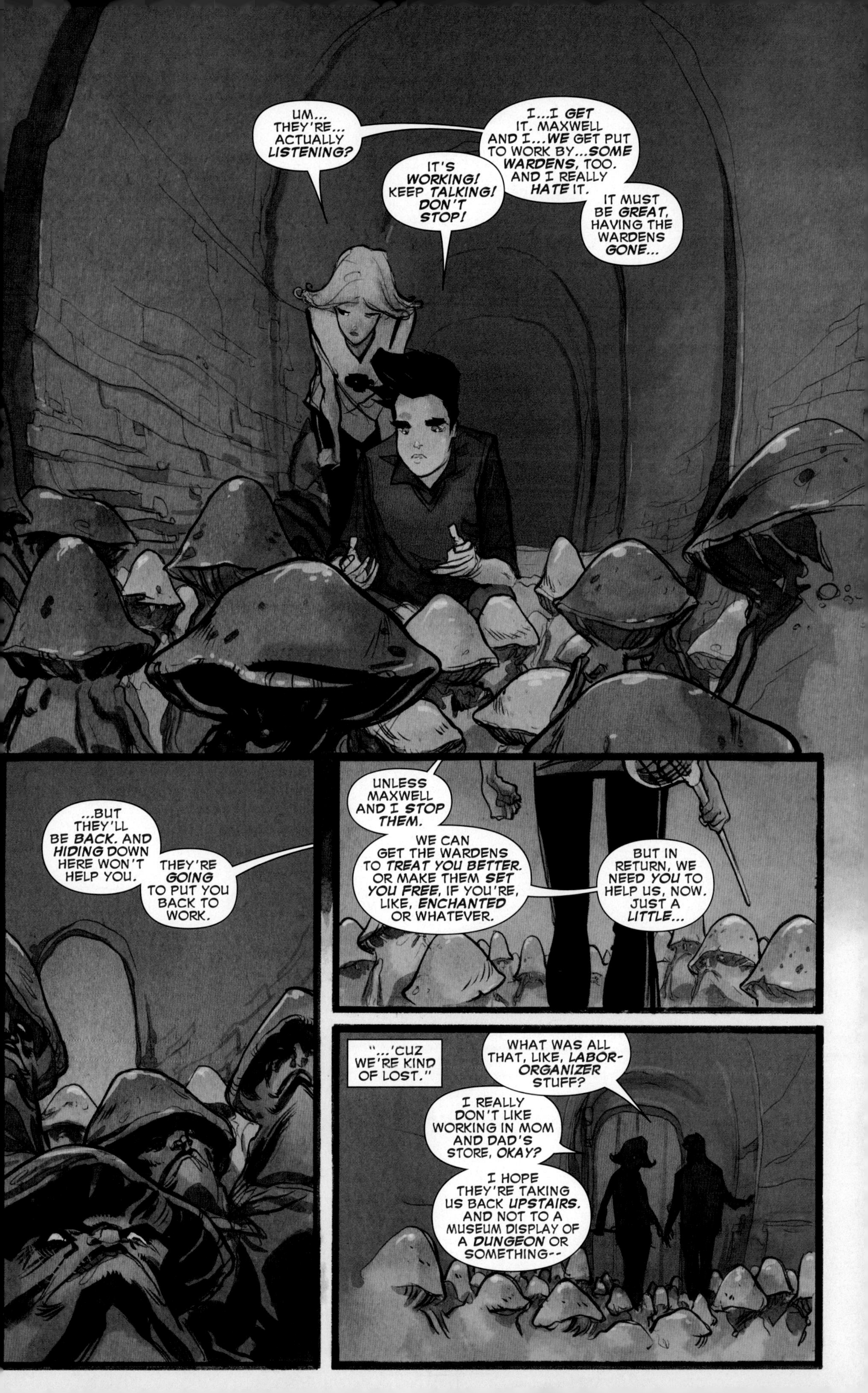

UM... THEY'RE... ACTUALLY LISTENING?
IT'S WORKING! KEEP TALKING! DON'T STOP!
I...I GET IT. MAXWELL AND I...WE GET PUT TO WORK BY...SOME WARDENS, TOO. AND I REALLY HATE IT.
IT MUST BE GREAT, HAVING THE WARDENS GONE...
...BUT THEY'LL BE BACK. AND HIDING DOWN HERE WON'T HELP YOU.
THEY'RE GOING TO PUT YOU BACK TO WORK.
UNLESS MAXWELL AND I STOP THEM.
WE CAN GET THE WARDENS TO TREAT YOU BETTER. OR MAKE THEM SET YOU FREE, IF YOU'RE, LIKE, ENCHANTED OR WHATEVER.
BUT IN RETURN, WE NEED YOU TO HELP US, NOW. JUST A LITTLE...
"...'CUZ WE'RE KIND OF LOST."
WHAT WAS ALL THAT, LIKE, LABOR-ORGANIZER STUFF?
I REALLY DON'T LIKE WORKING IN MOM AND DAD'S STORE, OKAY?
I HOPE THEY'RE TAKING US BACK UPSTAIRS. AND NOT TO A MUSEUM DISPLAY OF A DUNGEON OR SOMETHING--

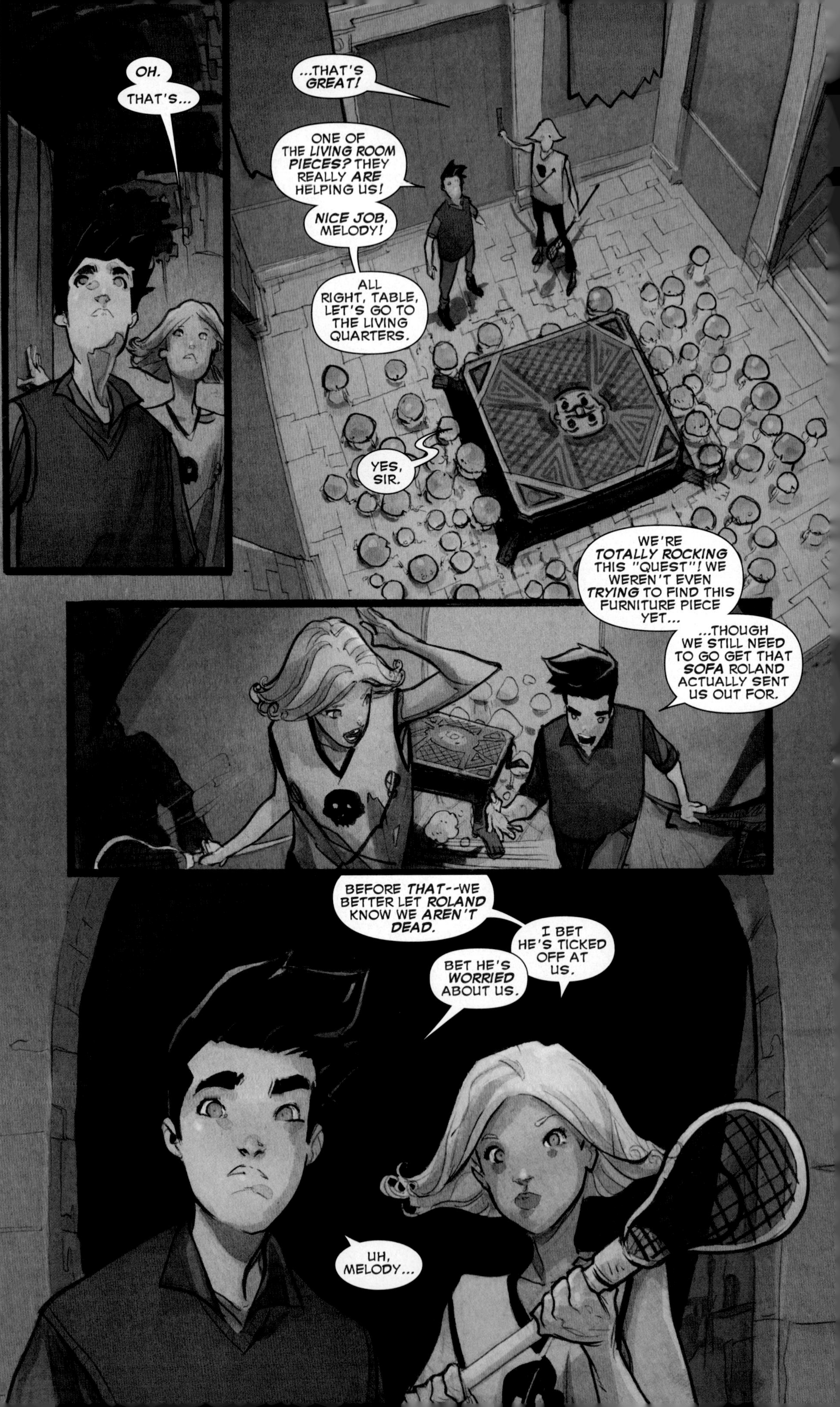
OH.
THAT'S...
...THAT'S GREAT!
ONE OF THE LIVING ROOM PIECES? THEY REALLY ARE HELPING US!
NICE JOB, MELODY!
ALL RIGHT, TABLE, LET'S GO TO THE LIVING QUARTERS.
YES, SIR.
WE'RE TOTALLY ROCKING THIS "QUEST"! WE WEREN'T EVEN TRYING TO FIND THIS FURNITURE PIECE YET...
...THOUGH WE STILL NEED TO GO GET THAT SOFA ROLAND ACTUALLY SENT US OUT FOR.
BEFORE THAT--WE BETTER LET ROLAND KNOW WE AREN'T DEAD.
I BET HE'S TICKED OFF AT US.
BET HE'S WORRIED ABOUT US.
UH, MELODY...

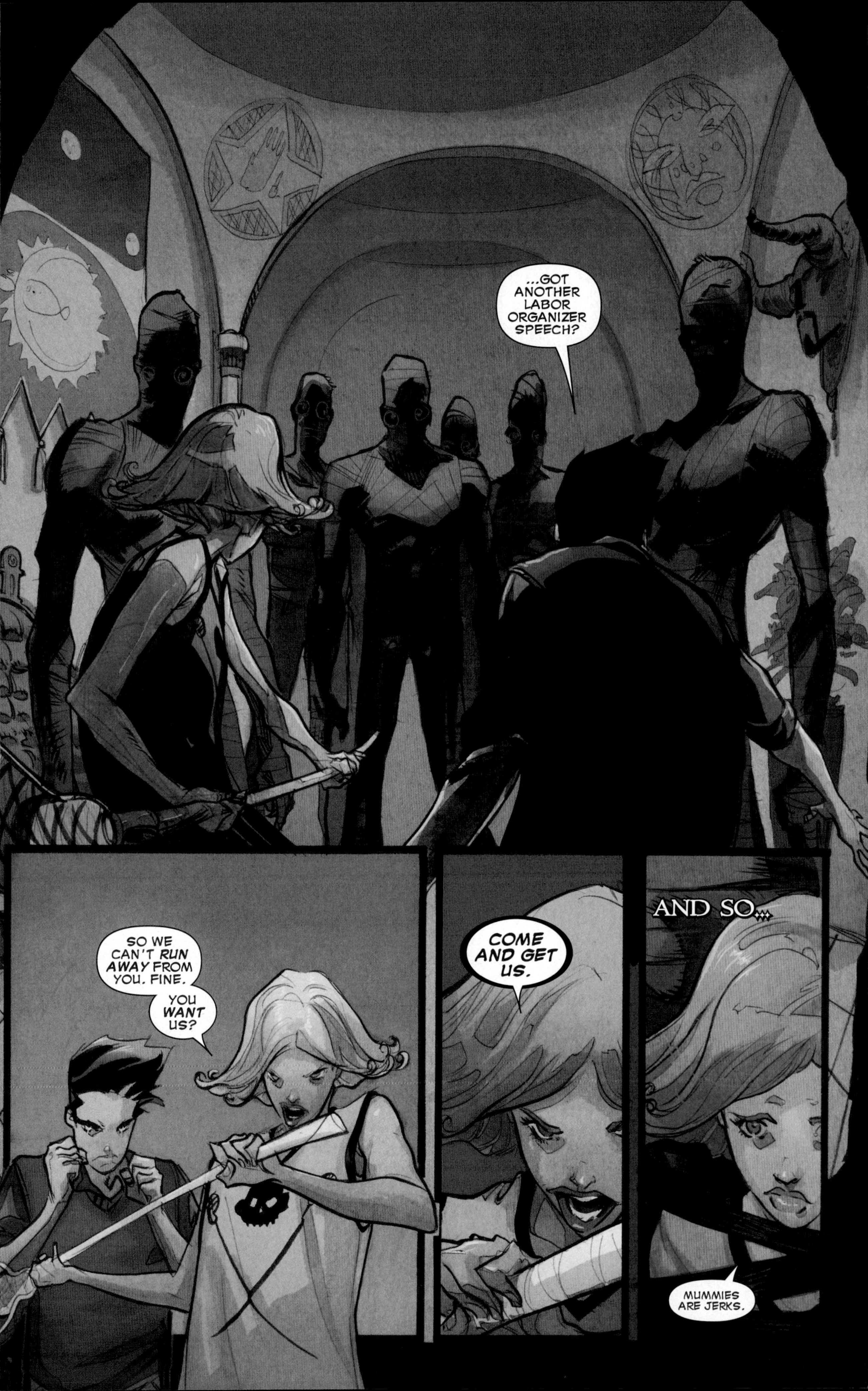
...GOT ANOTHER LABOR ORGANIZER SPEECH?
SO WE CAN'T RUN AWAY FROM YOU. FINE.
YOU WANT US?
COME AND GET US.
AND SO...
MUMMIES ARE JERKS.

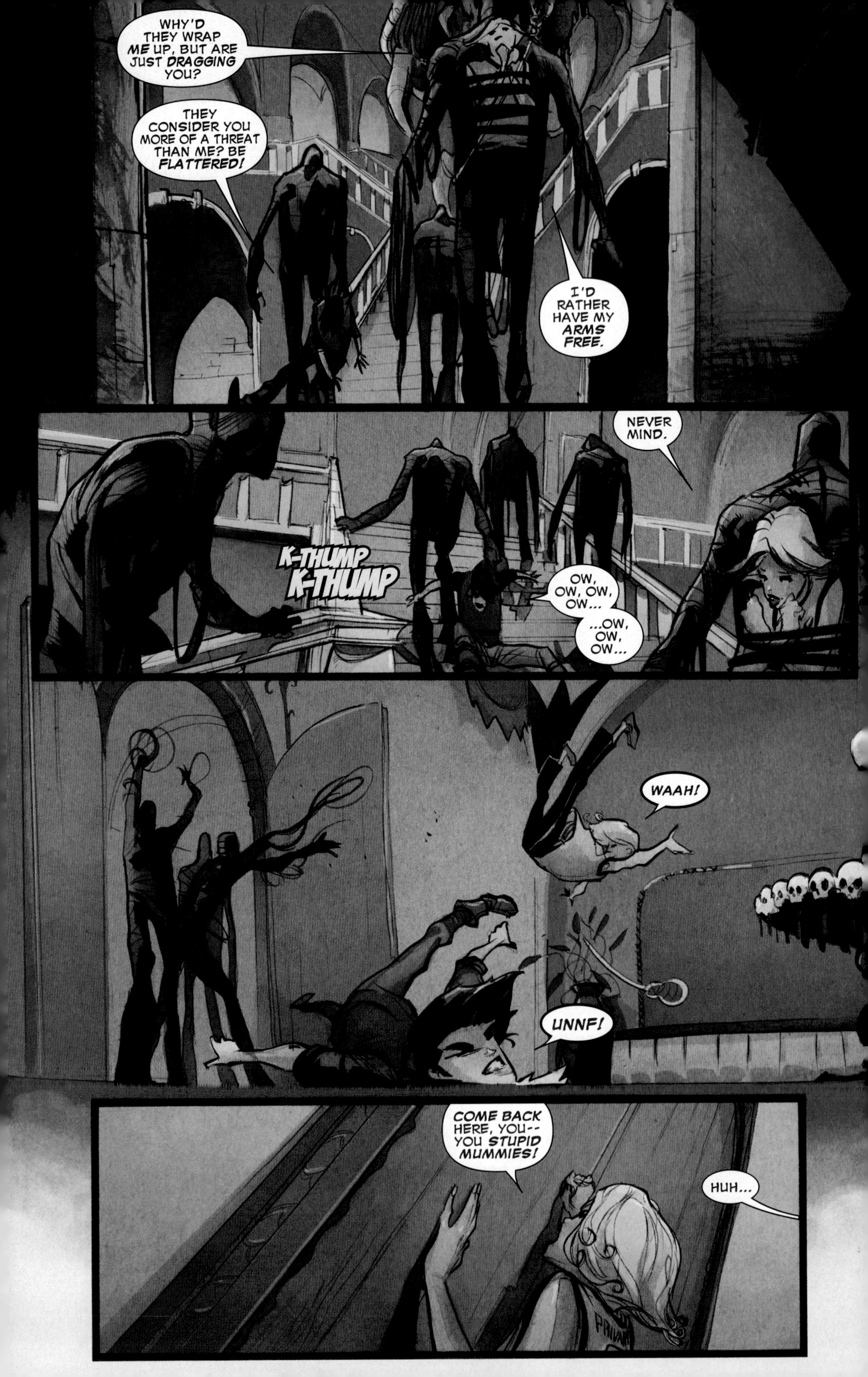
WHY'D THEY WRAP ME UP, BUT ARE JUST DRAGGING YOU?
THEY CONSIDER YOU MORE OF A THREAT THAN ME? BE FLATTERED!
I'D RATHER HAVE MY ARMS FREE.
NEVER MIND.
K-THUMP K-THUMP
OW, OW, OW, OW...
...OW, OW, OW...
WAAH!
UNNF!
COME BACK HERE, YOU-- YOU STUPID MUMMIES!
HUH...

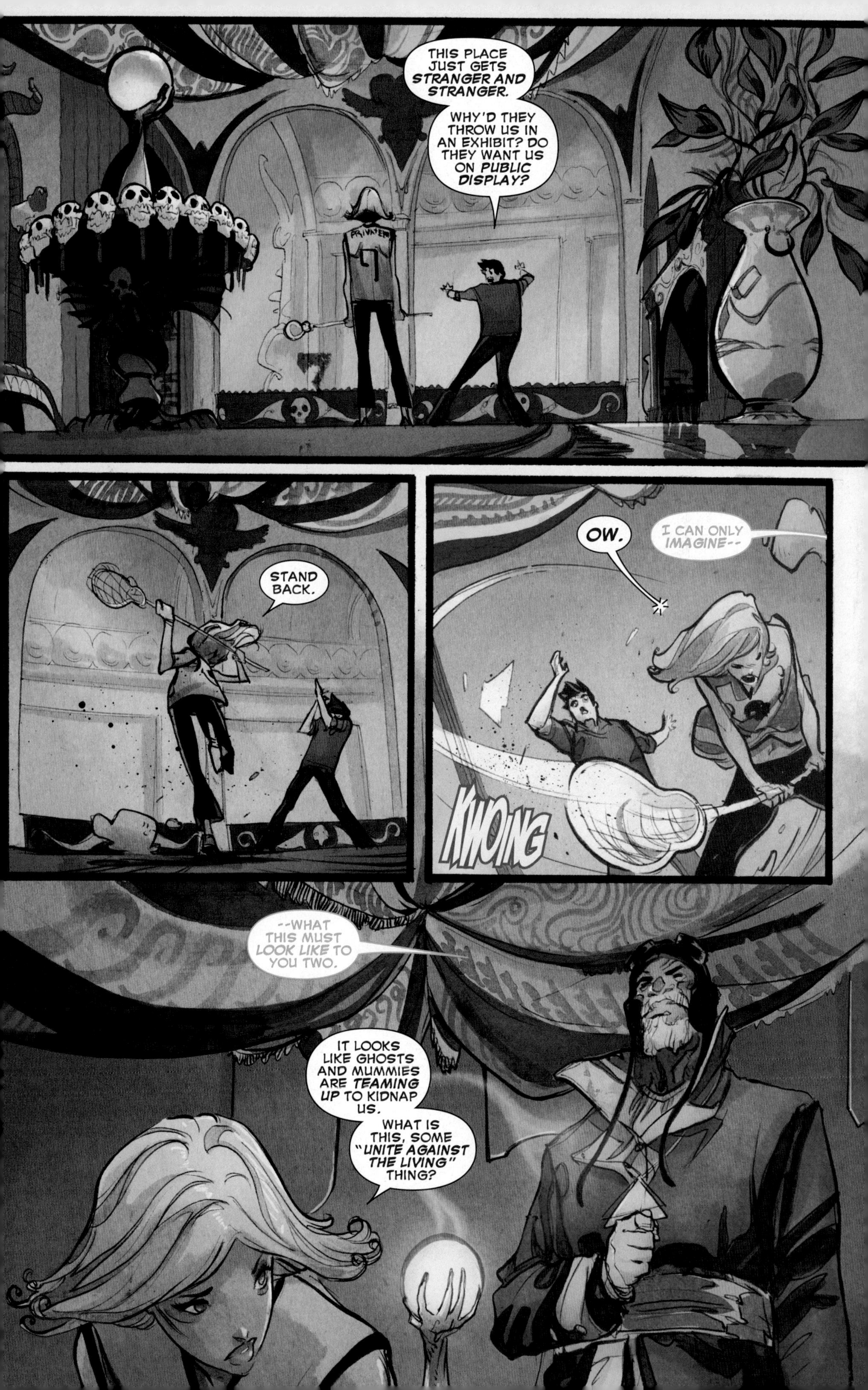
THIS PLACE JUST GETS STRANGER AND STRANGER.
WHY'D THEY THROW US IN AN EXHIBIT? DO THEY WANT US ON PUBLIC DISPLAY?
STAND BACK.
OW.
I CAN ONLY IMAGINE--
KWOING
--WHAT THIS MUST LOOK LIKE TO YOU TWO.
IT LOOKS LIKE GHOSTS AND MUMMIES ARE TEAMING UP TO KIDNAP US.
WHAT IS THIS, SOME "UNITE AGAINST THE LIVING" THING?

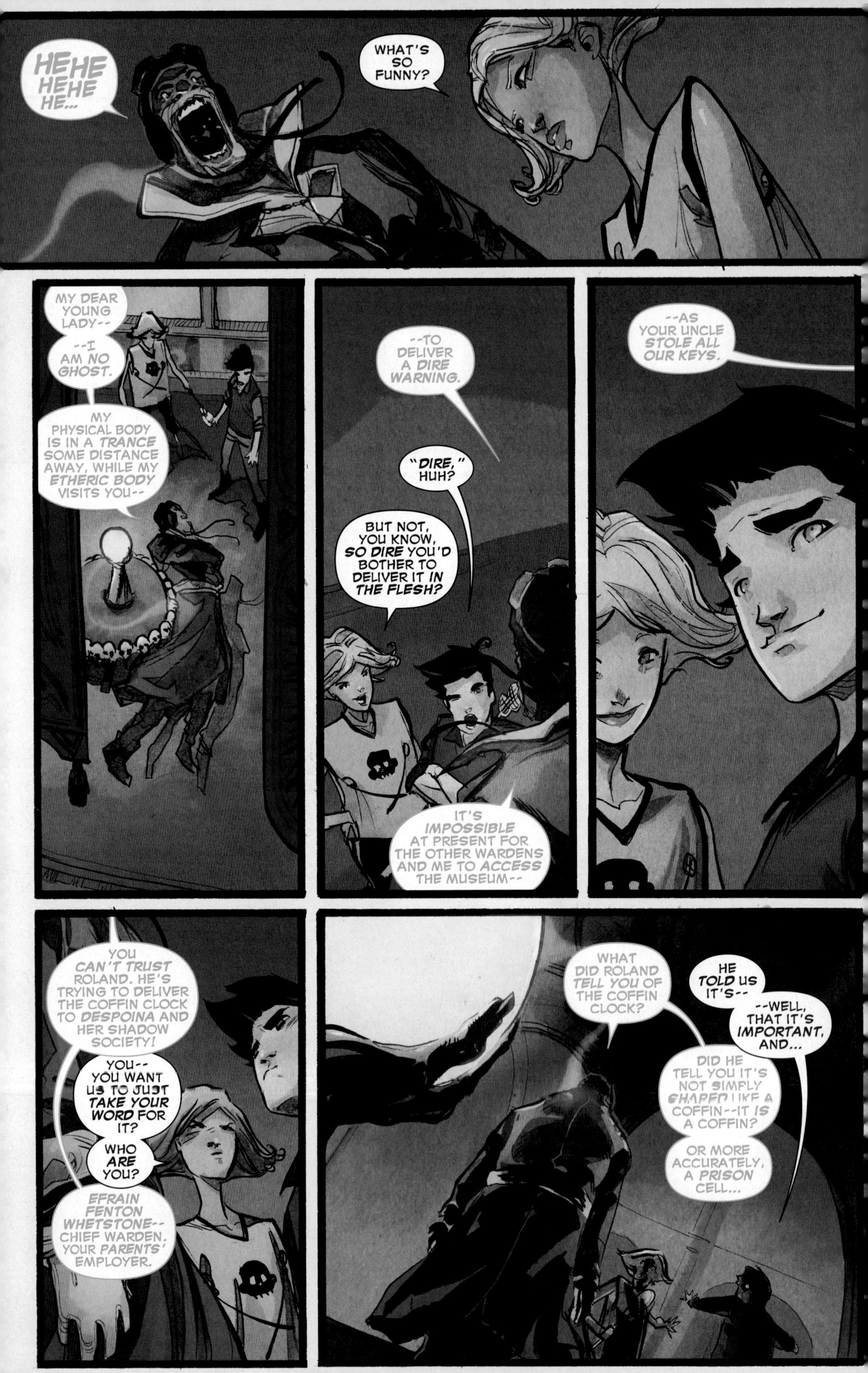
HEHE HEHE HE...
WHAT'S SO FUNNY?
MY DEAR YOUNG LADY--
--I AM NO GHOST.
MY PHYSICAL BODY IS IN A TRANCE SOME DISTANCE AWAY, WHILE MY ETHERIC BODY VISITS YOU--
--TO DELIVER A DIRE WARNING.
"DIRE," HUH?
BUT NOT, YOU KNOW, SO DIRE YOU'D BOTHER TO DELIVER IT IN THE FLESH?
IT'S IMPOSSIBLE AT PRESENT FOR THE OTHER WARDENS AND ME TO ACCESS THE MUSEUM--
--AS YOUR UNCLE STOLE ALL OUR KEYS.
YOU CAN'T TRUST ROLAND. HE'S TRYING TO DELIVER THE COFFIN CLOCK TO DESPOINA AND HER SHADOW SOCIETY!
YOU--YOU WANT US TO JUST TAKE YOUR WORD FOR IT?
WHO ARE YOU?
EFRAIN FENTON WHETSTONE--CHIEF WARDEN. YOUR PARENTS' EMPLOYER.
WHAT DID ROLAND TELL YOU OF THE COFFIN CLOCK?
HE TOLD US IT'S--
--WELL, THAT IT'S IMPORTANT, AND...
DID HE TELL YOU IT'S NOT SIMPLY SHAPED LIKE A COFFIN--IT IS A COFFIN?
OR MORE ACCURATELY, A PRISON CELL...

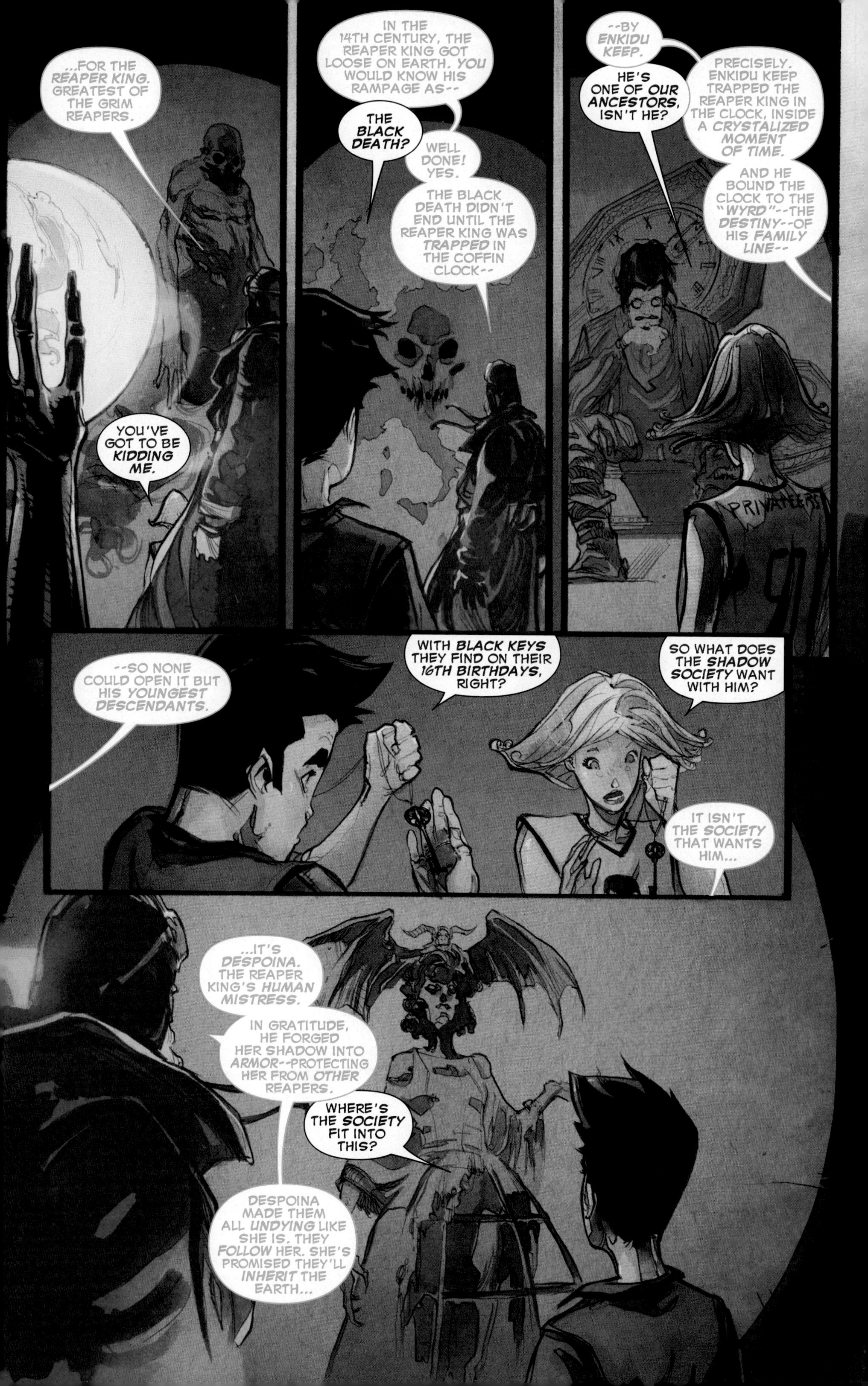
...FOR THE REAPER KING. GREATEST OF THE GRIM REAPERS.
YOU'VE GOT TO BE KIDDING ME.
IN THE 14TH CENTURY, THE REAPER KING GOT LOOSE ON EARTH. YOU WOULD KNOW HIS RAMPAGE AS--
THE BLACK DEATH?
WELL DONE! YES.
THE BLACK DEATH DIDN'T END UNTIL THE REAPER KING WAS TRAPPED IN THE COFFIN CLOCK--
--BY ENKIDU KEEP.
HE'S ONE OF OUR ANCESTORS, ISN'T HE?
PRECISELY. ENKIDU KEEP TRAPPED THE REAPER KING IN THE CLOCK, INSIDE A CRYSTALIZED MOMENT OF TIME.
AND HE BOUND THE CLOCK TO THE "WYRD"--THE DESTINY--OF HIS FAMILY LINE--
PRIVATEERS
--SO NONE COULD OPEN IT BUT HIS YOUNGEST DESCENDANTS.
WITH BLACK KEYS THEY FIND ON THEIR 16TH BIRTHDAYS, RIGHT?
SO WHAT DOES THE SHADOW SOCIETY WANT WITH HIM?
IT ISN'T THE SOCIETY THAT WANTS HIM...
...IT'S DESPOINA. THE REAPER KING'S HUMAN MISTRESS.
IN GRATITUDE, HE FORGED HER SHADOW INTO ARMOR--PROTECTING HER FROM OTHER REAPERS.
WHERE'S THE SOCIETY FIT INTO THIS?
DESPOINA MADE THEM ALL UNDYING LIKE SHE IS. THEY FOLLOW HER. SHE'S PROMISED THEY'LL INHERIT THE EARTH...

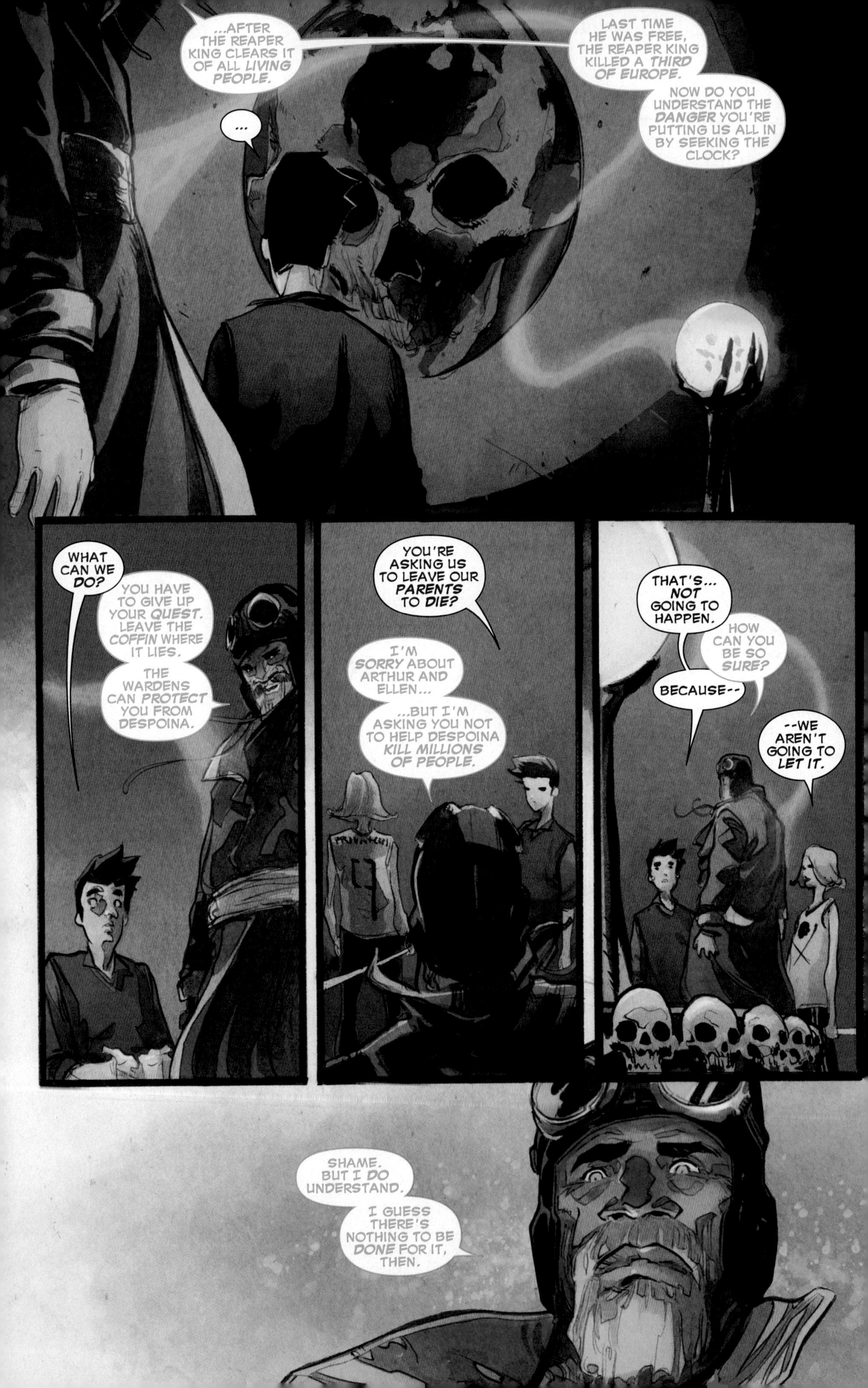
...AFTER THE REAPER KING CLEARS IT OF ALL LIVING PEOPLE.
LAST TIME HE WAS FREE, THE REAPER KING KILLED A THIRD OF EUROPE.
NOW DO YOU UNDERSTAND THE DANGER YOU'RE PUTTING US ALL IN BY SEEKING THE CLOCK?
...
WHAT CAN WE DO?
YOU HAVE TO GIVE UP YOUR QUEST. LEAVE THE COFFIN WHERE IT LIES.
THE WARDENS CAN PROTECT YOU FROM DESPOINA.
YOU'RE ASKING US TO LEAVE OUR PARENTS TO DIE?
I'M SORRY ABOUT ARTHUR AND ELLEN...
...BUT I'M ASKING YOU NOT TO HELP DESPOINA KILL MILLIONS OF PEOPLE.
THAT'S... NOT GOING TO HAPPEN.
HOW CAN YOU BE SO SURE?
BECAUSE--
--WE AREN'T GOING TO LET IT.
SHAME. BUT I DO UNDERSTAND.
I GUESS THERE'S NOTHING TO BE DONE FOR IT, THEN.

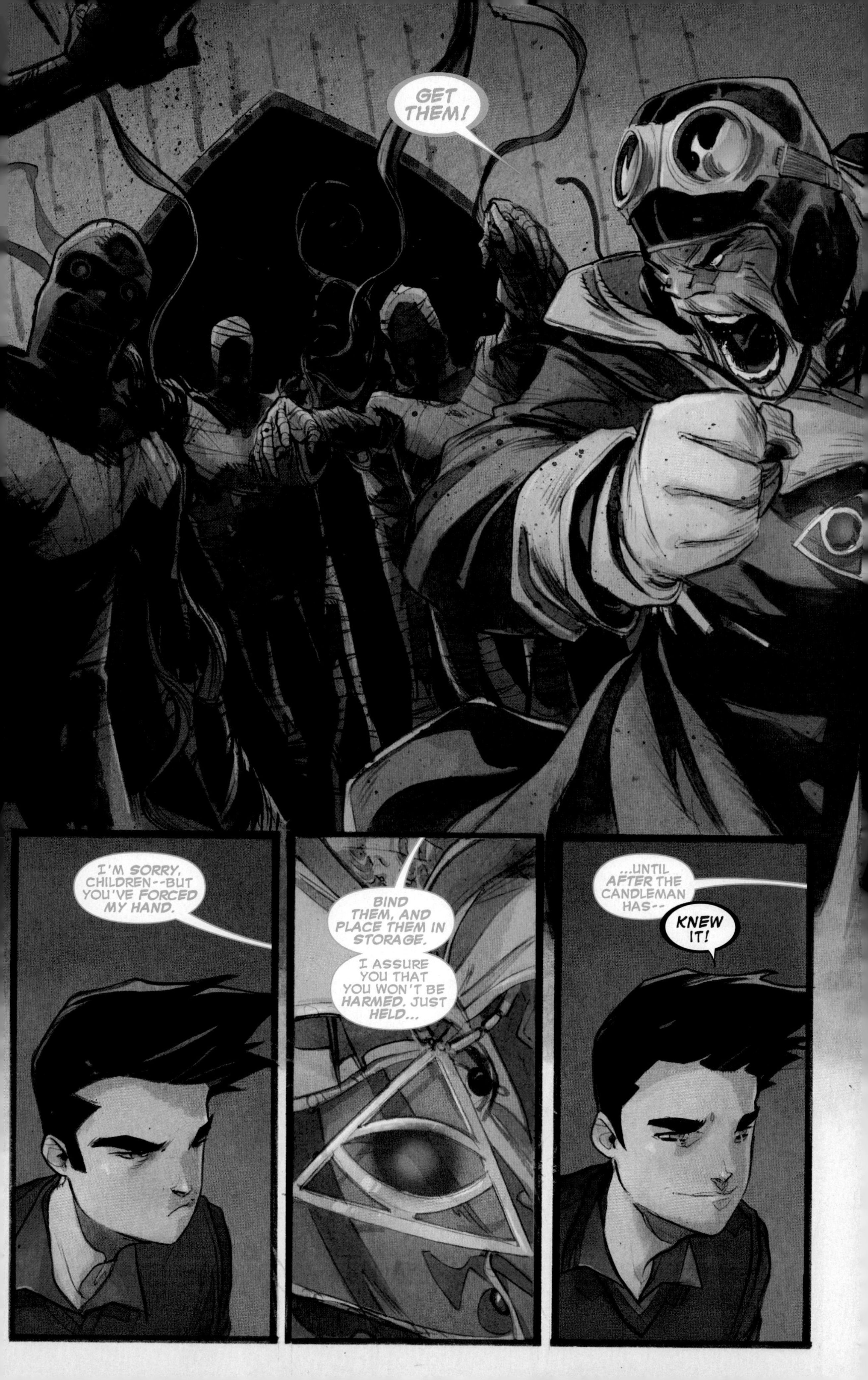
GET THEM!
I'M SORRY, CHILDREN--BUT YOU'VE FORCED MY HAND.
BIND THEM, AND PLACE THEM IN STORAGE.
I ASSURE YOU THAT YOU WON'T BE HARMED. JUST HELD...
...UNTIL AFTER THE CANDLEMAN HAS--
KNEW IT!

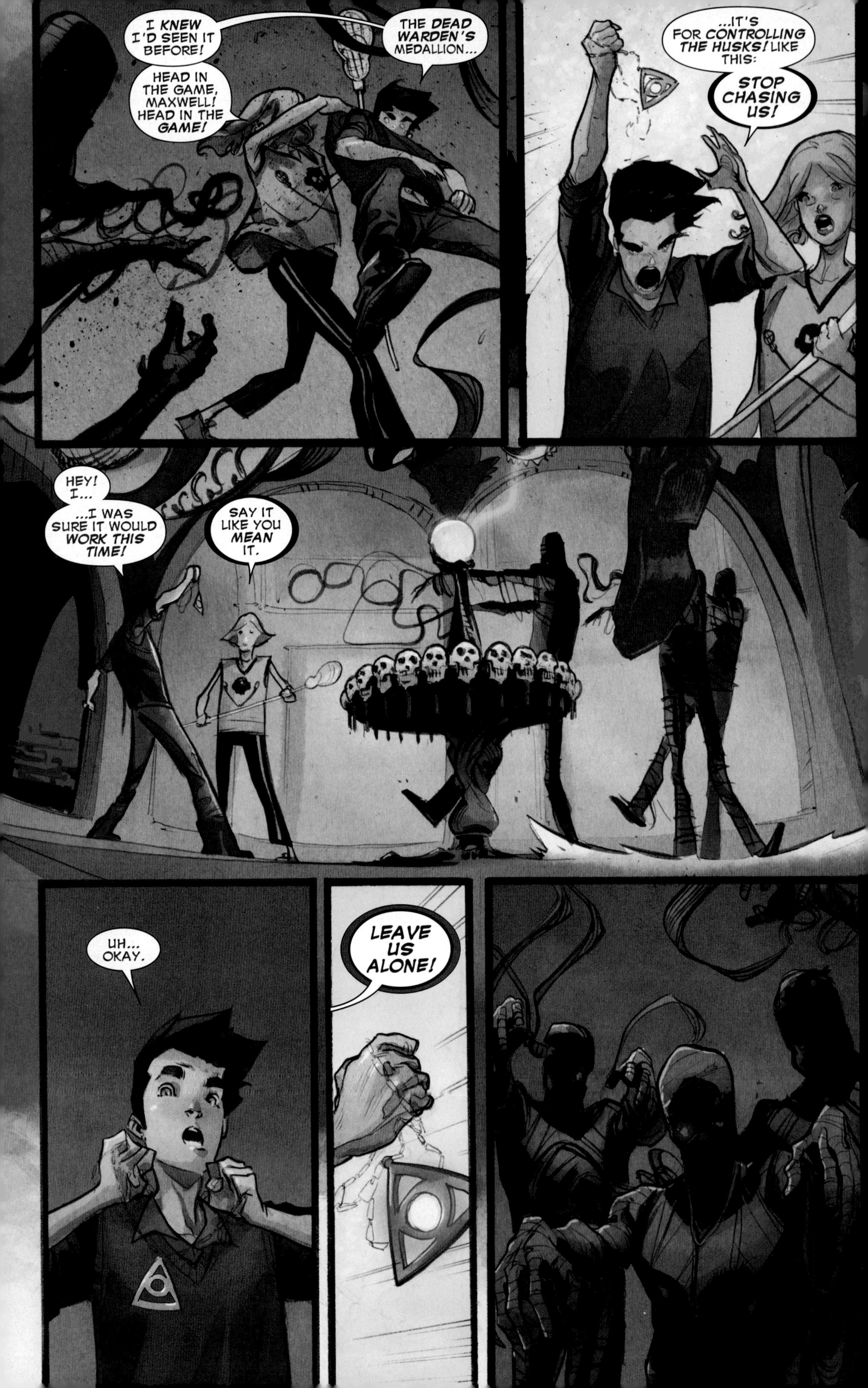
I KNEW I'D SEEN IT BEFORE!
THE DEAD WARDEN'S MEDALLION...
HEAD IN THE GAME, MAXWELL! HEAD IN THE GAME!
...IT'S FOR CONTROLLING THE HUSKS! LIKE THIS:
STOP CHASING US!
HEY! I...
...I WAS SURE IT WOULD WORK THIS TIME!
SAY IT LIKE YOU MEAN IT.
UH... OKAY.
LEAVE US ALONE!

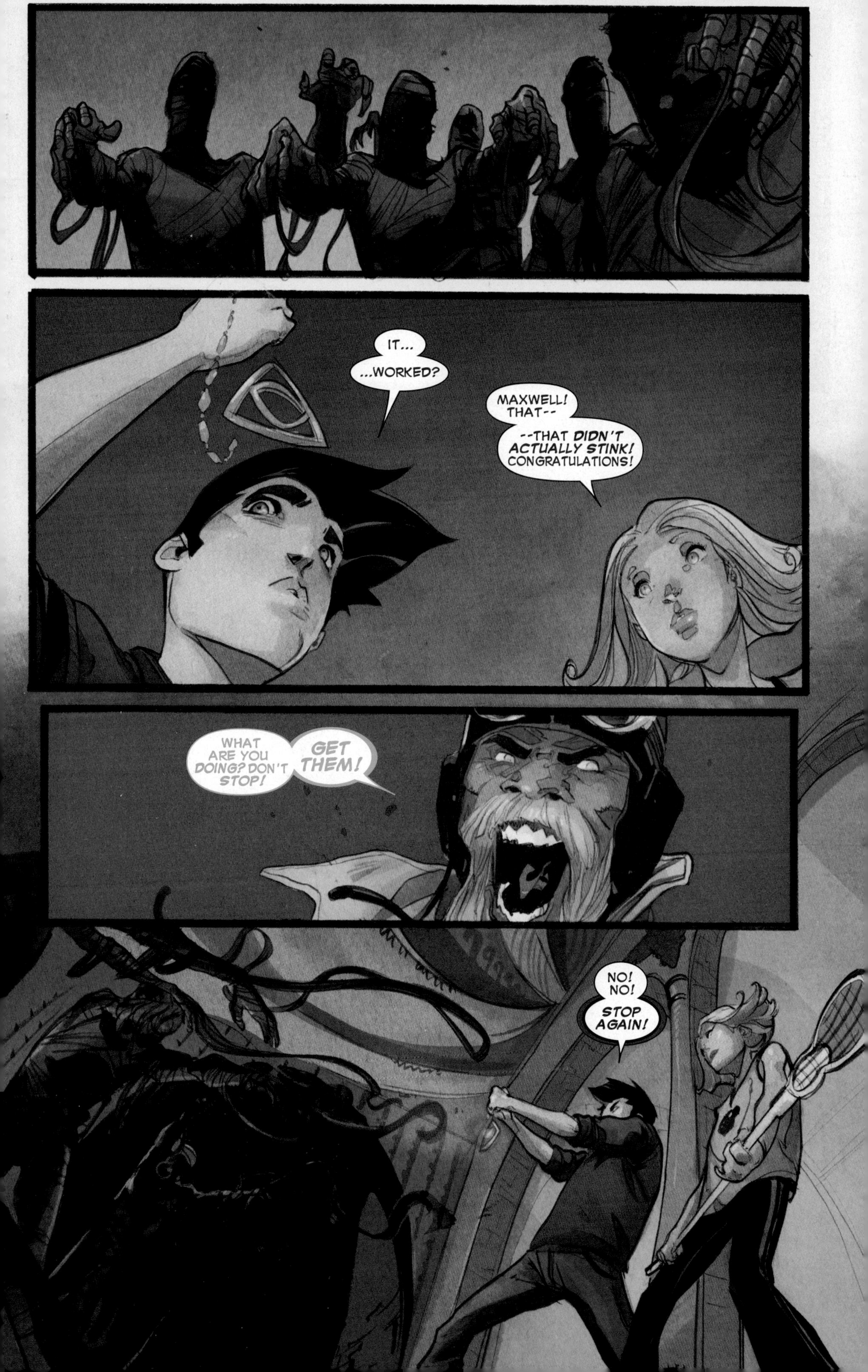
IT...
...WORKED?
MAXWELL! THAT--
--THAT DIDN'T ACTUALLY STINK! CONGRATULATIONS!
WHAT ARE YOU DOING? DON'T STOP!
GET THEM!
NO! NO!
STOP AGAIN!

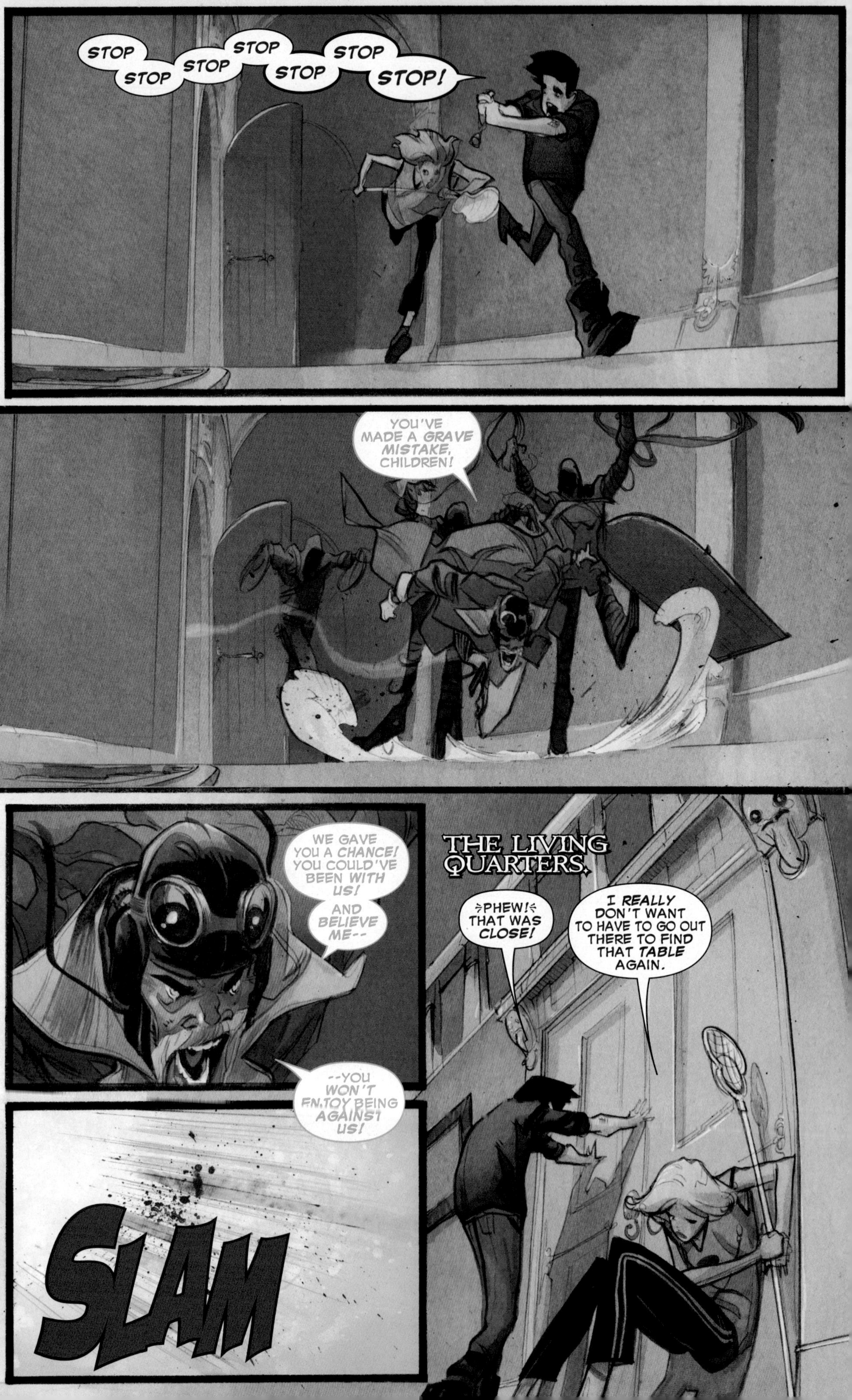
STOP
STOP
STOP
STOP
STOP
STOP
STOP!
YOU'VE MADE A GRAVE MISTAKE, CHILDREN!
WE GAVE YOU A CHANCE! YOU COULD'VE BEEN WITH US!
AND BELIEVE ME--
--YOU WON'T FN.TOY BEING AGAINST US!
SLAM
THE LIVING QUARTERS.
PHEW! THAT WAS CLOSE!
I REALLY DON'T WANT TO HAVE TO GO OUT THERE TO FIND THAT TABLE AGAIN.

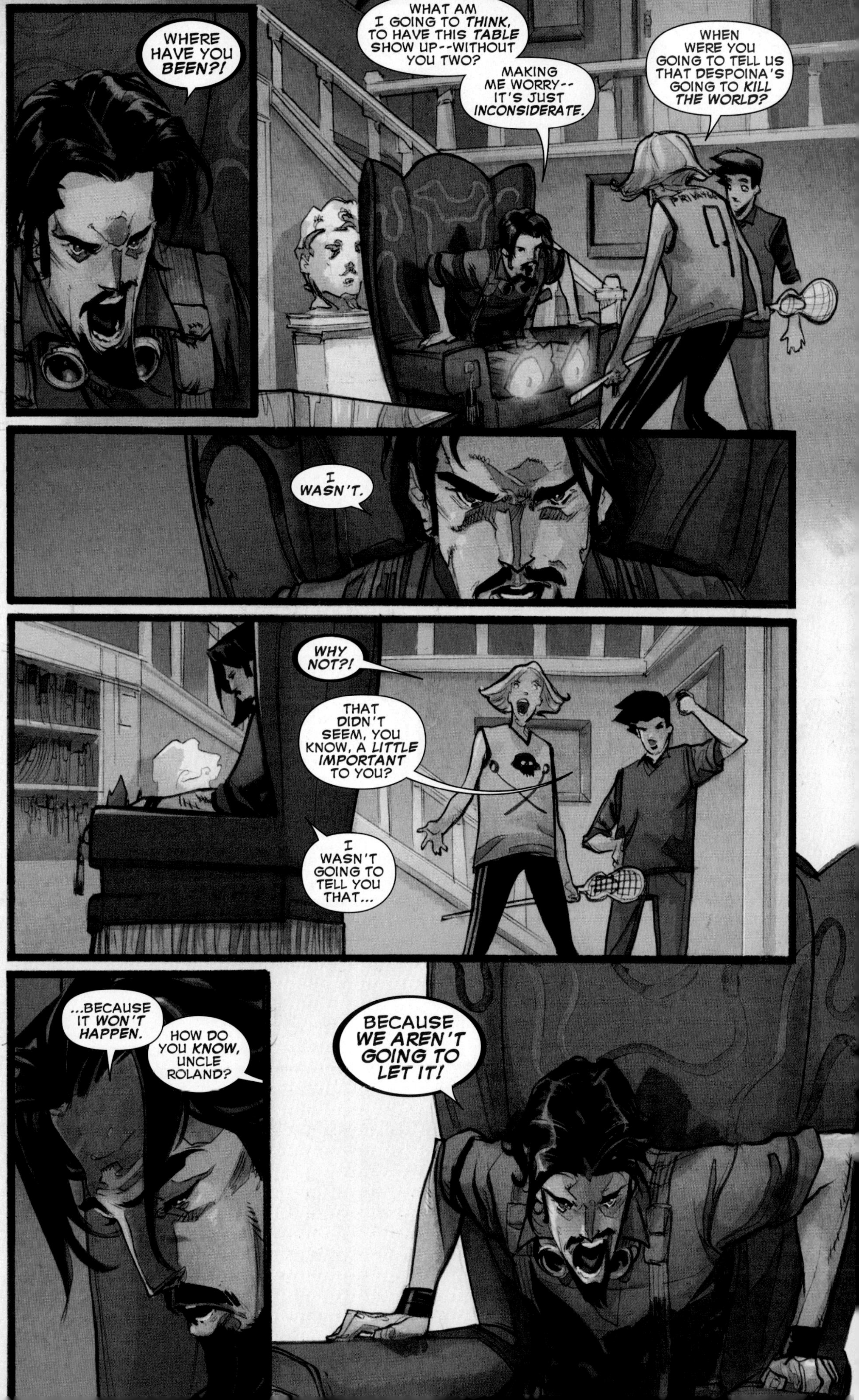
WHERE HAVE YOU BEEN?!
WHAT AM I GOING TO THINK, TO HAVE THIS TABLE SHOW UP--WITHOUT YOU TWO?
MAKING ME WORRY--IT'S JUST INCONSIDERATE.
WHEN WERE YOU GOING TO TELL US THAT DESPOINA'S GOING TO KILL THE WORLD?
I WASN'T.
WHY NOT?!
THAT DIDN'T SEEM, YOU KNOW, A LITTLE IMPORTANT TO YOU?
I WASN'T GOING TO TELL YOU THAT...
...BECAUSE IT WON'T HAPPEN.
HOW DO YOU KNOW, UNCLE ROLAND?
BECAUSE WE AREN'T GOING TO LET IT!

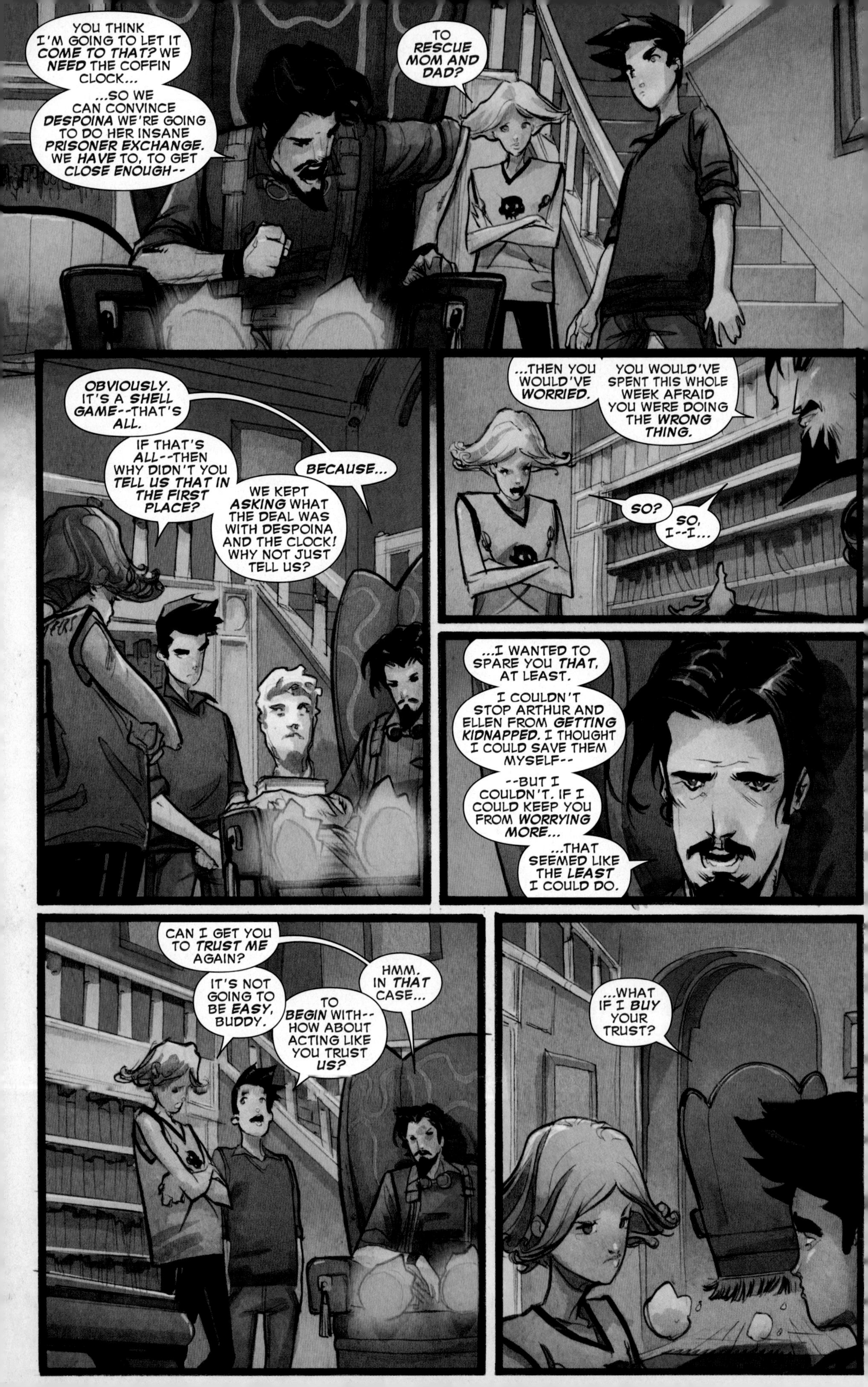
YOU THINK I'M GOING TO LET IT COME TO THAT? WE NEED THE COFFIN CLOCK...
...SO WE CAN CONVINCE DESPOINA WE'RE GOING TO DO HER INSANE PRISONER EXCHANGE. WE HAVE TO, TO GET CLOSE ENOUGH--
TO RESCUE MOM AND DAD?
OBVIOUSLY. IT'S A SHELL GAME--THAT'S ALL.
IF THAT'S ALL--THEN WHY DIDN'T YOU TELL US THAT IN THE FIRST PLACE?
WE KEPT ASKING WHAT THE DEAL WAS WITH DESPOINA AND THE CLOCK! WHY NOT JUST TELL US?
BECAUSE...
...THEN YOU WOULD'VE WORRIED.
YOU WOULD'VE SPENT THIS WHOLE WEEK AFRAID YOU WERE DOING THE WRONG THING.
SO?
SO, I--I...
...I WANTED TO SPARE YOU THAT, AT LEAST.
I COULDN'T STOP ARTHUR AND ELLEN FROM GETTING KIDNAPPED. I THOUGHT I COULD SAVE THEM MYSELF--
--BUT I COULDN'T. IF I COULD KEEP YOU FROM WORRYING MORE...
...THAT SEEMED LIKE THE LEAST I COULD DO.
CAN I GET YOU TO TRUST ME AGAIN?
IT'S NOT GOING TO BE EASY, BUDDY.
TO BEGIN WITH--HOW ABOUT ACTING LIKE YOU TRUST US?
HMM. IN THAT CASE...
...WHAT IF I BUY YOUR TRUST?

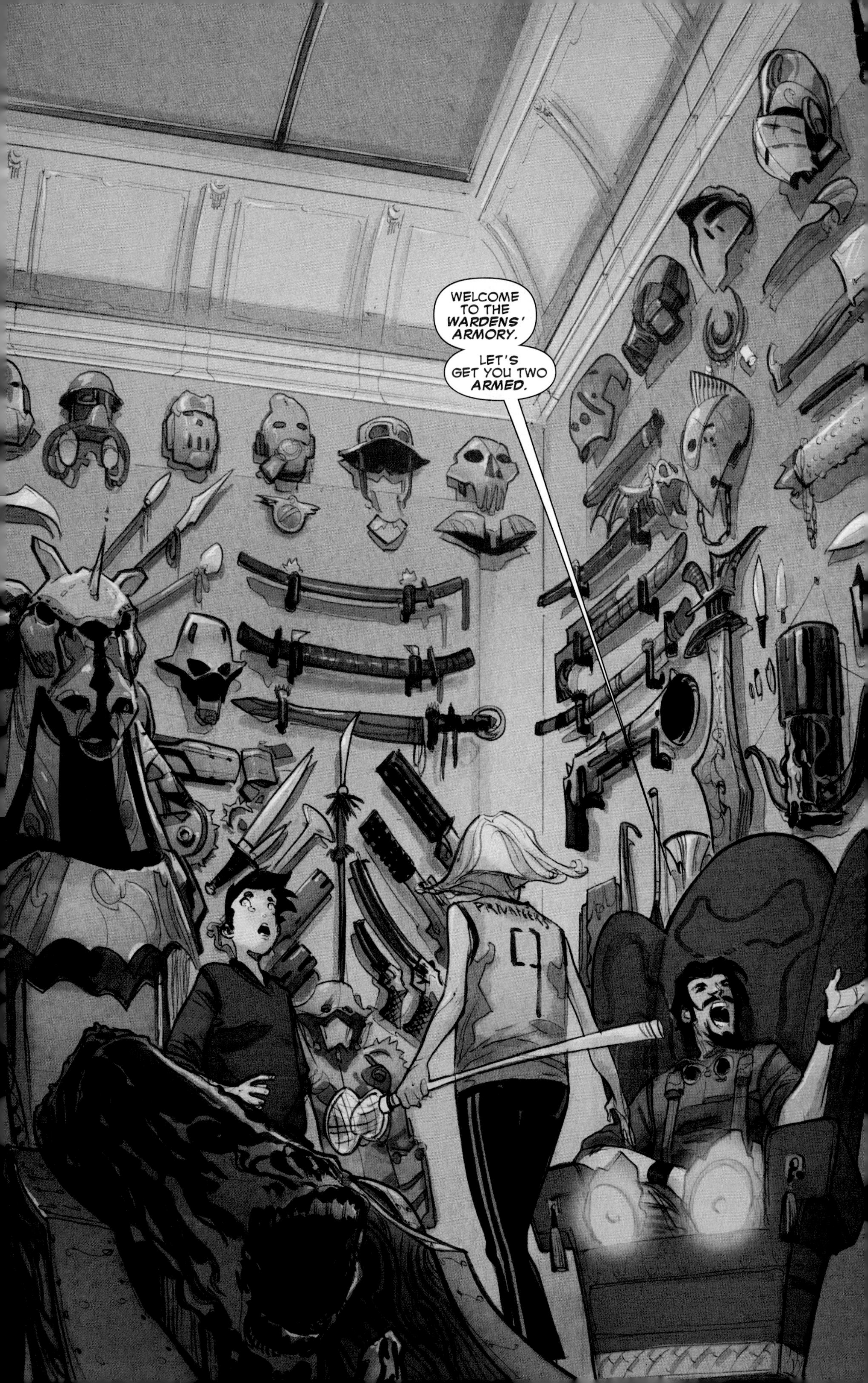
WELCOME TO THE WARDENS' ARMORY.
LET'S GET YOU TWO ARMED.
PRIVATEERS

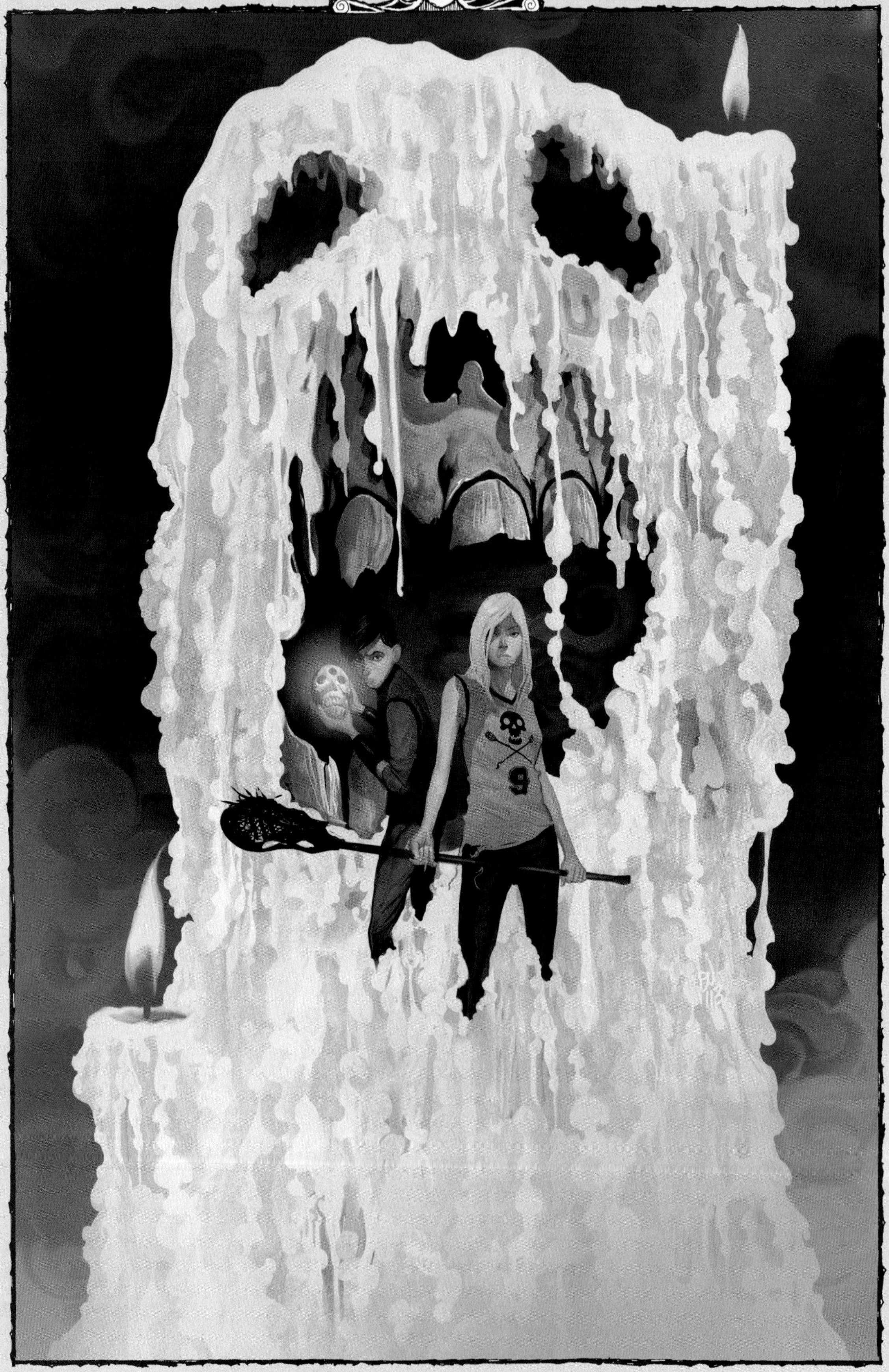

4

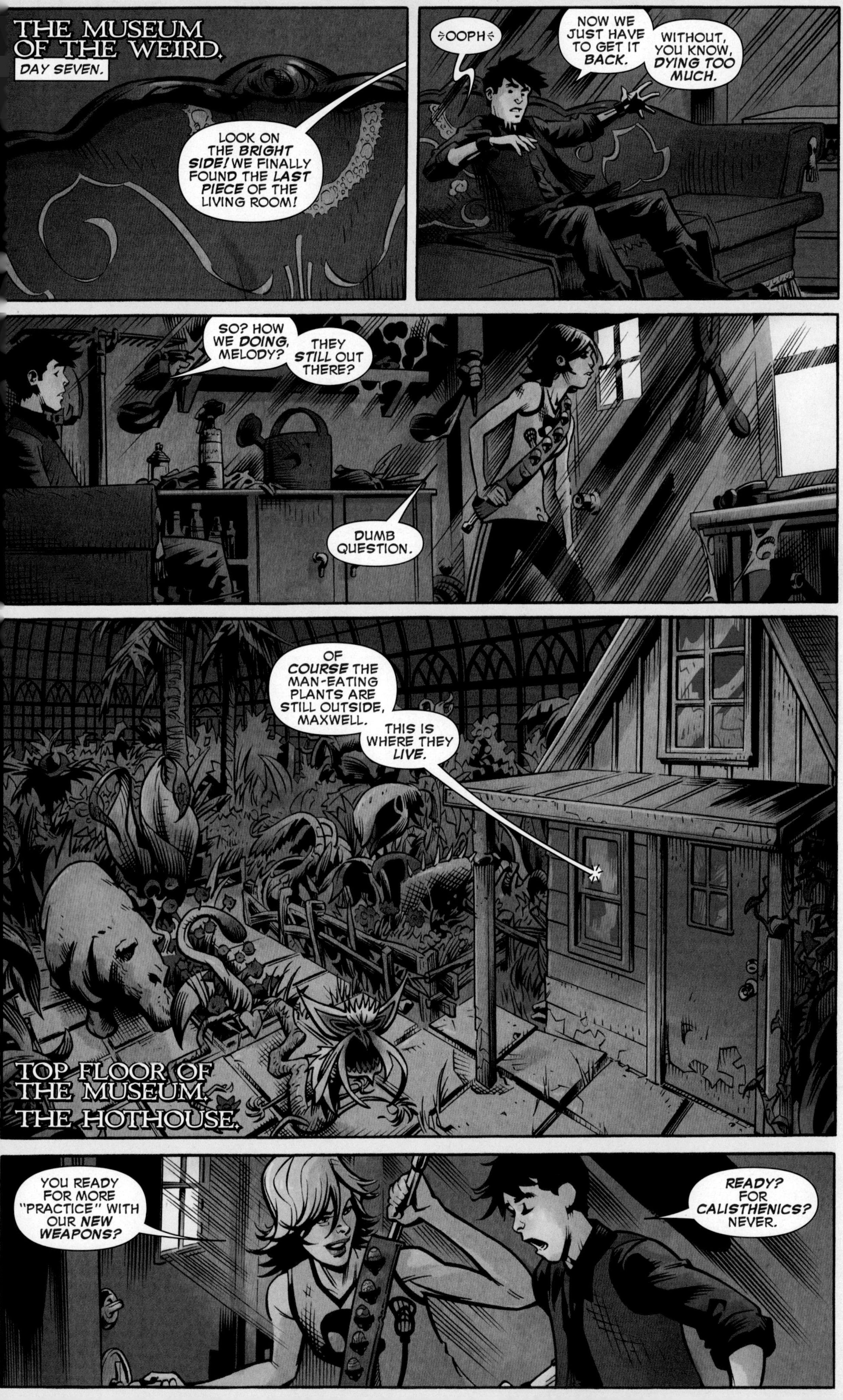
THE MUSEUM OF THE WEIRD.
DAY SEVEN.
LOOK ON THE BRIGHT SIDE! WE FINALLY FOUND THE LAST PIECE OF THE LIVING ROOM!
OOPH
NOW WE JUST HAVE TO GET IT BACK.
WITHOUT, YOU KNOW, DYING TOO MUCH.
SO? HOW WE DOING, MELODY?
THEY STILL OUT THERE?
DUMB QUESTION.
OF COURSE THE MAN-EATING PLANTS ARE STILL OUTSIDE, MAXWELL.
THIS IS WHERE THEY LIVE.
TOP FLOOR OF THE MUSEUM. THE HOTHOUSE.
YOU READY FOR MORE "PRACTICE" WITH OUR NEW WEAPONS?
READY? FOR CALISTHENICS? NEVER.

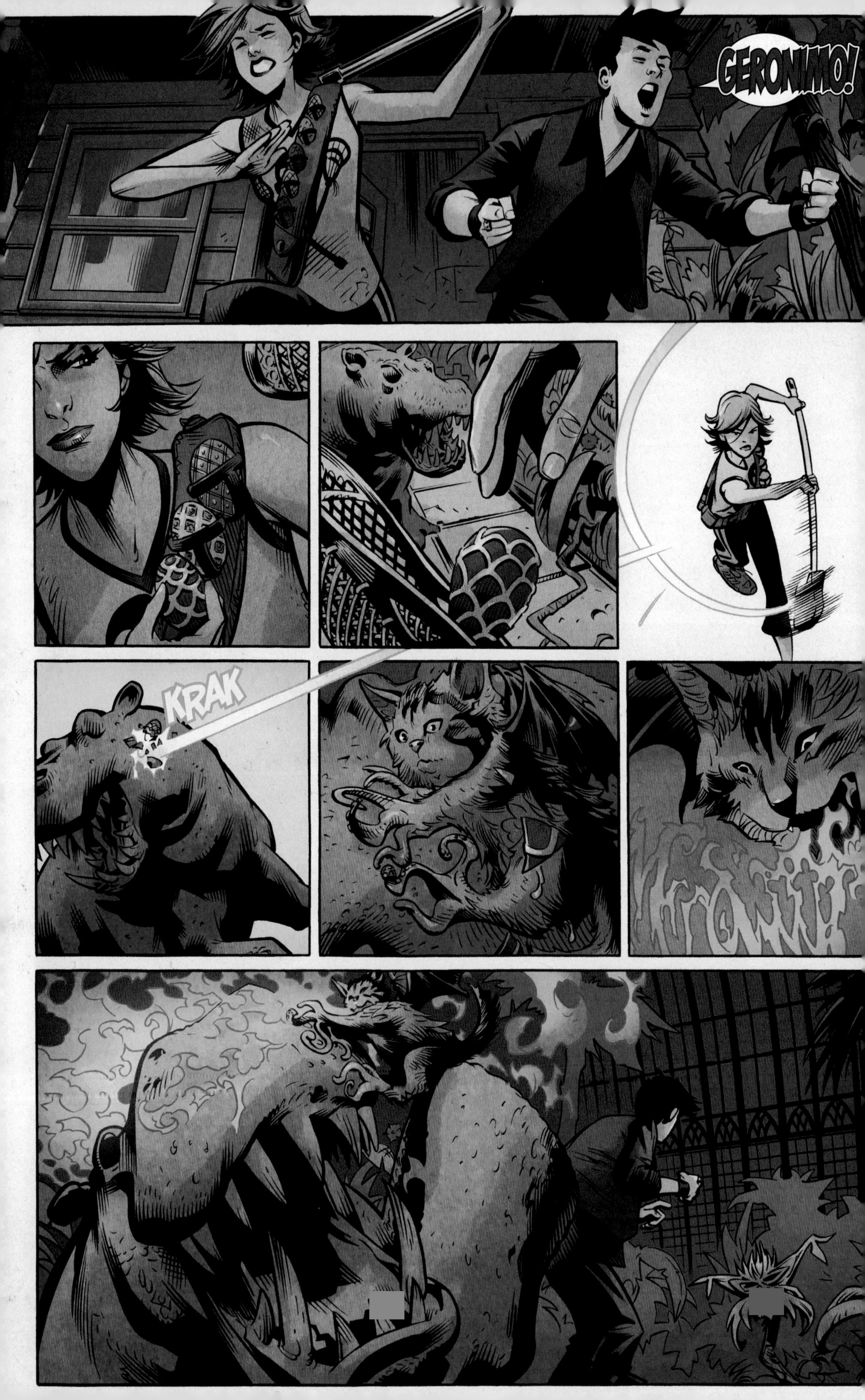

GERONIMO!
KRAK

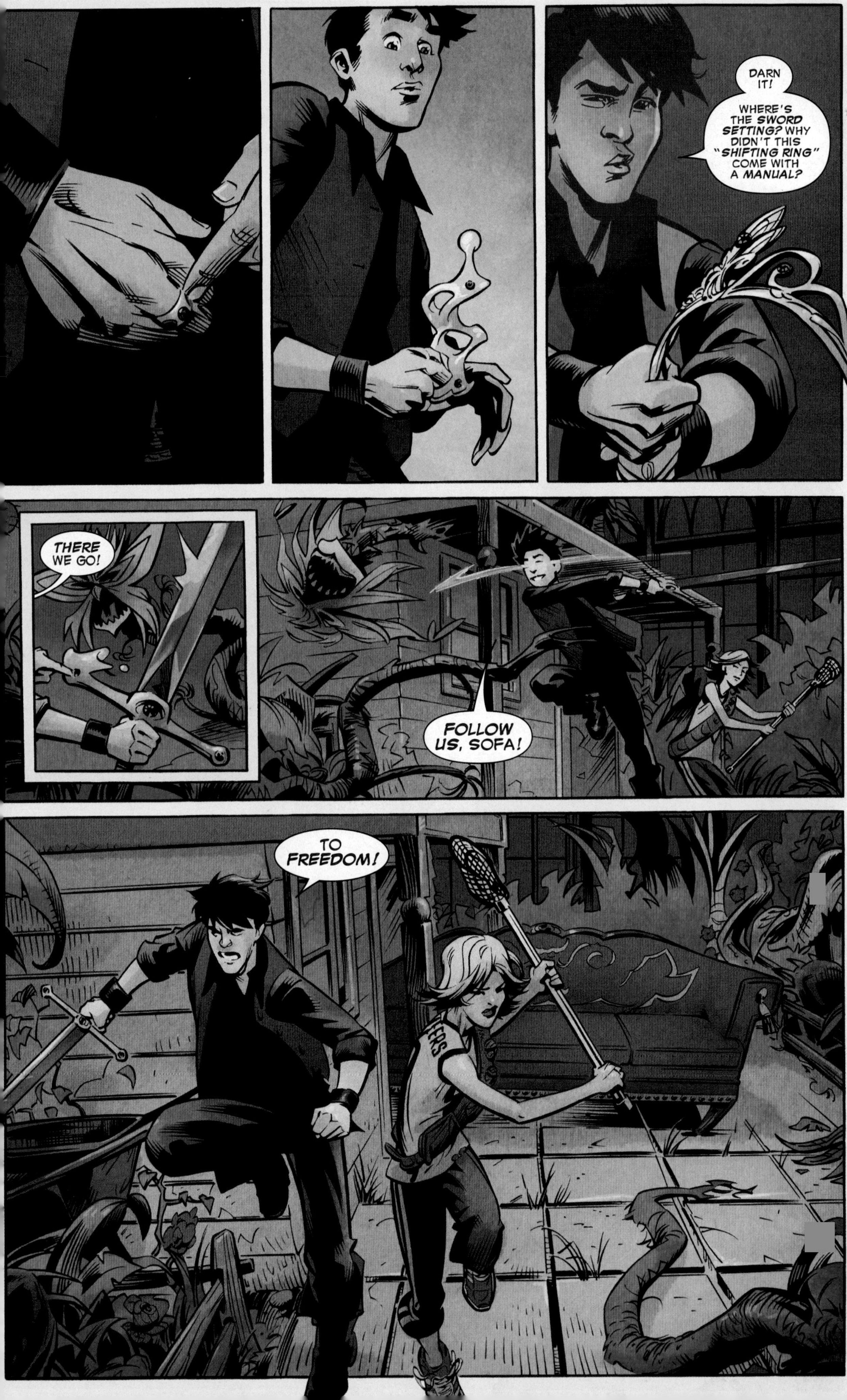
DARN IT!
WHERE'S THE SWORD SETTING? WHY DIDN'T THIS "SHIFTING RING" COME WITH A MANUAL?
THERE WE GO!
FOLLOW US, SOFA!
TO FREEDOM!

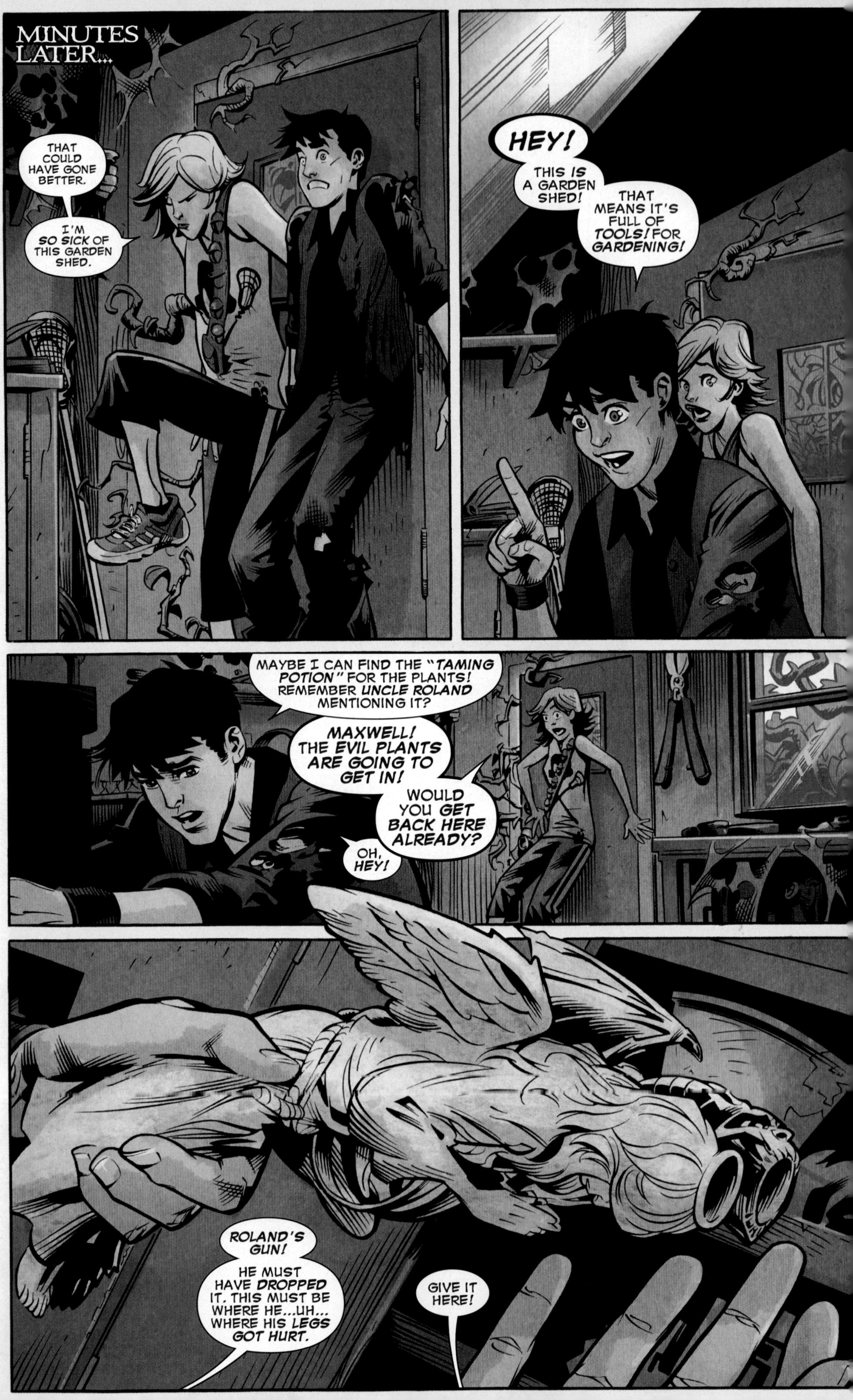

MINUTES LATER...
THAT COULD HAVE GONE BETTER.
I'M SO SICK OF THIS GARDEN SHED.
HEY!
THIS IS A GARDEN SHED!
THAT MEANS IT'S FULL OF TOOLS! FOR GARDENING!
MAYBE I CAN FIND THE "TAMING POTION" FOR THE PLANTS! REMEMBER UNCLE ROLAND MENTIONING IT?
MAXWELL! THE EVIL PLANTS ARE GOING TO GET IN!
WOULD YOU GET BACK HERE ALREADY?
OH, HEY!
ROLAND'S GUN!
HE MUST HAVE DROPPED IT. THIS MUST BE WHERE HE...UH... WHERE HIS LEGS GOT HURT.
GIVE IT HERE!

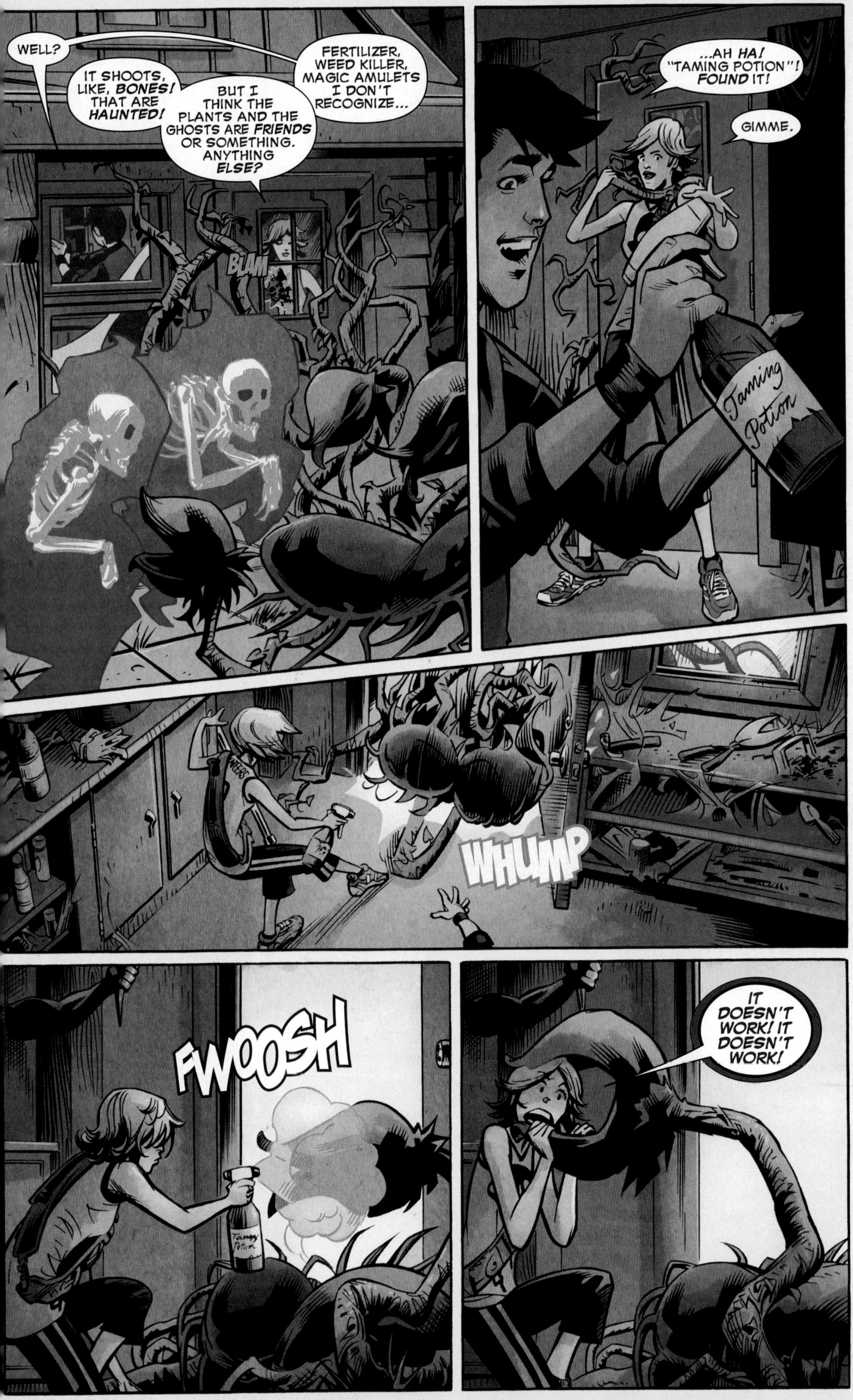
WELL?
IT SHOOTS, LIKE, BONES! THAT ARE HAUNTED!
BUT I THINK THE PLANTS AND THE GHOSTS ARE FRIENDS OR SOMETHING. ANYTHING ELSE?
FERTILIZER, WEED KILLER, MAGIC AMULETS I DON'T RECOGNIZE...
BLAM
...AH HA! "TAMING POTION"! FOUND IT!
GIMME.
Taming Potion
WHUMP
FWOOSH
IT DOESN'T WORK! IT DOESN'T WORK!

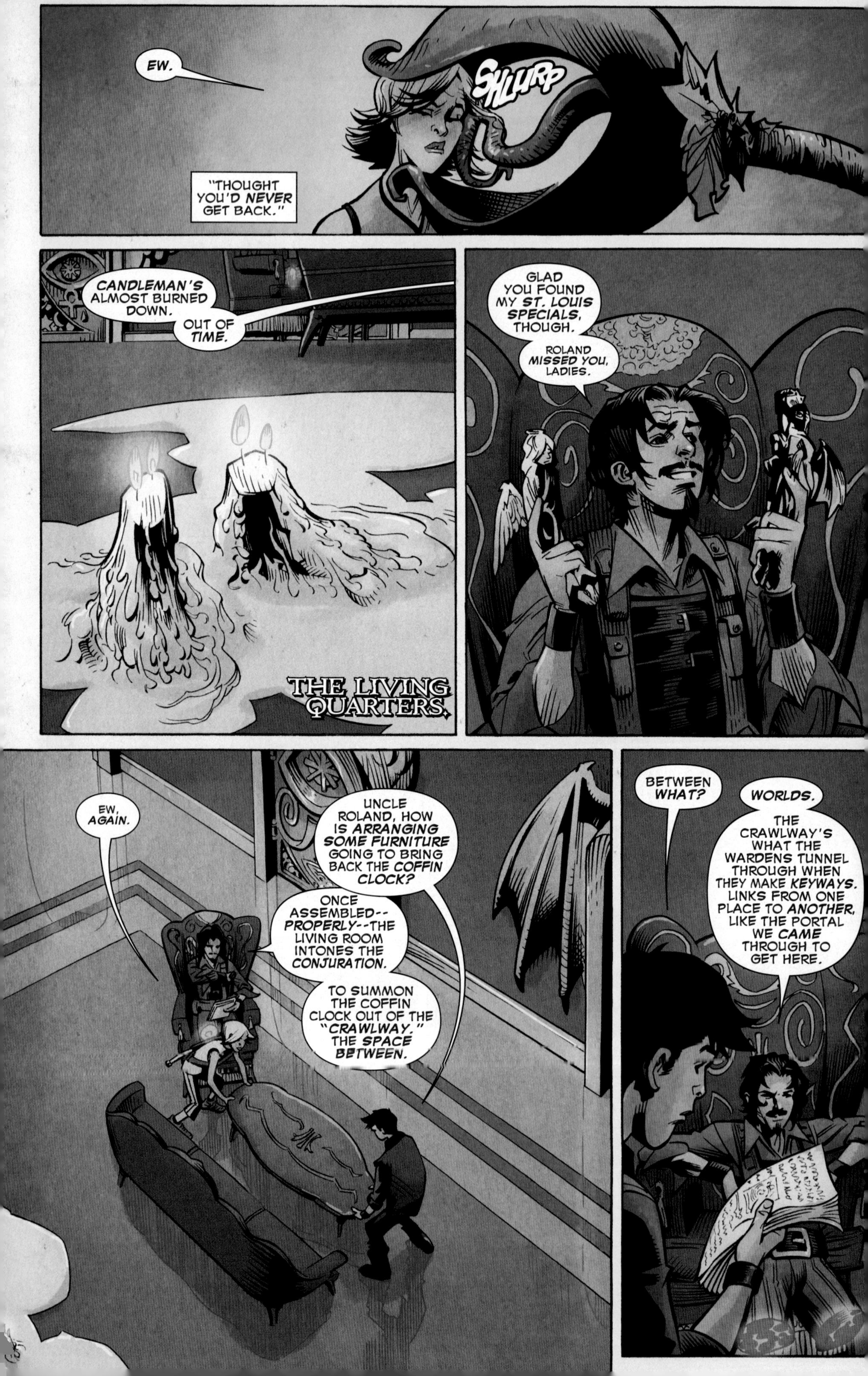
EW.
SHLURP
"THOUGHT YOU'D NEVER GET BACK."
CANDLEMAN'S ALMOST BURNED DOWN.
OUT OF TIME.
THE LIVING QUARTERS.
GLAD YOU FOUND MY ST. LOUIS SPECIALS, THOUGH.
ROLAND MISSED YOU, LADIES.
EW, AGAIN.
UNCLE ROLAND, HOW IS ARRANGING SOME FURNITURE GOING TO BRING BACK THE COFFIN CLOCK?
ONCE ASSEMBLED--PROPERLY--THE LIVING ROOM INTONES THE CONJURATION.
TO SUMMON THE COFFIN CLOCK OUT OF THE "CRAWLWAY." THE SPACE BETWEEN.
BETWEEN WHAT?
WORLDS.
THE CRAWLWAY'S WHAT THE WARDENS TUNNEL THROUGH WHEN THEY MAKE KEYWAYS. LINKS FROM ONE PLACE TO ANOTHER, LIKE THE PORTAL WE CAME THROUGH TO GET HERE.

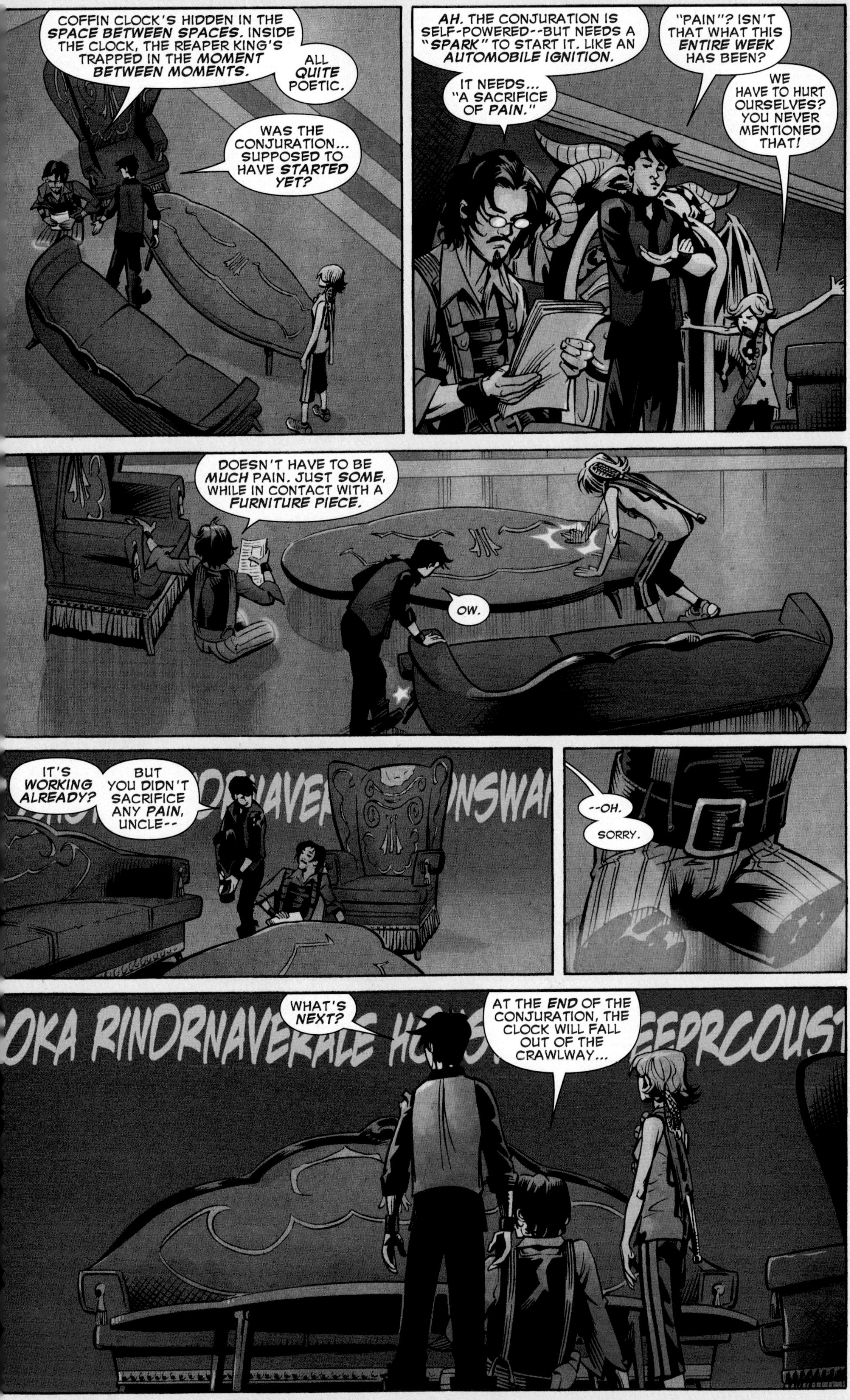
COFFIN CLOCK'S HIDDEN IN THE SPACE BETWEEN SPACES. INSIDE THE CLOCK, THE REAPER KING'S TRAPPED IN THE MOMENT BETWEEN MOMENTS.
ALL QUITE POETIC.
WAS THE CONJURATION... SUPPOSED TO HAVE STARTED YET?
AH. THE CONJURATION IS SELF-POWERED--BUT NEEDS A "SPARK" TO START IT. LIKE AN AUTOMOBILE IGNITION.
IT NEEDS... "A SACRIFICE OF PAIN."
"PAIN"? ISN'T THAT WHAT THIS ENTIRE WEEK HAS BEEN?
WE HAVE TO HURT OURSELVES? YOU NEVER MENTIONED THAT!
DOESN'T HAVE TO BE MUCH PAIN. JUST SOME, WHILE IN CONTACT WITH A FURNITURE PIECE.
OW.
IT'S WORKING ALREADY?
BUT YOU DIDN'T SACRIFICE ANY PAIN, UNCLE--
--OH.
SORRY.
WHAT'S NEXT?
AT THE END OF THE CONJURATION, THE CLOCK WILL FALL OUT OF THE CRAWLWAY...

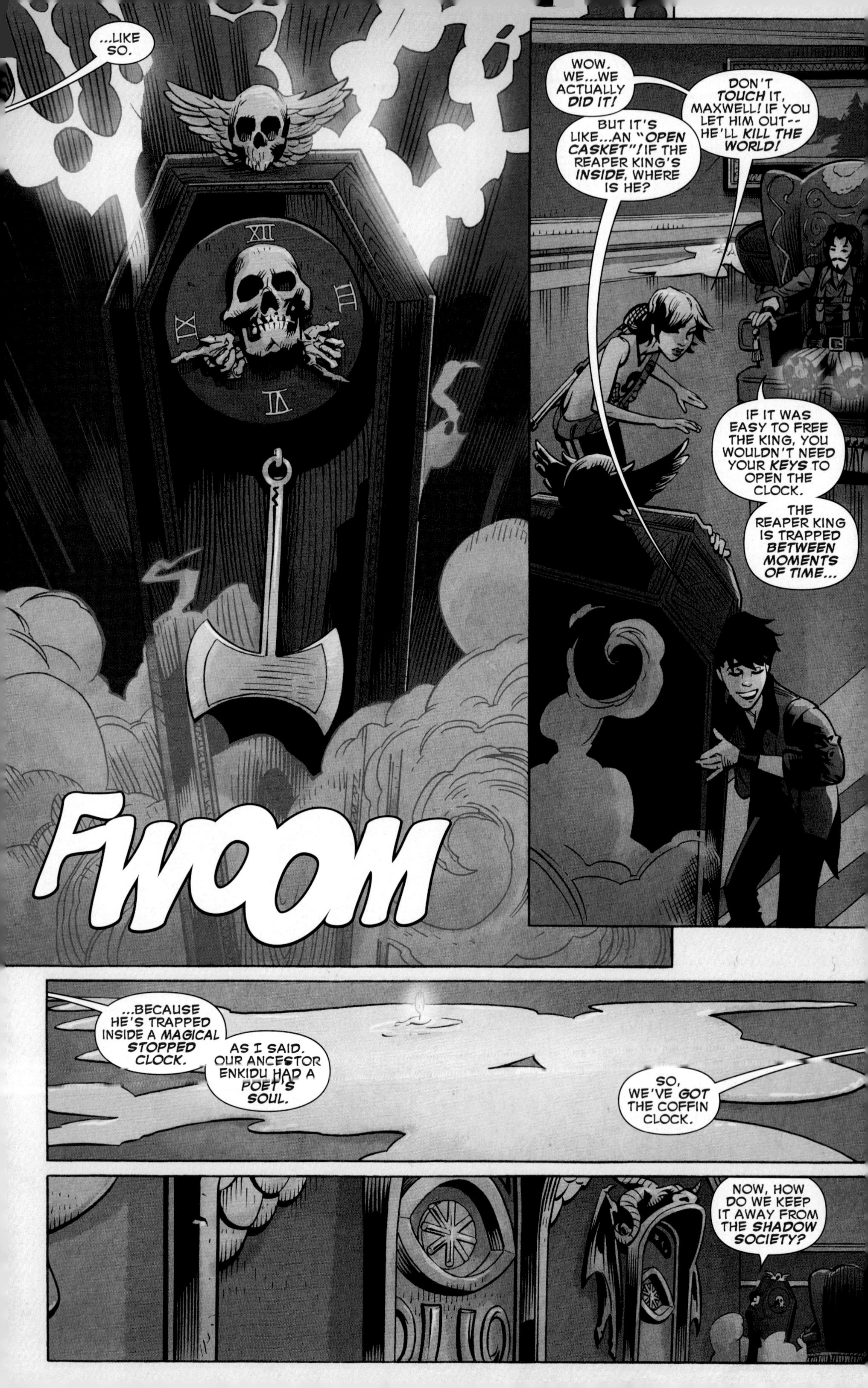
...LIKE SO.
WOW. WE...WE ACTUALLY DID IT!
BUT IT'S LIKE...AN "OPEN CASKET"! IF THE REAPER KING'S INSIDE, WHERE IS HE?
DON'T TOUCH IT, MAXWELL! IF YOU LET HIM OUT-- HE'LL KILL THE WORLD!
IF IT WAS EASY TO FREE THE KING, YOU WOULDN'T NEED YOUR KEYS TO OPEN THE CLOCK.
THE REAPER KING IS TRAPPED BETWEEN MOMENTS OF TIME...
FWOOM
...BECAUSE HE'S TRAPPED INSIDE A MAGICAL STOPPED CLOCK.
AS I SAID. OUR ANCESTOR ENKIDU HAD A POET'S SOUL.
SO, WE'VE GOT THE COFFIN CLOCK.
NOW, HOW DO WE KEEP IT AWAY FROM THE SHADOW SOCIETY?

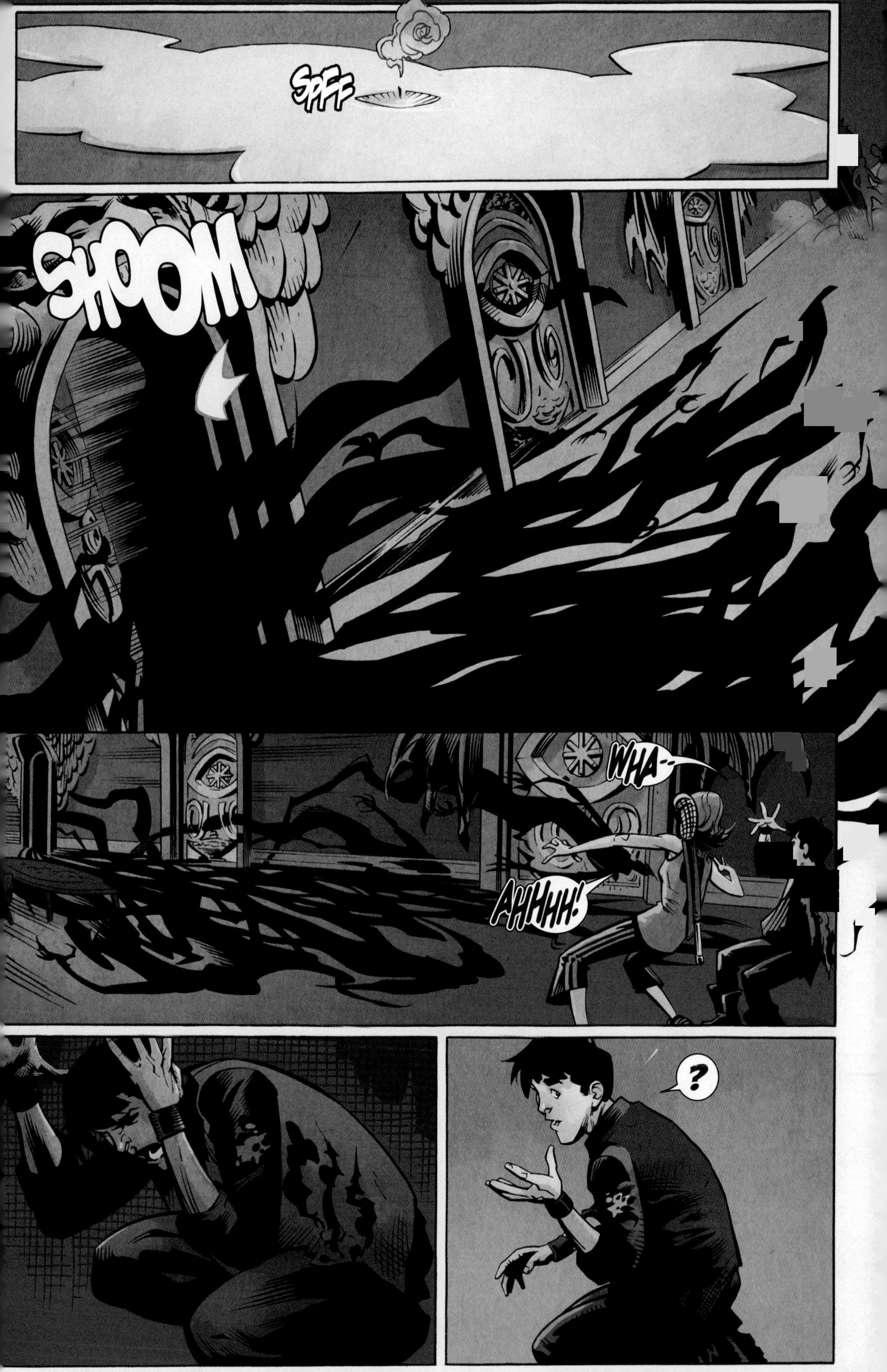
SPFF
SHOOM
WHA--
AHHHH!
?

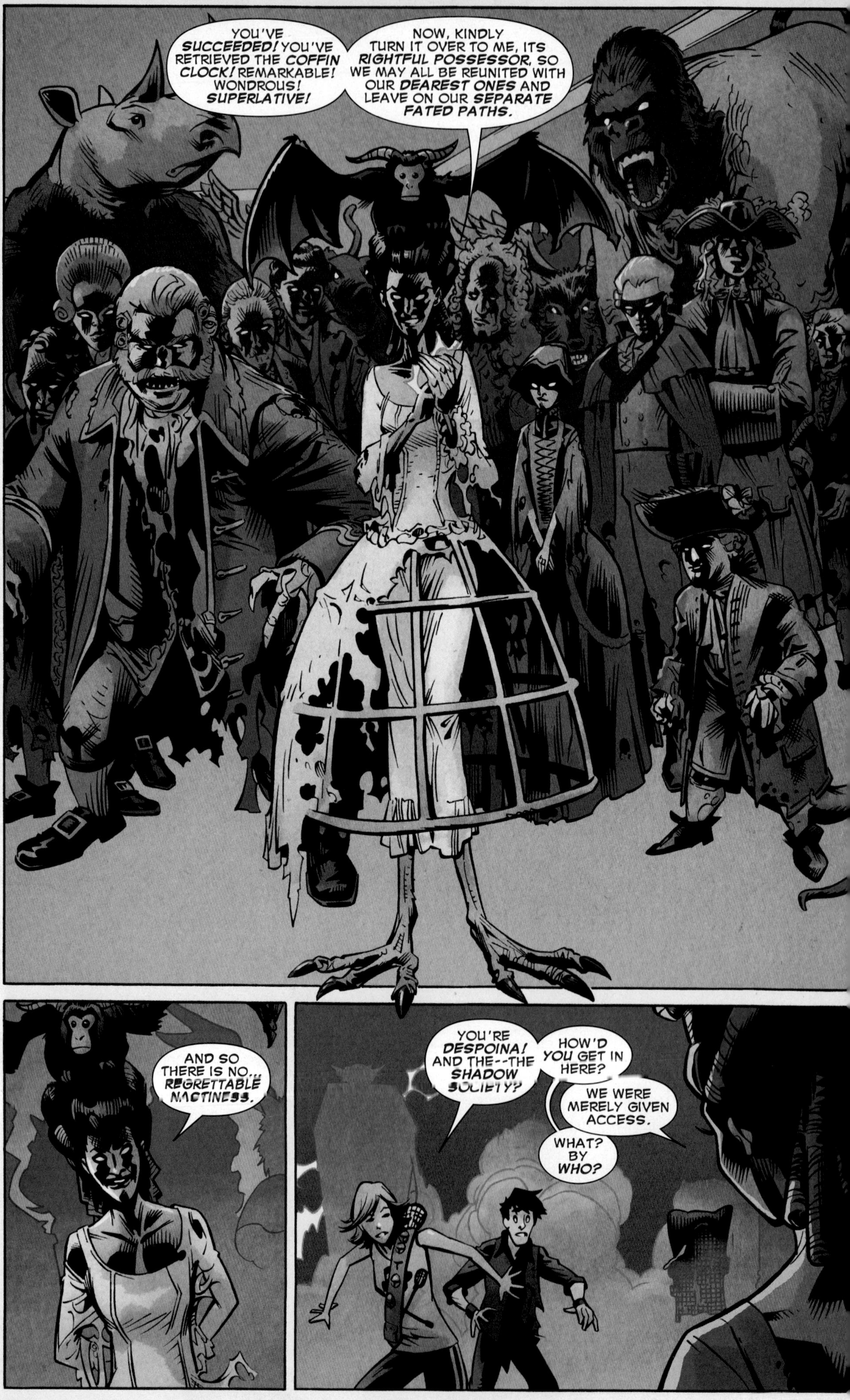
YOU'VE SUCCEEDED! YOU'VE RETRIEVED THE COFFIN CLOCK! REMARKABLE! WONDROUS! SUPERLATIVE!
NOW, KINDLY TURN IT OVER TO ME, ITS RIGHTFUL POSSESSOR, SO WE MAY ALL BE REUNITED WITH OUR DEAREST ONES AND LEAVE ON OUR SEPARATE FATED PATHS.
AND SO THERE IS NO... REGRETTABLE NASTINESS.
YOU'RE DESPOINA! AND THE--THE SHADOW SOCIETY?
HOW'D YOU GET IN HERE?
WE WERE MERELY GIVEN ACCESS.
WHAT? BY WHO?

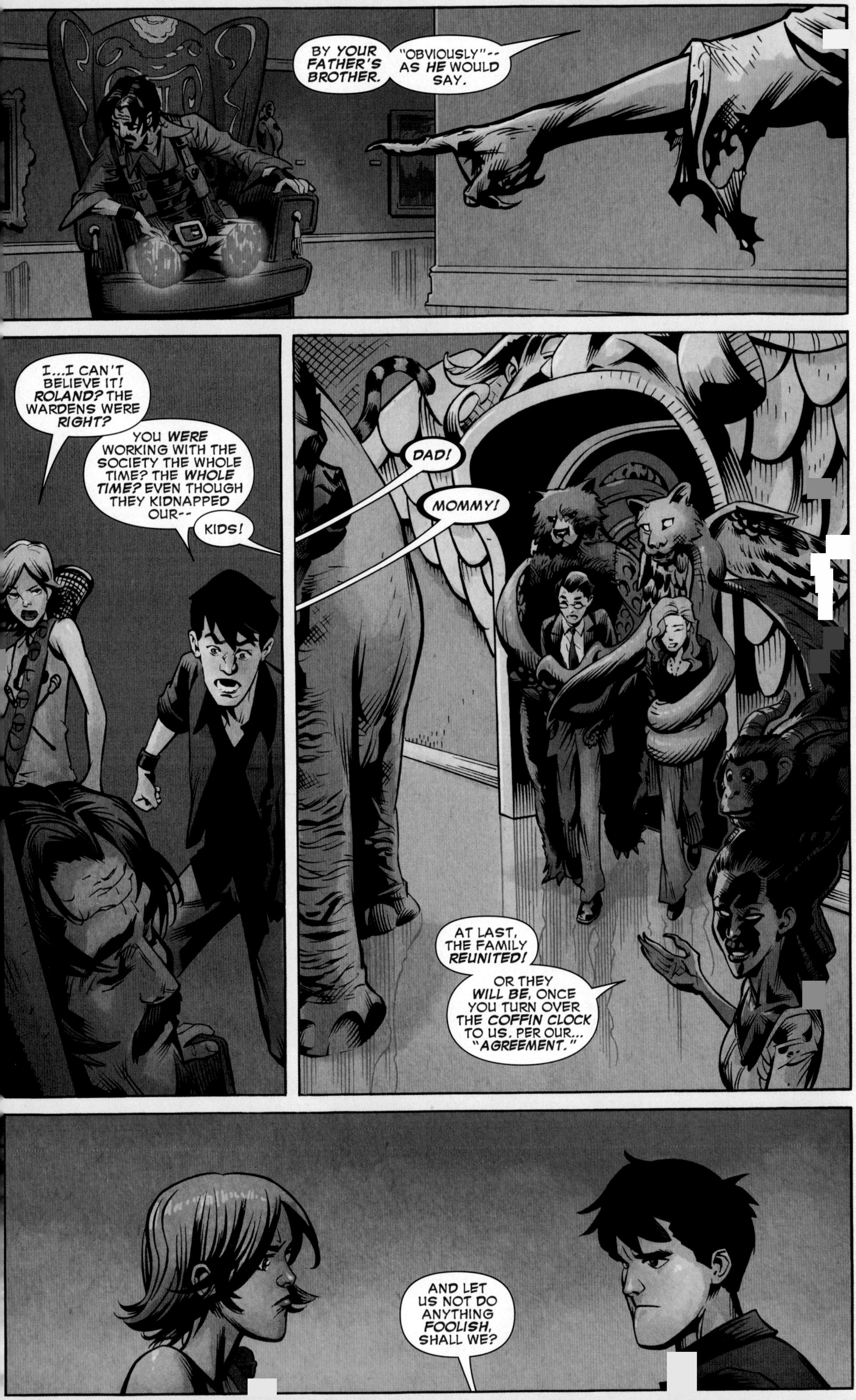
BY YOUR FATHER'S BROTHER.
"OBVIOUSLY"-- AS HE WOULD SAY.
I...I CAN'T BELIEVE IT! ROLAND? THE WARDENS WERE RIGHT?
YOU WERE WORKING WITH THE SOCIETY THE WHOLE TIME? THE WHOLE TIME? EVEN THOUGH THEY KIDNAPPED OUR--
KIDS!
DAD!
MOMMY!
AT LAST, THE FAMILY REUNITED!
OR THEY WILL BE, ONCE YOU TURN OVER THE COFFIN CLOCK TO US. PER OUR... "AGREEMENT."
AND LET US NOT DO ANYTHING FOOLISH, SHALL WE?

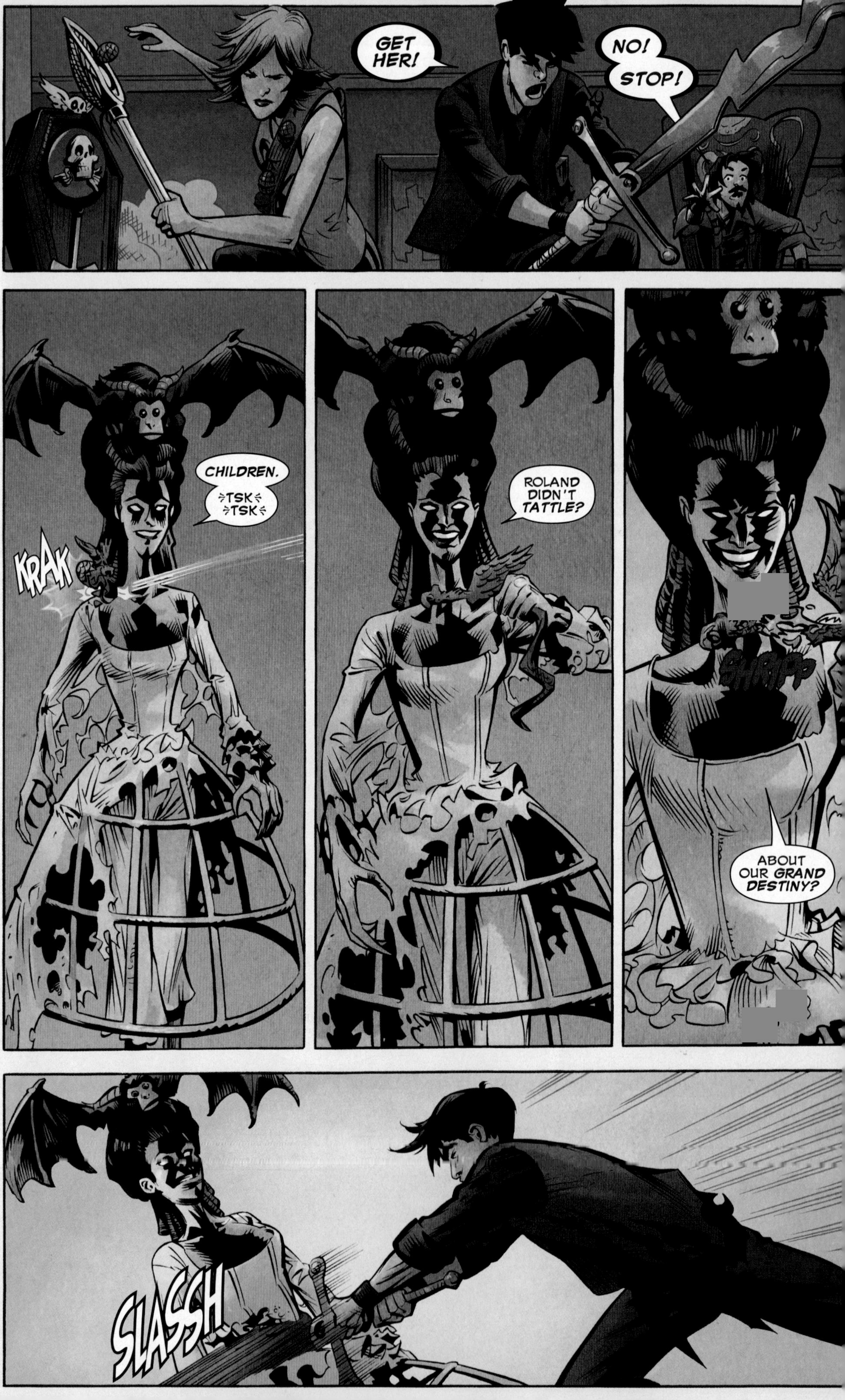
GET HER!
NO! STOP!
CHILDREN. ⁂TSK ⁂TSK
KRAK
ROLAND DIDN'T TATTLE?
SHRIPP
ABOUT OUR GRAND DESTINY?
SLASSH

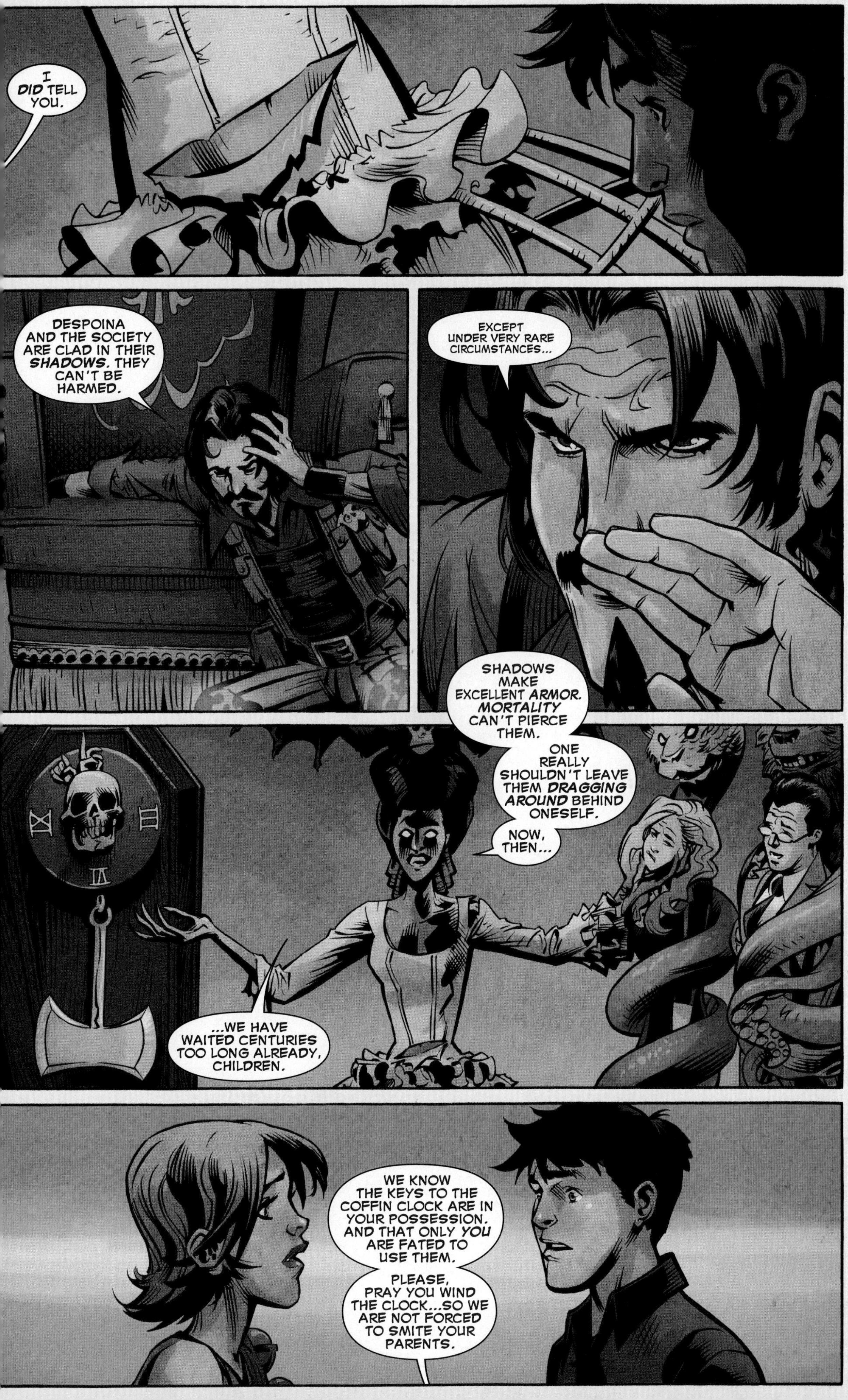
I DID TELL YOU.
DESPOINA AND THE SOCIETY ARE CLAD IN THEIR SHADOWS. THEY CAN'T BE HARMED.
EXCEPT UNDER VERY RARE CIRCUMSTANCES...
SHADOWS MAKE EXCELLENT ARMOR. MORTALITY CAN'T PIERCE THEM.
ONE REALLY SHOULDN'T LEAVE THEM DRAGGING AROUND BEHIND ONESELF.
NOW, THEN...
...WE HAVE WAITED CENTURIES TOO LONG ALREADY, CHILDREN.
WE KNOW THE KEYS TO THE COFFIN CLOCK ARE IN YOUR POSSESSION. AND THAT ONLY YOU ARE FATED TO USE THEM.
PLEASE, PRAY YOU WIND THE CLOCK...SO WE ARE NOT FORCED TO SMITE YOUR PARENTS.

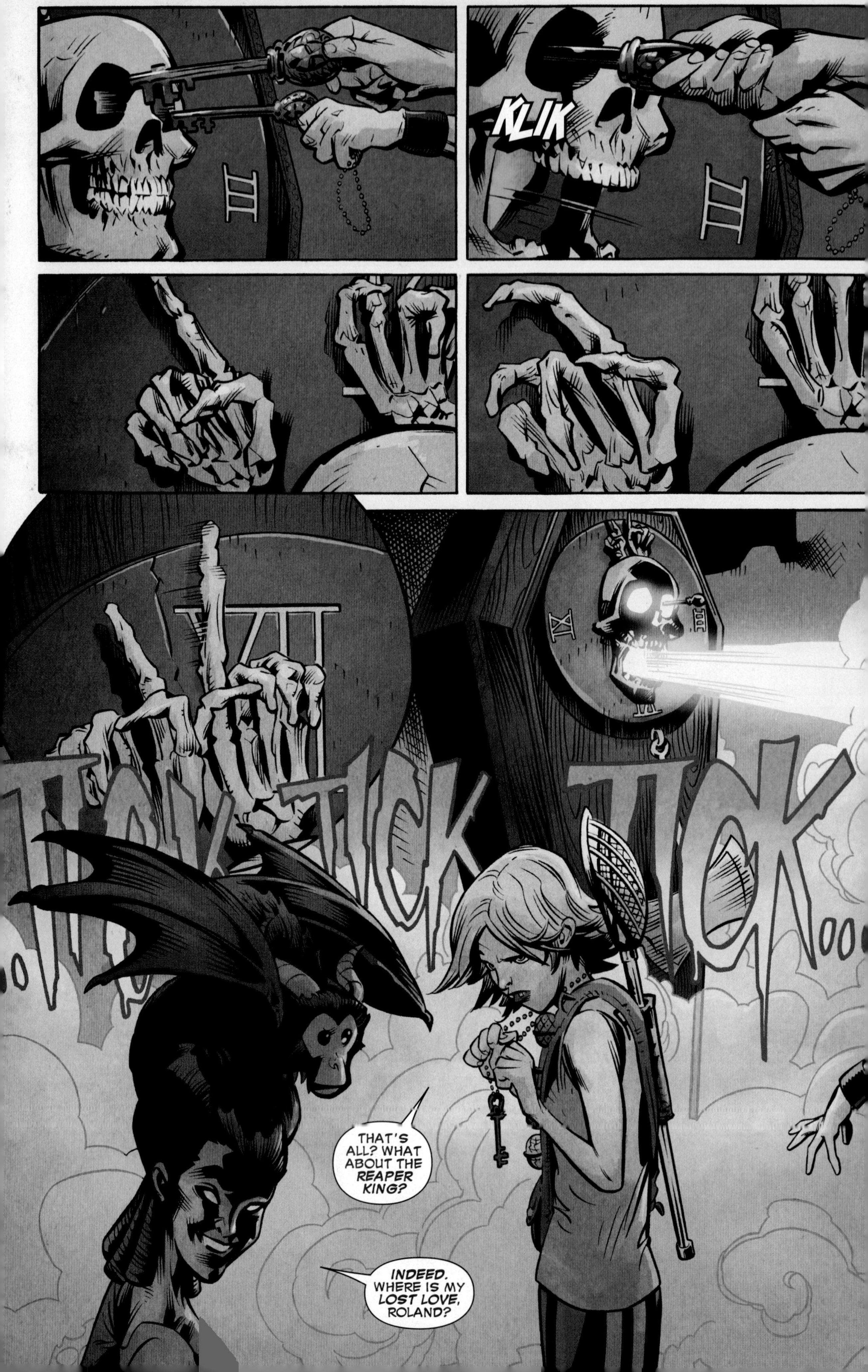
KLIK
...TICK... TICK... TICK...
THAT'S ALL? WHAT ABOUT THE *REAPER KING*?
INDEED. WHERE IS MY *LOST LOVE,* ROLAND?

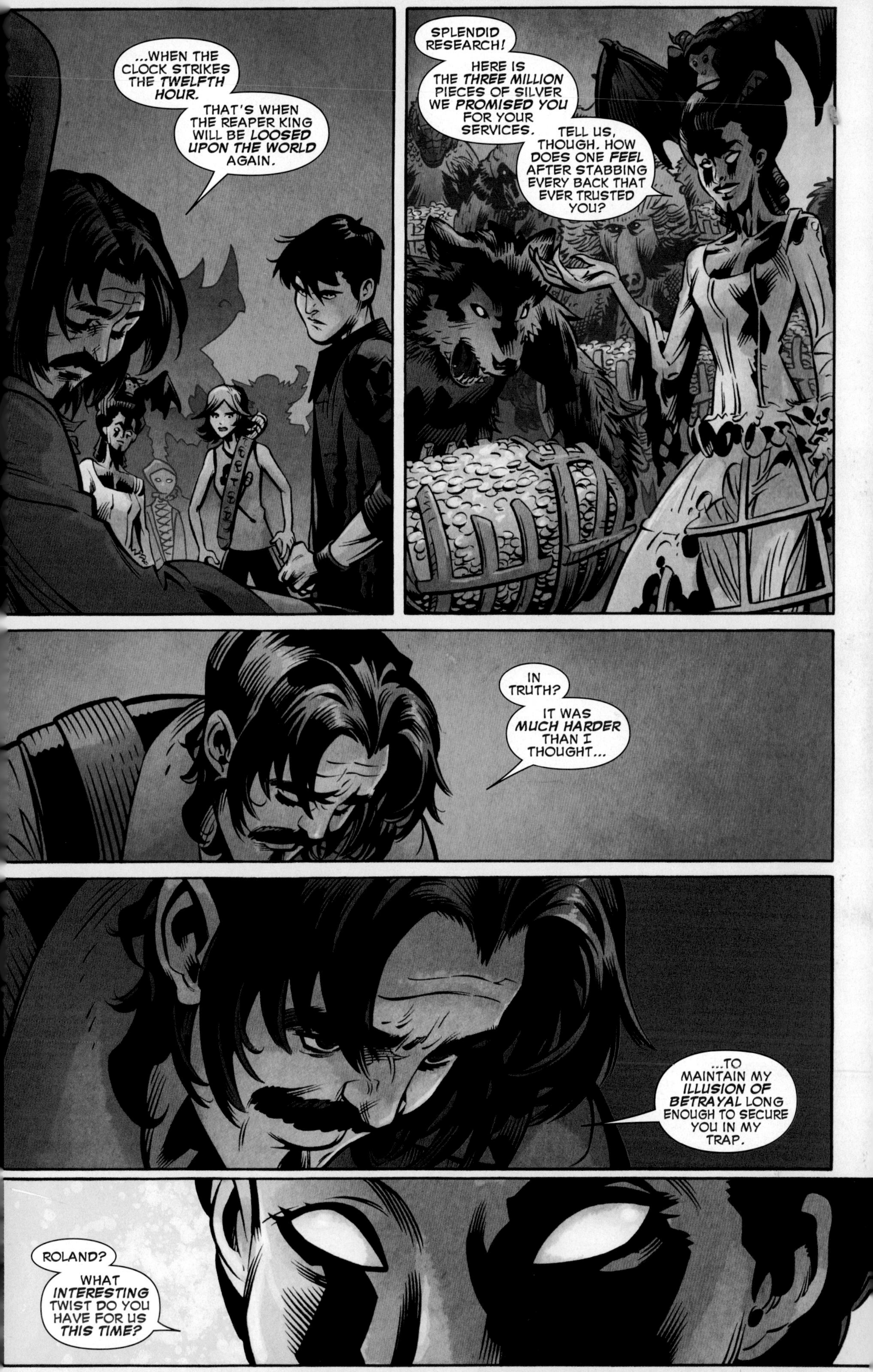
...WHEN THE CLOCK STRIKES THE TWELFTH HOUR.
THAT'S WHEN THE REAPER KING WILL BE LOOSED UPON THE WORLD AGAIN.
SPLENDID RESEARCH!
HERE IS THE THREE MILLION PIECES OF SILVER WE PROMISED YOU FOR YOUR SERVICES.
TELL US, THOUGH. HOW DOES ONE FEEL AFTER STABBING EVERY BACK THAT EVER TRUSTED YOU?
IN TRUTH?
IT WAS MUCH HARDER THAN I THOUGHT...
...TO MAINTAIN MY ILLUSION OF BETRAYAL LONG ENOUGH TO SECURE YOU IN MY TRAP.
ROLAND?
WHAT INTERESTING TWIST DO YOU HAVE FOR US THIS TIME?

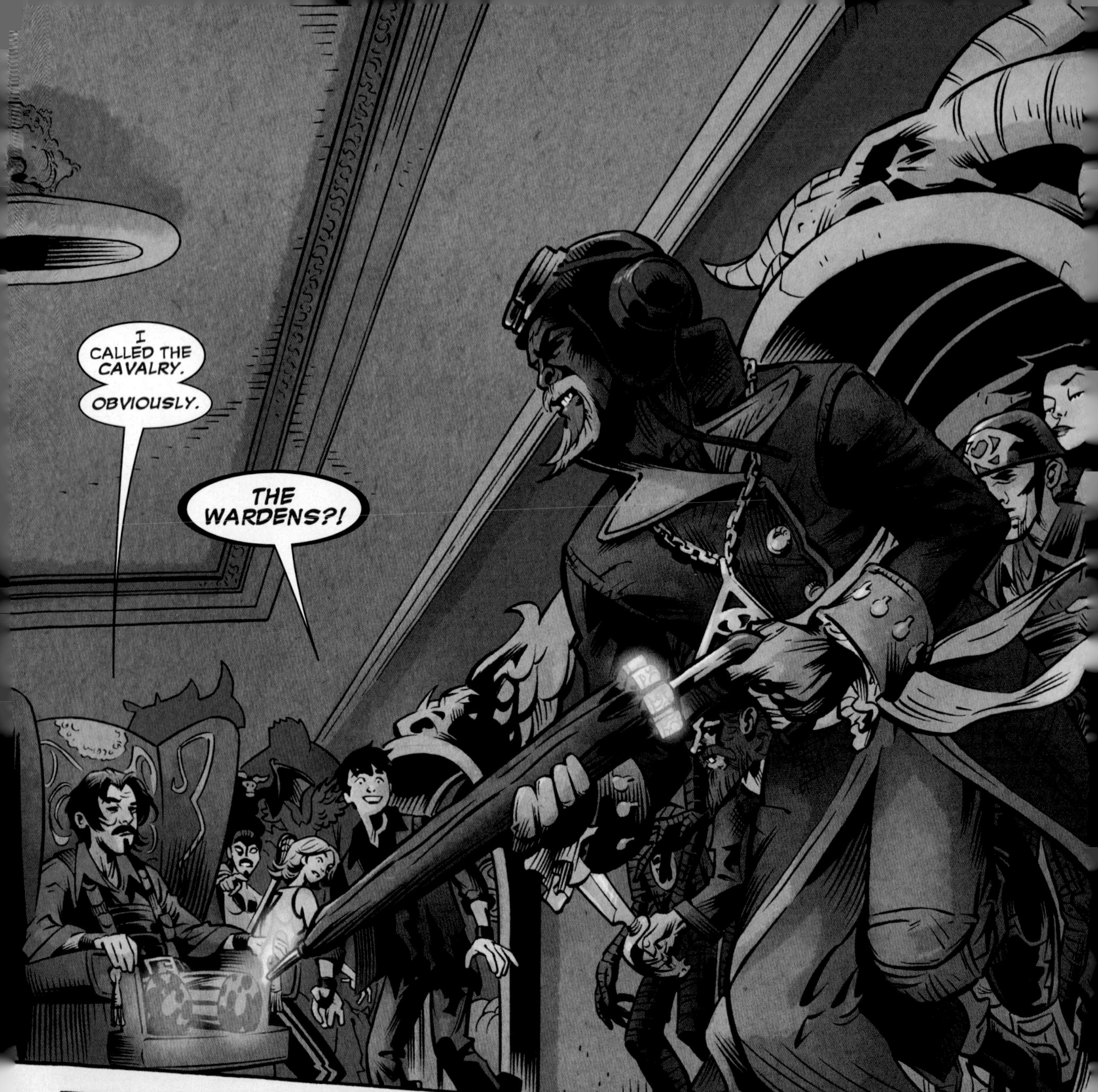

I CALLED THE CAVALRY.
OBVIOUSLY.
THE WARDENS?!

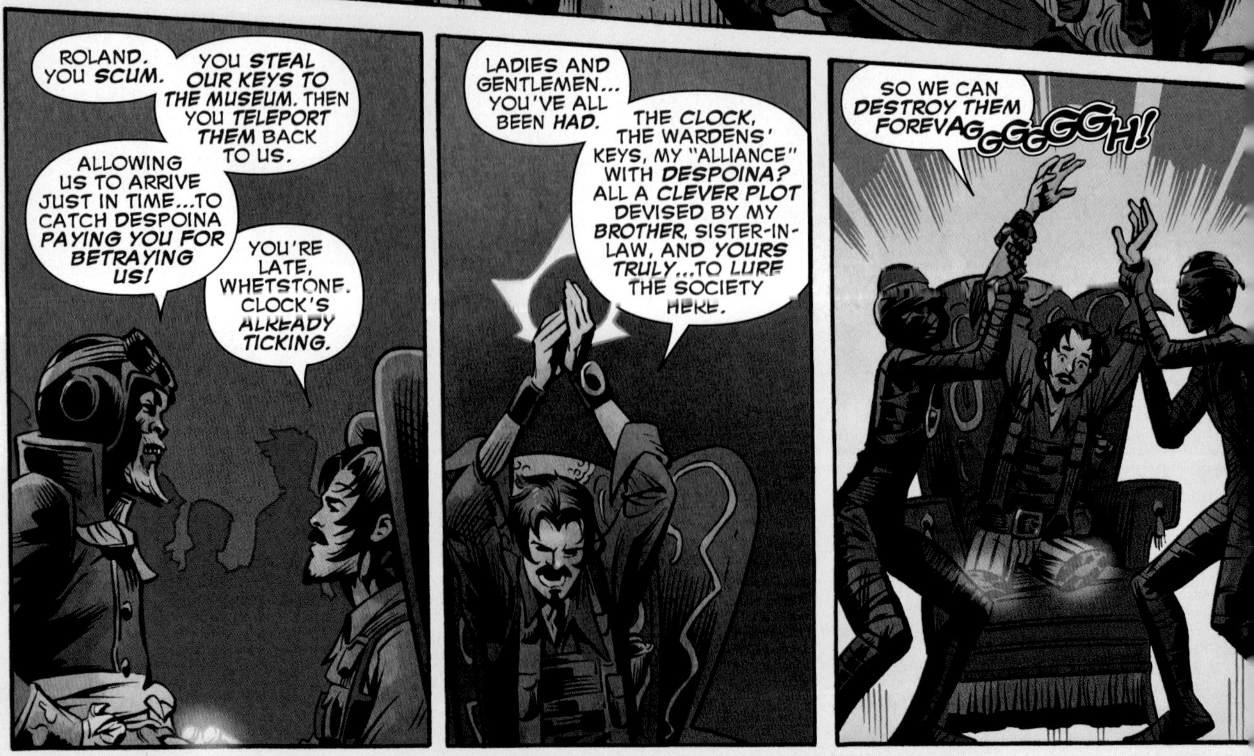

ROLAND. YOU SCUM.
YOU STEAL OUR KEYS TO THE MUSEUM. THEN YOU TELEPORT THEM BACK TO US.
ALLOWING US TO ARRIVE JUST IN TIME...TO CATCH DESPOINA PAYING YOU FOR BETRAYING US!
YOU'RE LATE, WHETSTONE. CLOCK'S ALREADY TICKING.
LADIES AND GENTLEMEN... YOU'VE ALL BEEN HAD.
THE CLOCK, THE WARDENS' KEYS, MY "ALLIANCE" WITH DESPOINA? ALL A CLEVER PLOT DEVISED BY MY BROTHER, SISTER-IN-LAW, AND YOURS TRULY...TO LURE THE SOCIETY HERE.
SO WE CAN DESTROY THEM FOREVAGGGGGGH!

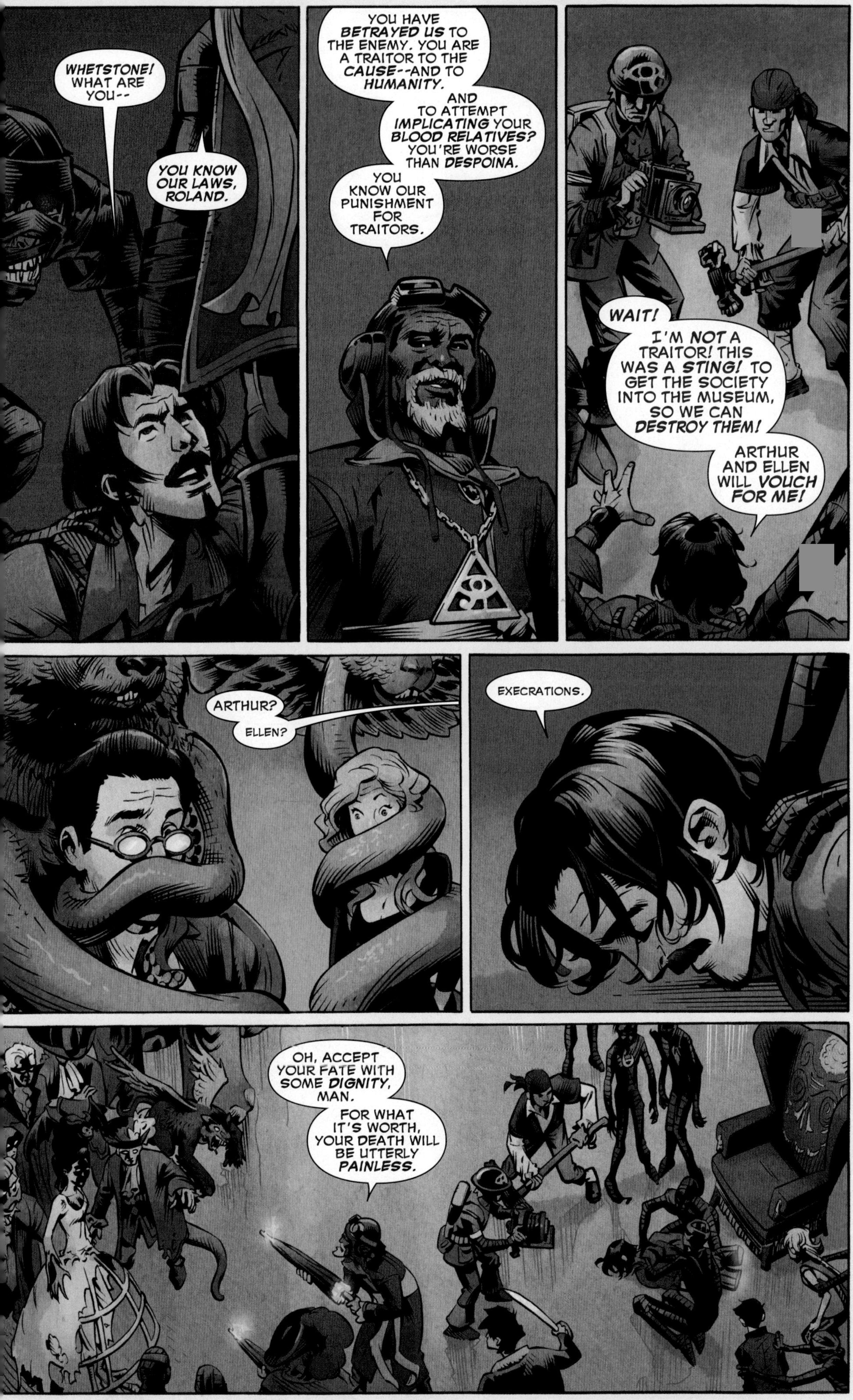
WHETSTONE! WHAT ARE YOU--
YOU KNOW OUR LAWS, ROLAND.
YOU HAVE BETRAYED US TO THE ENEMY. YOU ARE A TRAITOR TO THE CAUSE--AND TO HUMANITY.
AND TO ATTEMPT IMPLICATING YOUR BLOOD RELATIVES? YOU'RE WORSE THAN DESPOINA.
YOU KNOW OUR PUNISHMENT FOR TRAITORS.
WAIT!
I'M NOT A TRAITOR! THIS WAS A STING! TO GET THE SOCIETY INTO THE MUSEUM, SO WE CAN DESTROY THEM!
ARTHUR AND ELLEN WILL VOUCH FOR ME!
ARTHUR?
ELLEN?
EXECRATIONS.
OH, ACCEPT YOUR FATE WITH SOME DIGNITY, MAN.
FOR WHAT IT'S WORTH, YOUR DEATH WILL BE UTTERLY PAINLESS.

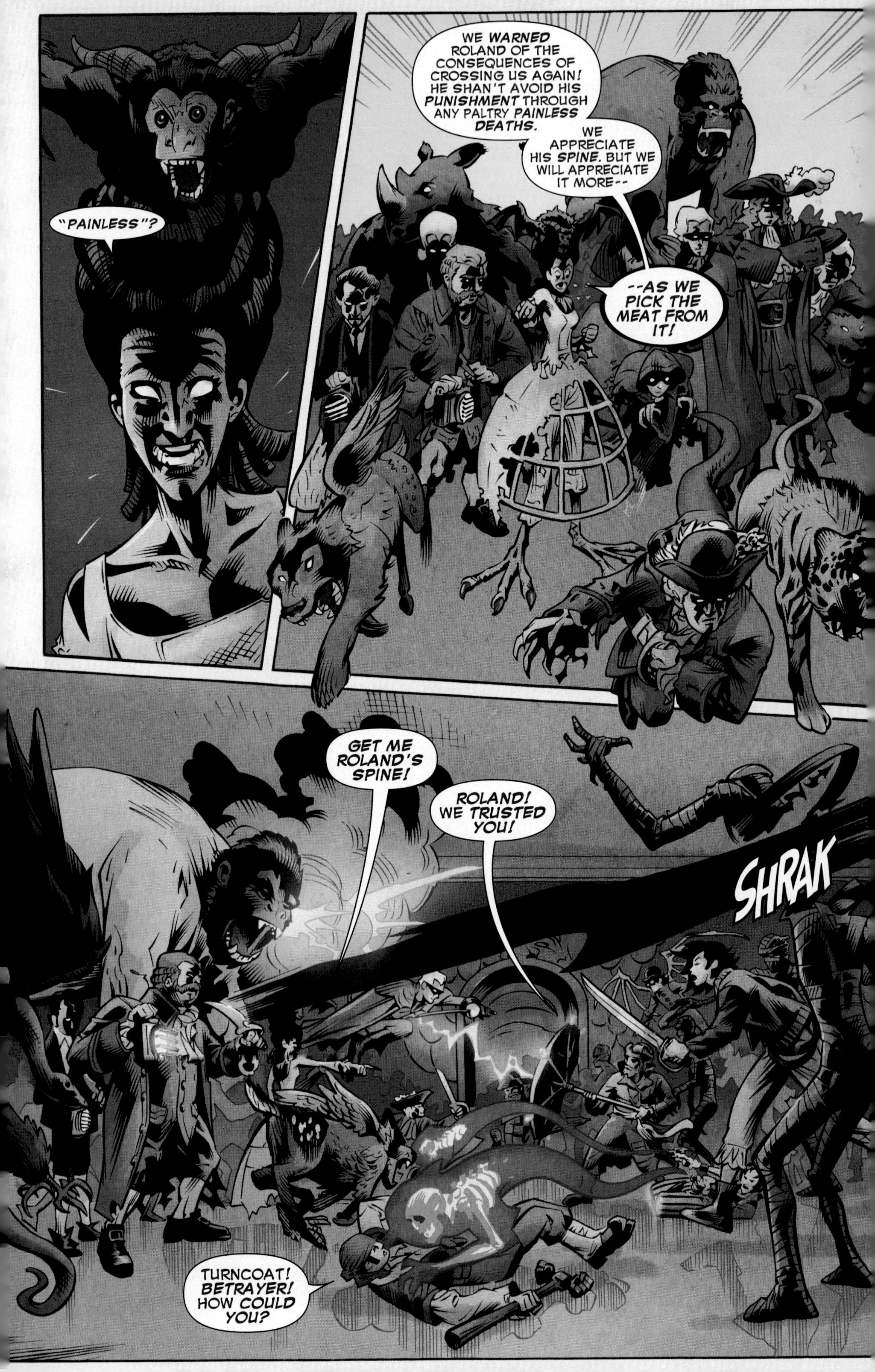
"PAINLESS"?
WE WARNED ROLAND OF THE CONSEQUENCES OF CROSSING US AGAIN! HE SHAN'T AVOID HIS PUNISHMENT THROUGH ANY PALTRY PAINLESS DEATHS.
WE APPRECIATE HIS SPINE. BUT WE WILL APPRECIATE IT MORE--
--AS WE PICK THE MEAT FROM IT!
GET ME ROLAND'S SPINE!
ROLAND! WE TRUSTED YOU!
SHRAK
TURNCOAT! BETRAYER! HOW COULD YOU?

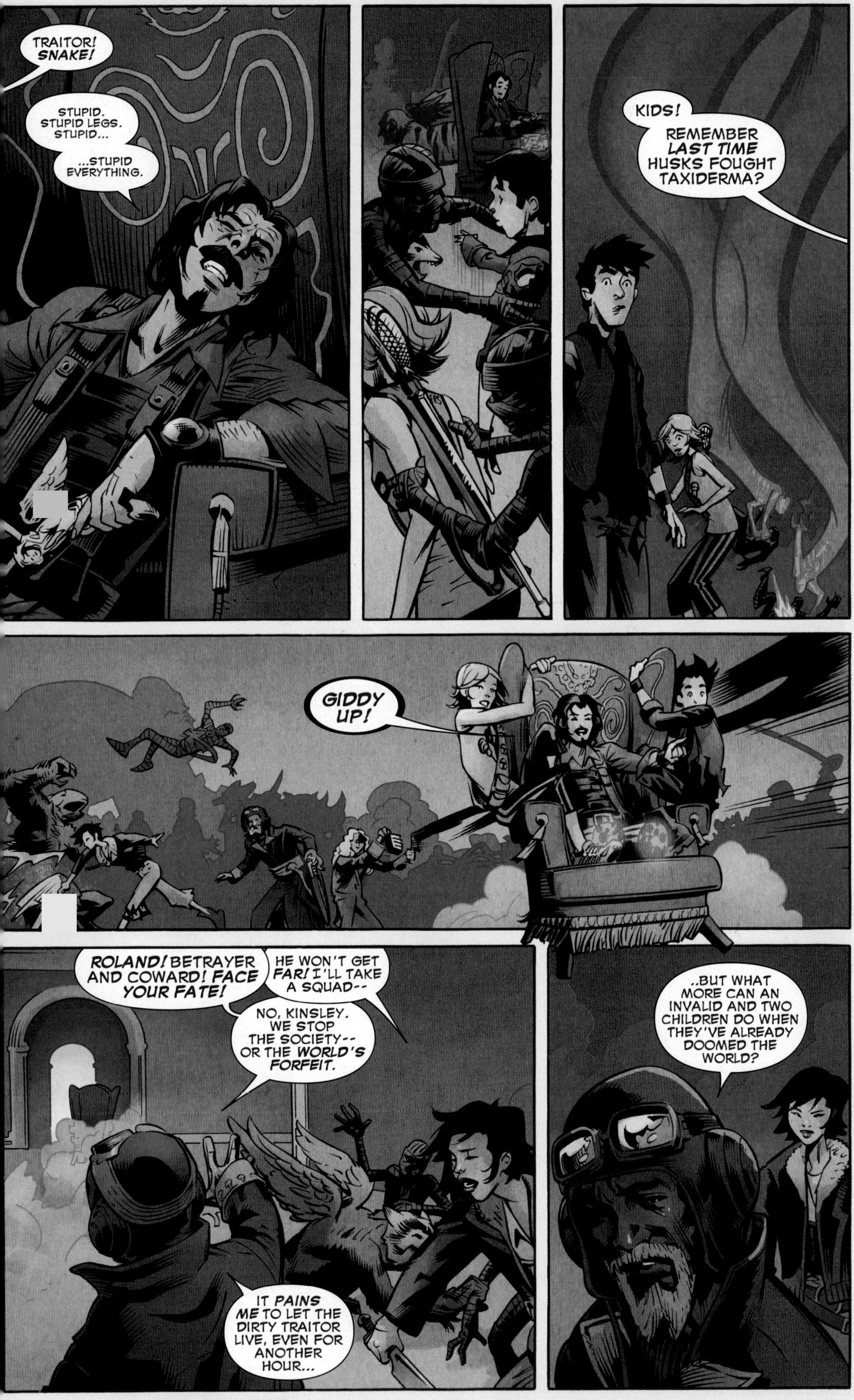
TRAITOR! SNAKE!
STUPID. STUPID LEGS. STUPID...
...STUPID EVERYTHING.
KIDS!
REMEMBER LAST TIME HUSKS FOUGHT TAXIDERMA?
GIDDY UP!
ROLAND! BETRAYER AND COWARD! FACE YOUR FATE!
HE WON'T GET FAR! I'LL TAKE A SQUAD--
NO, KINSLEY. WE STOP THE SOCIETY-- OR THE WORLD'S FORFEIT.
IT PAINS ME TO LET THE DIRTY TRAITOR LIVE, EVEN FOR ANOTHER HOUR...
..BUT WHAT MORE CAN AN INVALID AND TWO CHILDREN DO WHEN THEY'VE ALREADY DOOMED THE WORLD?

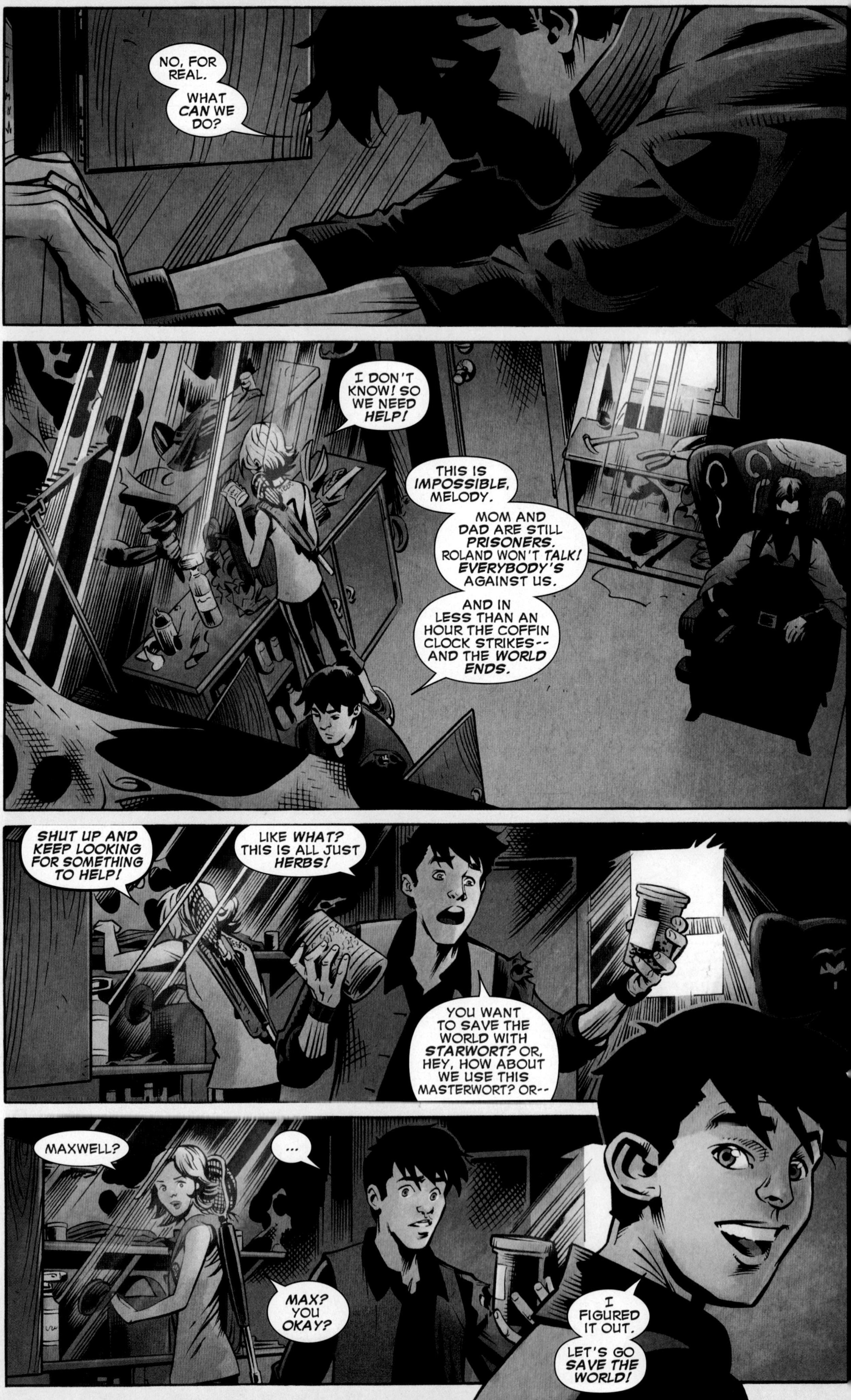
NO, FOR REAL.
WHAT CAN WE DO?
I DON'T KNOW! SO WE NEED HELP!
THIS IS IMPOSSIBLE, MELODY.
MOM AND DAD ARE STILL PRISONERS. ROLAND WON'T TALK! EVERYBODY'S AGAINST US.
AND IN LESS THAN AN HOUR THE COFFIN CLOCK STRIKES-- AND THE WORLD ENDS.
SHUT UP AND KEEP LOOKING FOR SOMETHING TO HELP!
LIKE WHAT? THIS IS ALL JUST HERBS!
YOU WANT TO SAVE THE WORLD WITH STARWORT? OR, HEY, HOW ABOUT WE USE THIS MASTERWORT? OR--
MAXWELL?
...
MAX? YOU OKAY?
I FIGURED IT OUT.
LET'S GO SAVE THE WORLD!

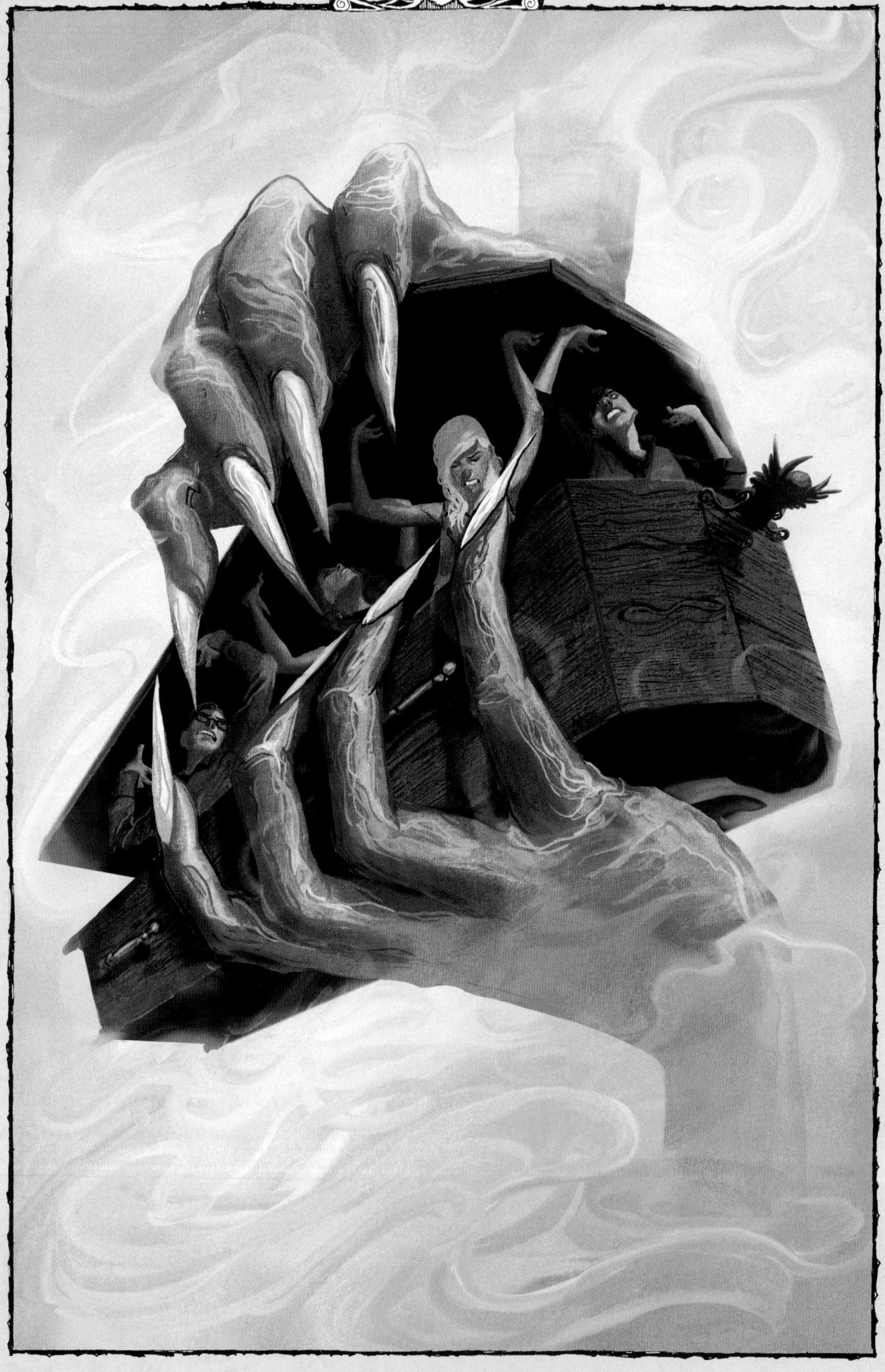

5

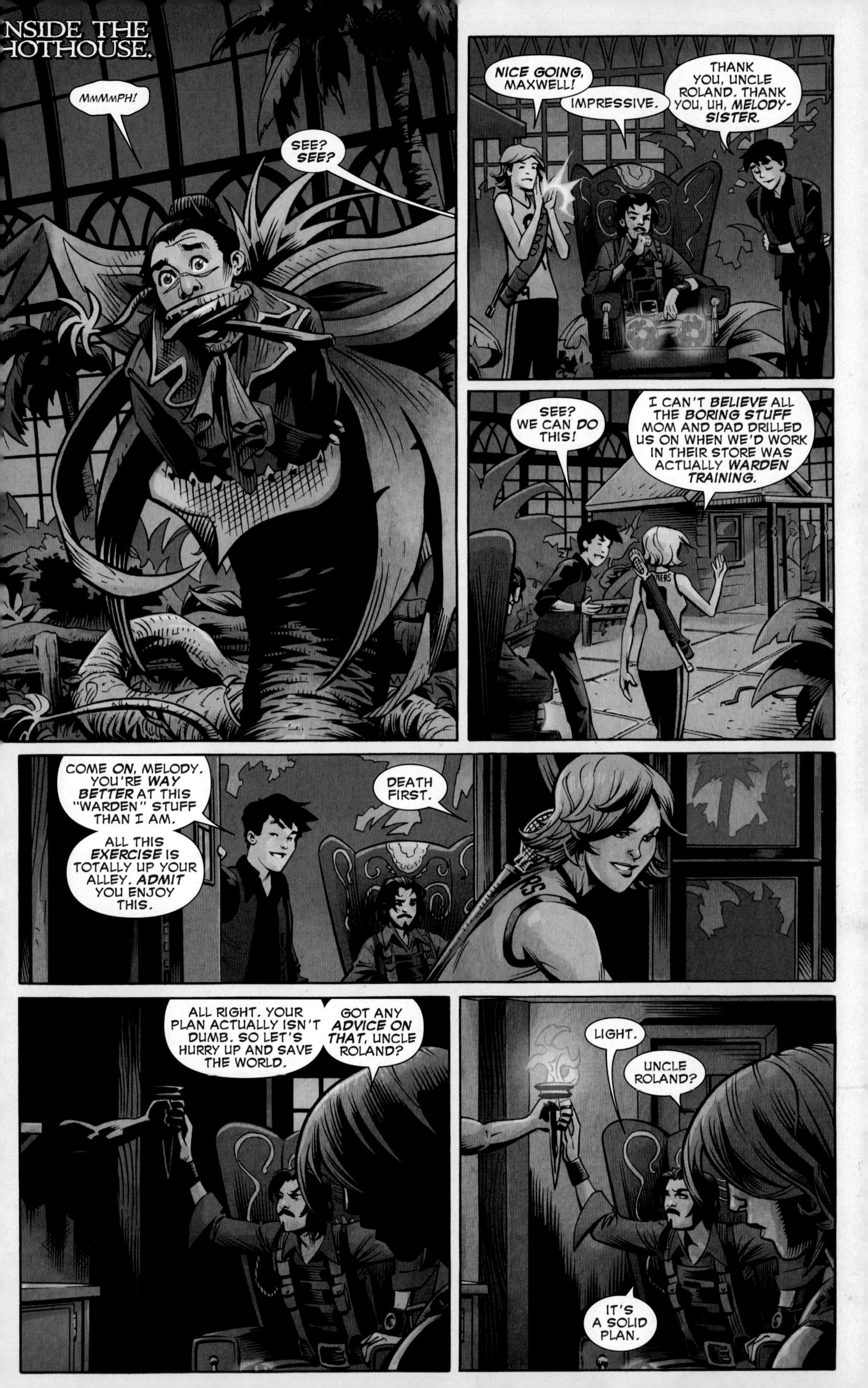
NSIDE THE
HOTHOUSE.
MMMMPH!
SEE? SEE?
NICE GOING, MAXWELL!
IMPRESSIVE.
THANK YOU, UNCLE ROLAND. THANK YOU, UH, MELODY-SISTER.
SEE? WE CAN DO THIS!
I CAN'T BELIEVE ALL THE BORING STUFF MOM AND DAD DRILLED US ON WHEN WE'D WORK IN THEIR STORE WAS ACTUALLY WARDEN TRAINING.
COME ON, MELODY. YOU'RE WAY BETTER AT THIS "WARDEN" STUFF THAN I AM.
ALL THIS EXERCISE IS TOTALLY UP YOUR ALLEY. ADMIT YOU ENJOY THIS.
DEATH FIRST.
ALL RIGHT. YOUR PLAN ACTUALLY ISN'T DUMB. SO LET'S HURRY UP AND SAVE THE WORLD.
GOT ANY ADVICE ON THAT, UNCLE ROLAND?
LIGHT.
UNCLE ROLAND?
IT'S A SOLID PLAN.

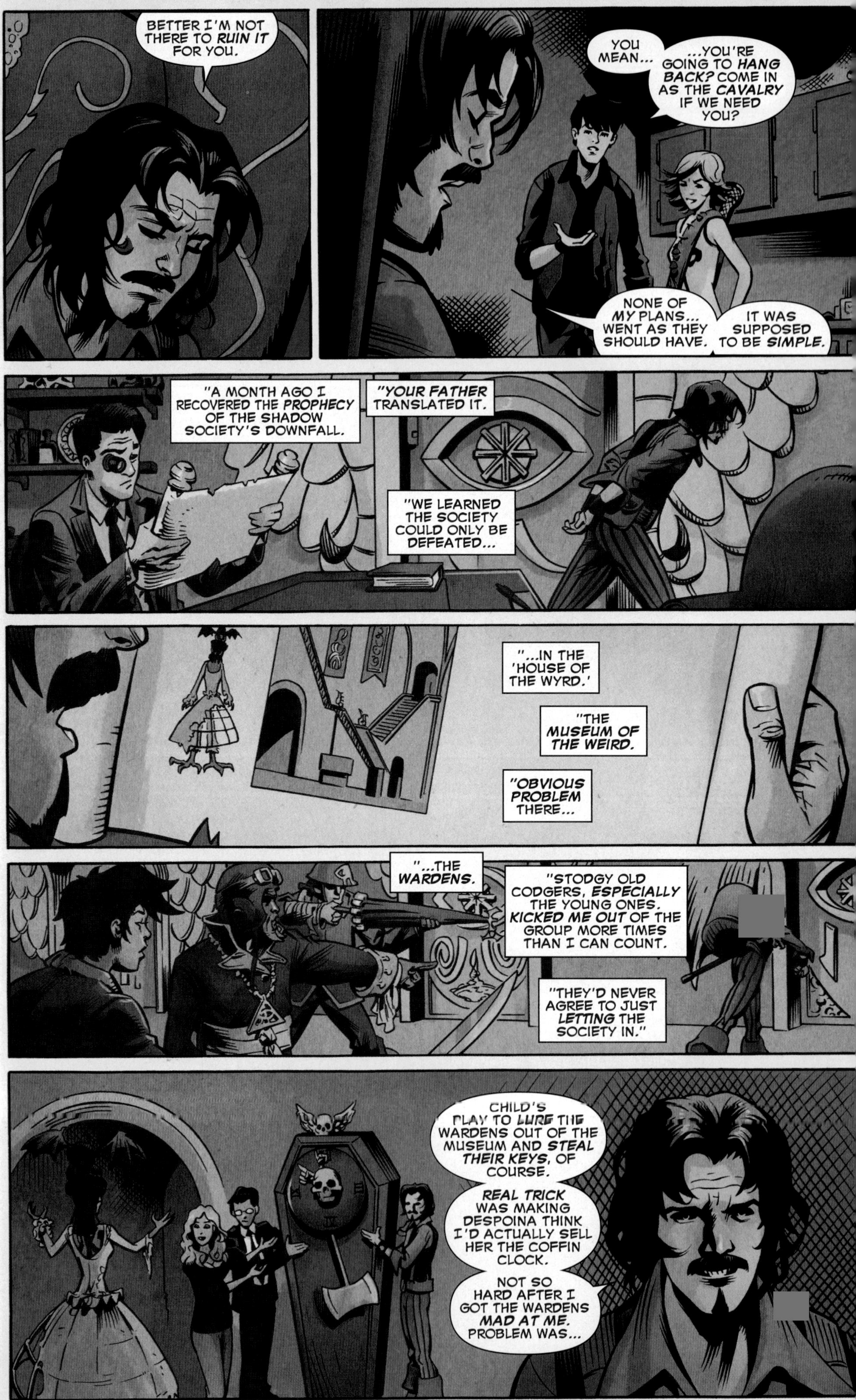
BETTER I'M NOT THERE TO RUIN IT FOR YOU.
YOU MEAN...
...YOU'RE GOING TO HANG BACK? COME IN AS THE CAVALRY IF WE NEED YOU?
NONE OF MY PLANS... WENT AS THEY SHOULD HAVE.
IT WAS SUPPOSED TO BE SIMPLE.
"A MONTH AGO I RECOVERED THE PROPHECY OF THE SHADOW SOCIETY'S DOWNFALL.
"YOUR FATHER TRANSLATED IT.
"WE LEARNED THE SOCIETY COULD ONLY BE DEFEATED...
"...IN THE 'HOUSE OF THE WYRD.'
"THE MUSEUM OF THE WEIRD.
"OBVIOUS PROBLEM THERE...
"...THE WARDENS.
"STODGY OLD CODGERS, ESPECIALLY THE YOUNG ONES. KICKED ME OUT OF THE GROUP MORE TIMES THAN I CAN COUNT.
"THEY'D NEVER AGREE TO JUST LETTING THE SOCIETY IN."
CHILD'S PLAY TO LURE THE WARDENS OUT OF THE MUSEUM AND STEAL THEIR KEYS, OF COURSE.
REAL TRICK WAS MAKING DESPOINA THINK I'D ACTUALLY SELL HER THE COFFIN CLOCK.
NOT SO HARD AFTER I GOT THE WARDENS MAD AT ME. PROBLEM WAS...

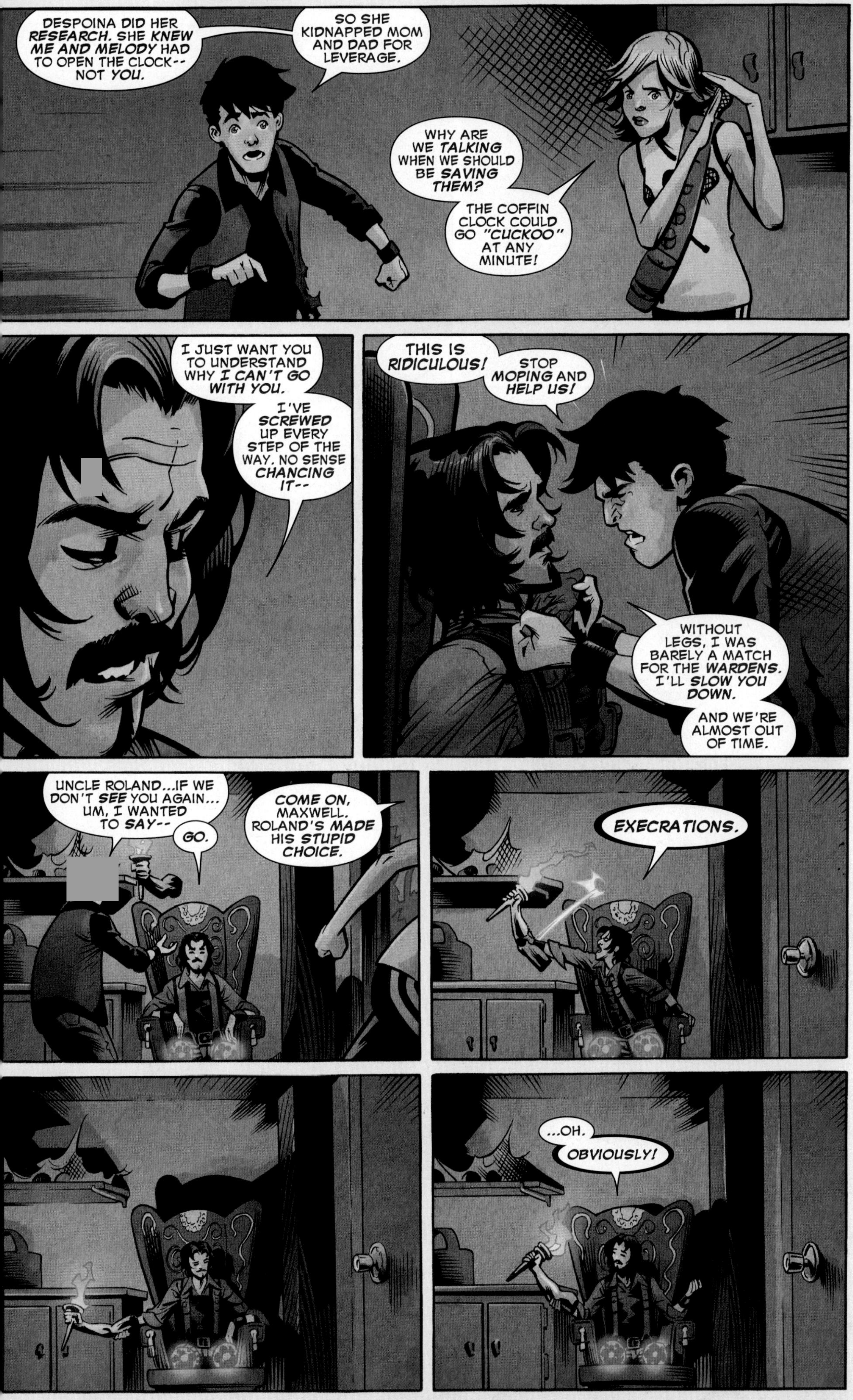
DESPOINA DID HER RESEARCH. SHE KNEW ME AND MELODY HAD TO OPEN THE CLOCK-- NOT YOU.
SO SHE KIDNAPPED MOM AND DAD FOR LEVERAGE.
WHY ARE WE TALKING WHEN WE SHOULD BE SAVING THEM?
THE COFFIN CLOCK COULD GO "CUCKOO" AT ANY MINUTE!
I JUST WANT YOU TO UNDERSTAND WHY I CAN'T GO WITH YOU.
I'VE SCREWED UP EVERY STEP OF THE WAY. NO SENSE CHANCING IT--
THIS IS RIDICULOUS!
STOP MOPING AND HELP US!
WITHOUT LEGS, I WAS BARELY A MATCH FOR THE WARDENS. I'LL SLOW YOU DOWN.
AND WE'RE ALMOST OUT OF TIME.
UNCLE ROLAND...IF WE DON'T SEE YOU AGAIN... UM, I WANTED TO SAY--
GO.
COME ON, MAXWELL. ROLAND'S MADE HIS STUPID CHOICE.
EXECRATIONS.
...OH.
OBVIOUSLY!

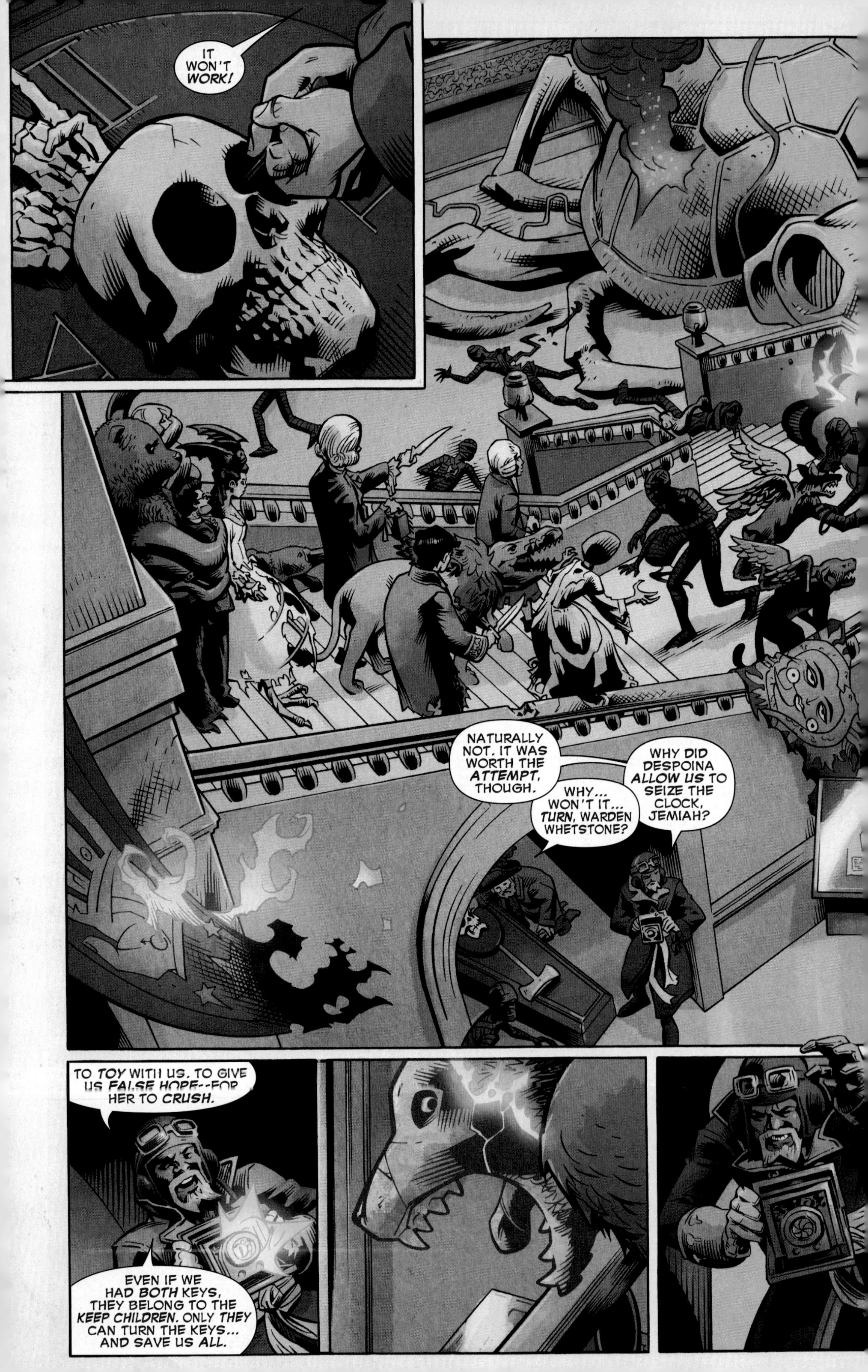
IT WON'T WORK!
NATURALLY NOT. IT WAS WORTH THE ATTEMPT, THOUGH.
WHY DID DESPOINA ALLOW US TO SEIZE THE CLOCK, JEMIAH?
WHY... WON'T IT... TURN, WARDEN WHETSTONE?
TO TOY WITH US. TO GIVE US FALSE HOPE--FOR HER TO CRUSH.
EVEN IF WE HAD BOTH KEYS, THEY BELONG TO THE KEEP CHILDREN. ONLY THEY CAN TURN THE KEYS... AND SAVE US ALL.

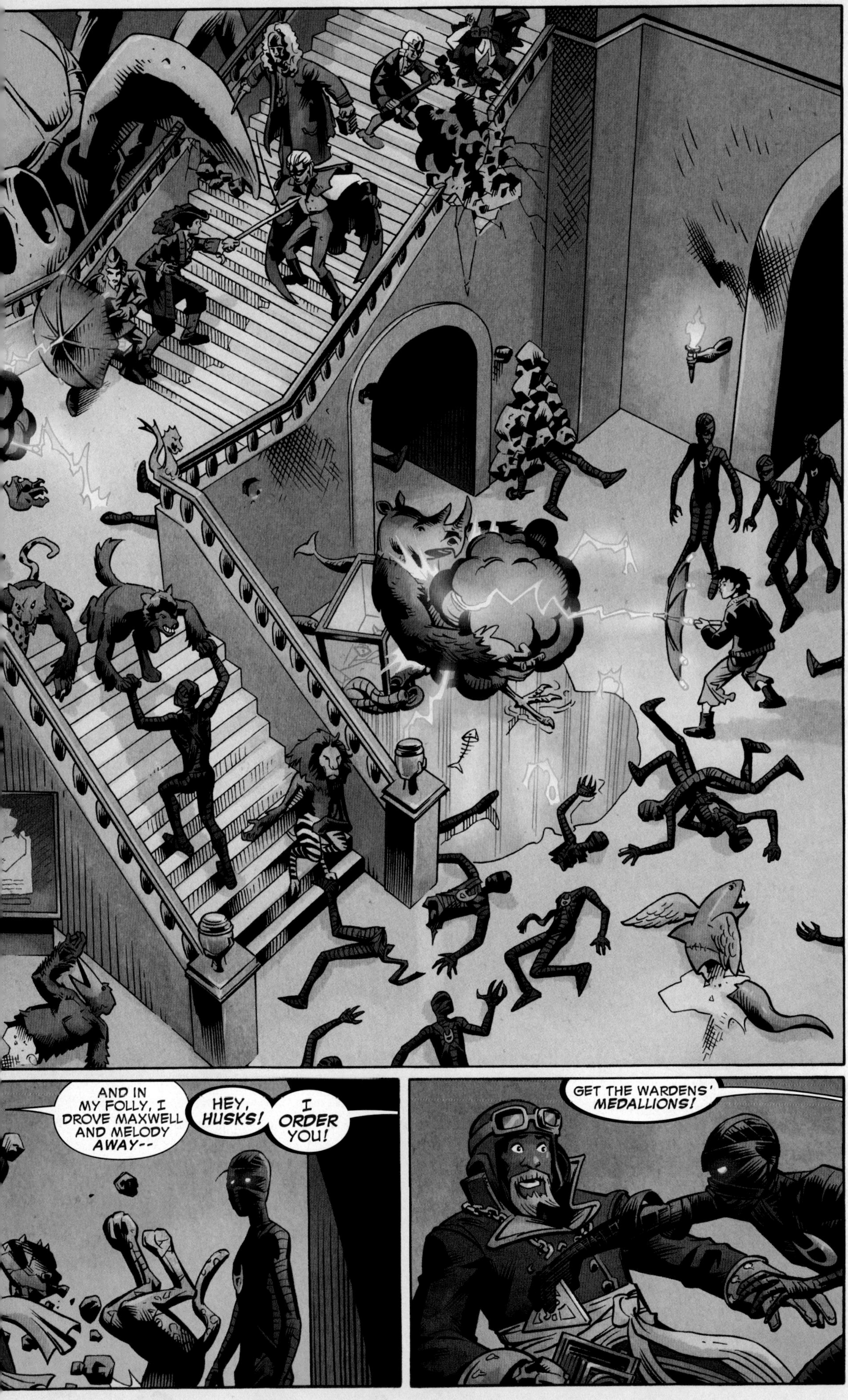
AND IN MY FOLLY, I DROVE MAXWELL AND MELODY AWAY--
HEY, HUSKS!
I ORDER YOU!
GET THE WARDENS' MEDALLIONS!

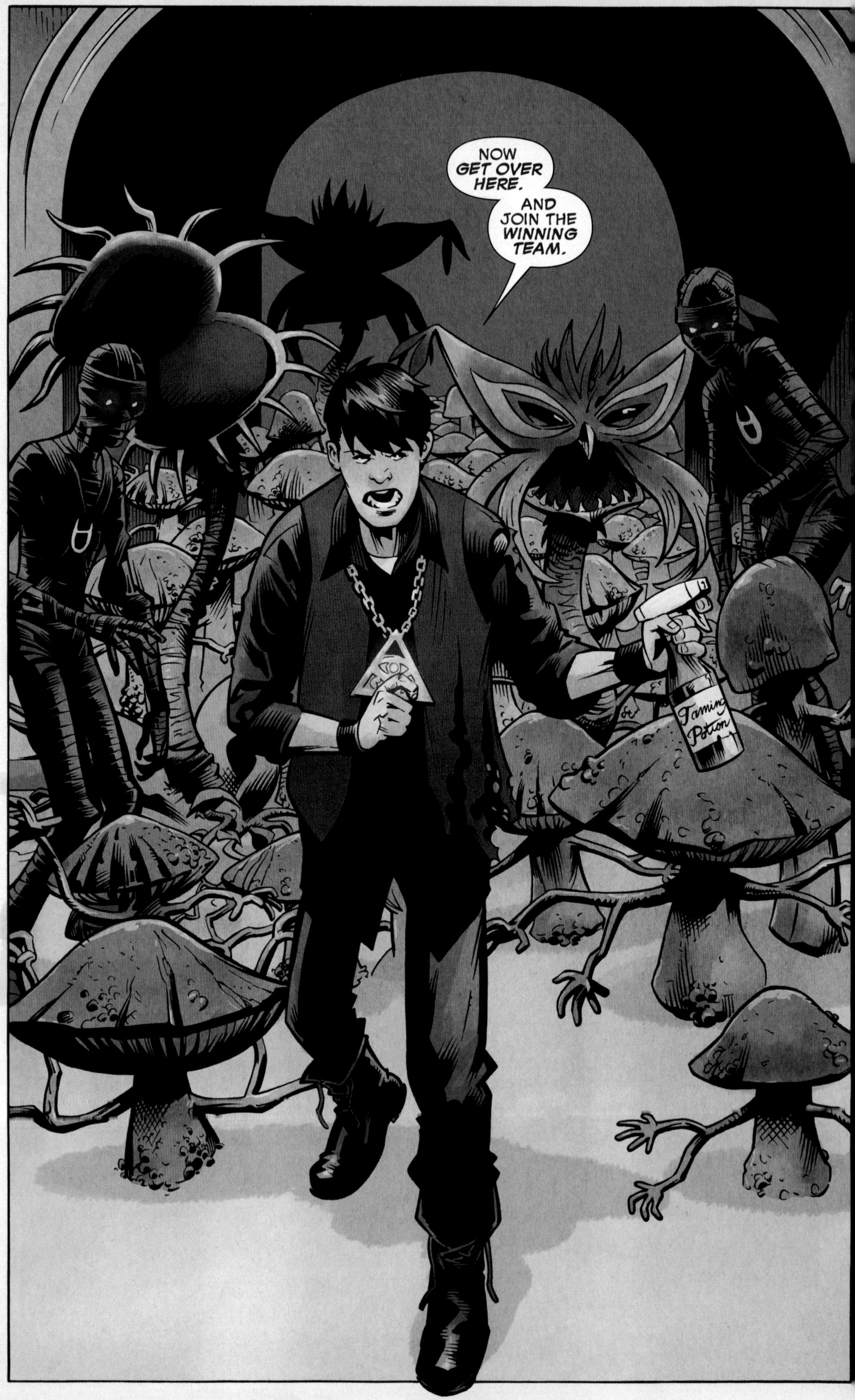
NOW GET OVER HERE.
AND JOIN THE WINNING TEAM.
Taming Potion

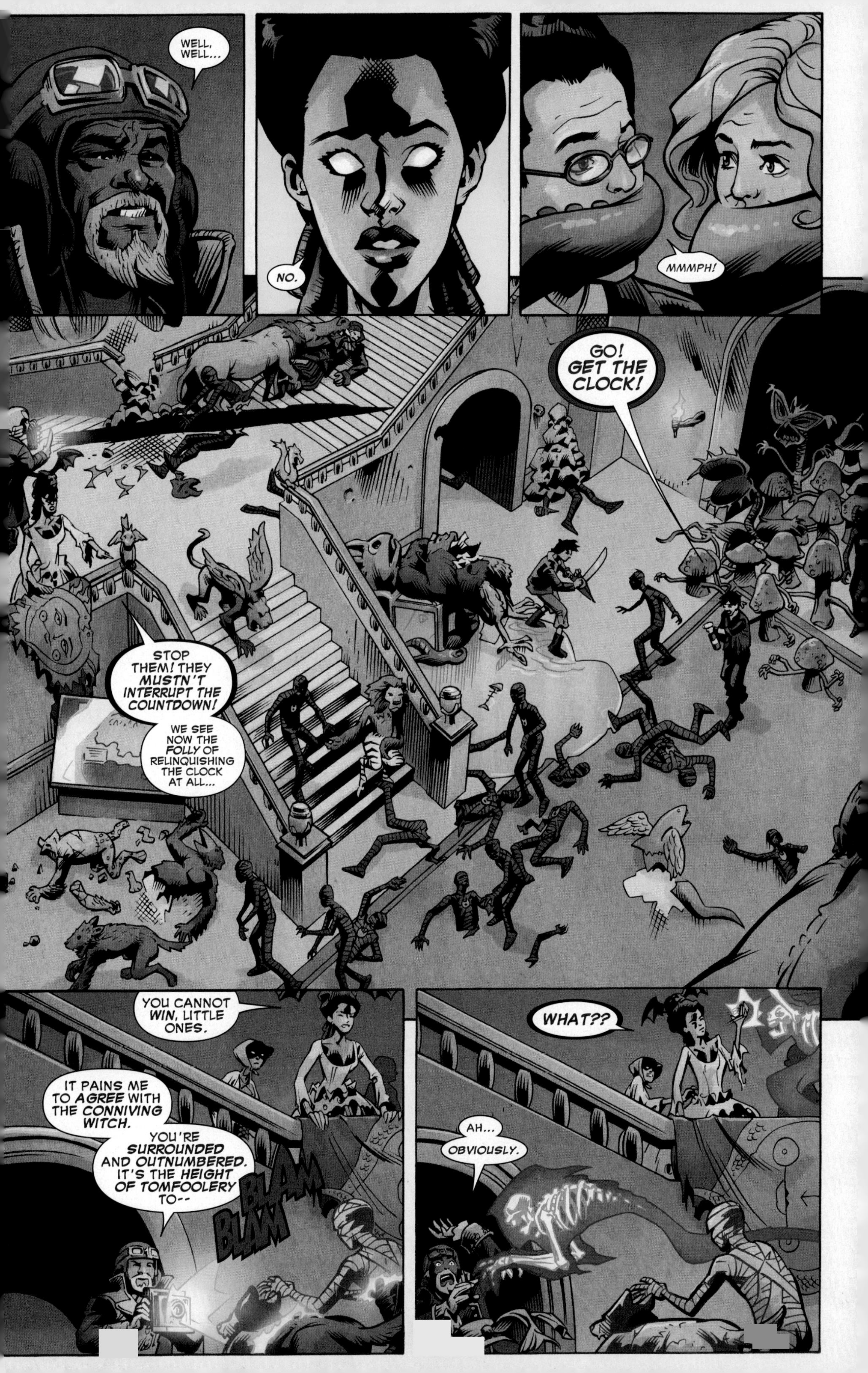

WELL, WELL...
NO.
MMMPH!
GO! GET THE CLOCK!
STOP THEM! THEY MUSTN'T INTERRUPT THE COUNTDOWN!
WE SEE NOW THE FOLLY OF RELINQUISHING THE CLOCK AT ALL...
YOU CANNOT WIN, LITTLE ONES.
IT PAINS ME TO AGREE WITH THE CONNIVING WITCH.
YOU'RE SURROUNDED AND OUTNUMBERED. IT'S THE HEIGHT OF TOMFOOLERY TO--
BLAM
BLAM
WHAT??
AH... OBVIOUSLY.

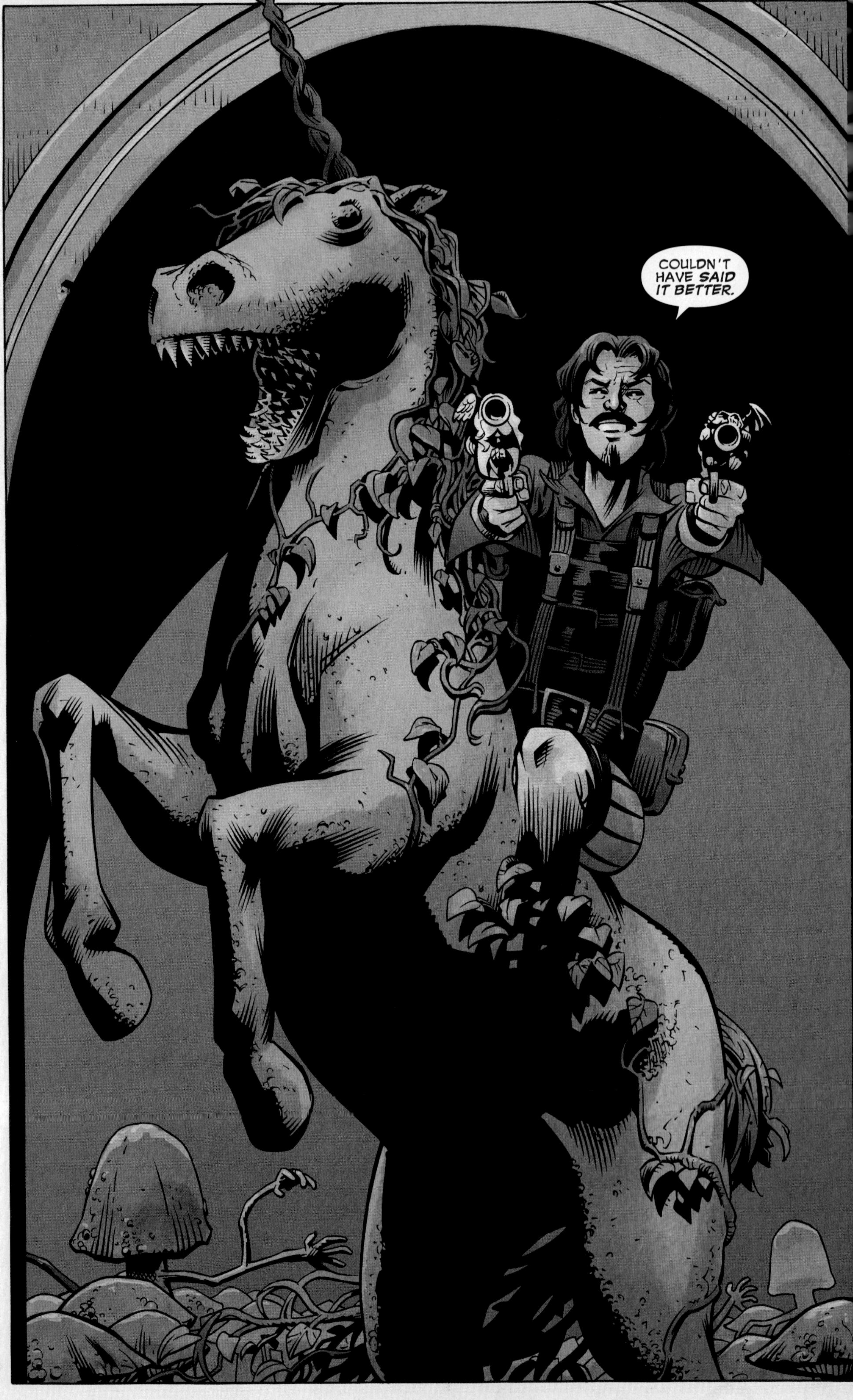
COULDN'T HAVE SAID IT BETTER.

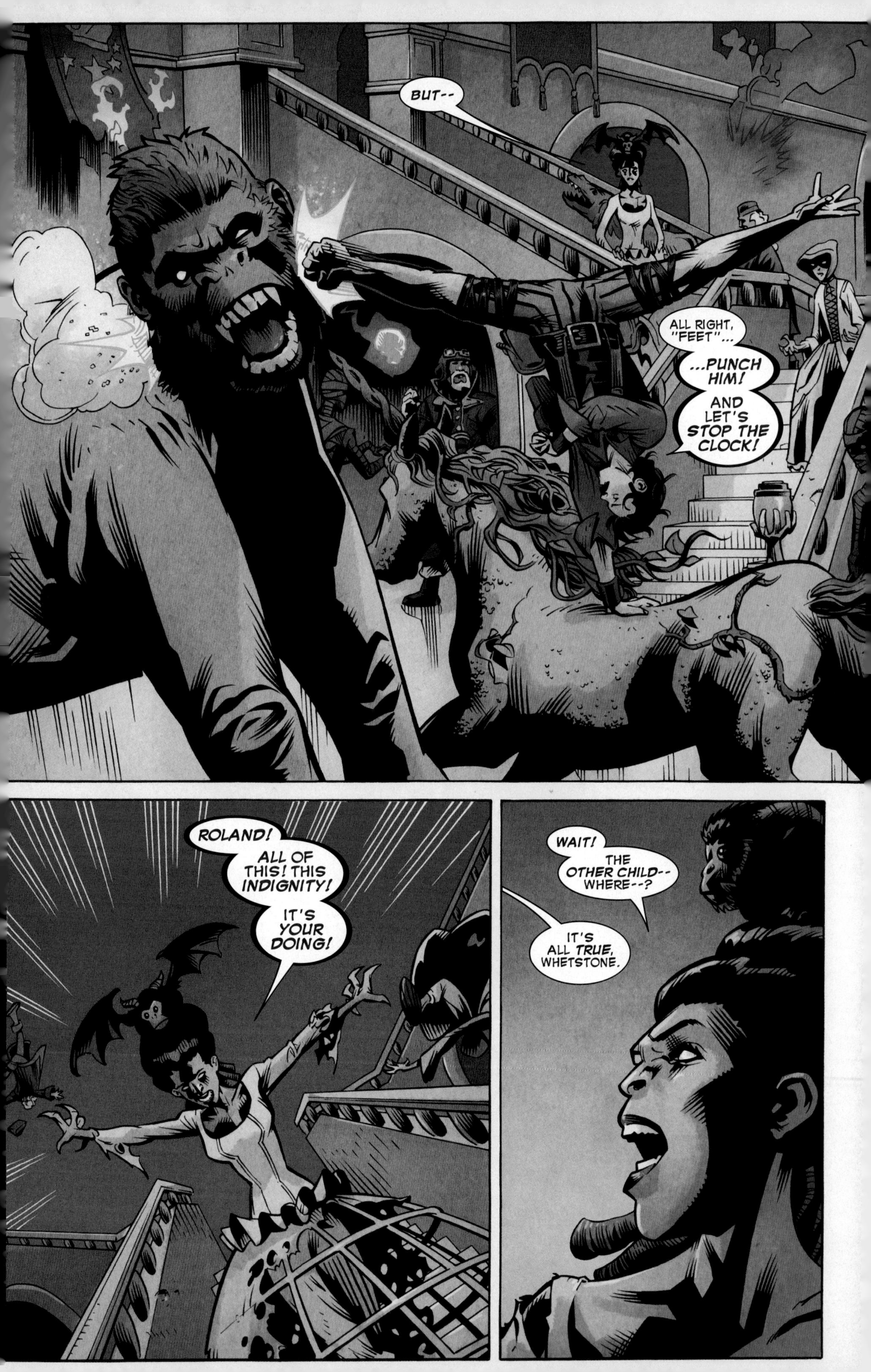
BUT--
ALL RIGHT, "FEET"...
...PUNCH HIM!
AND LET'S STOP THE CLOCK!
ROLAND!
ALL OF THIS! THIS INDIGNITY!
IT'S YOUR DOING!
WAIT!
THE OTHER CHILD-- WHERE--?
IT'S ALL TRUE, WHETSTONE.

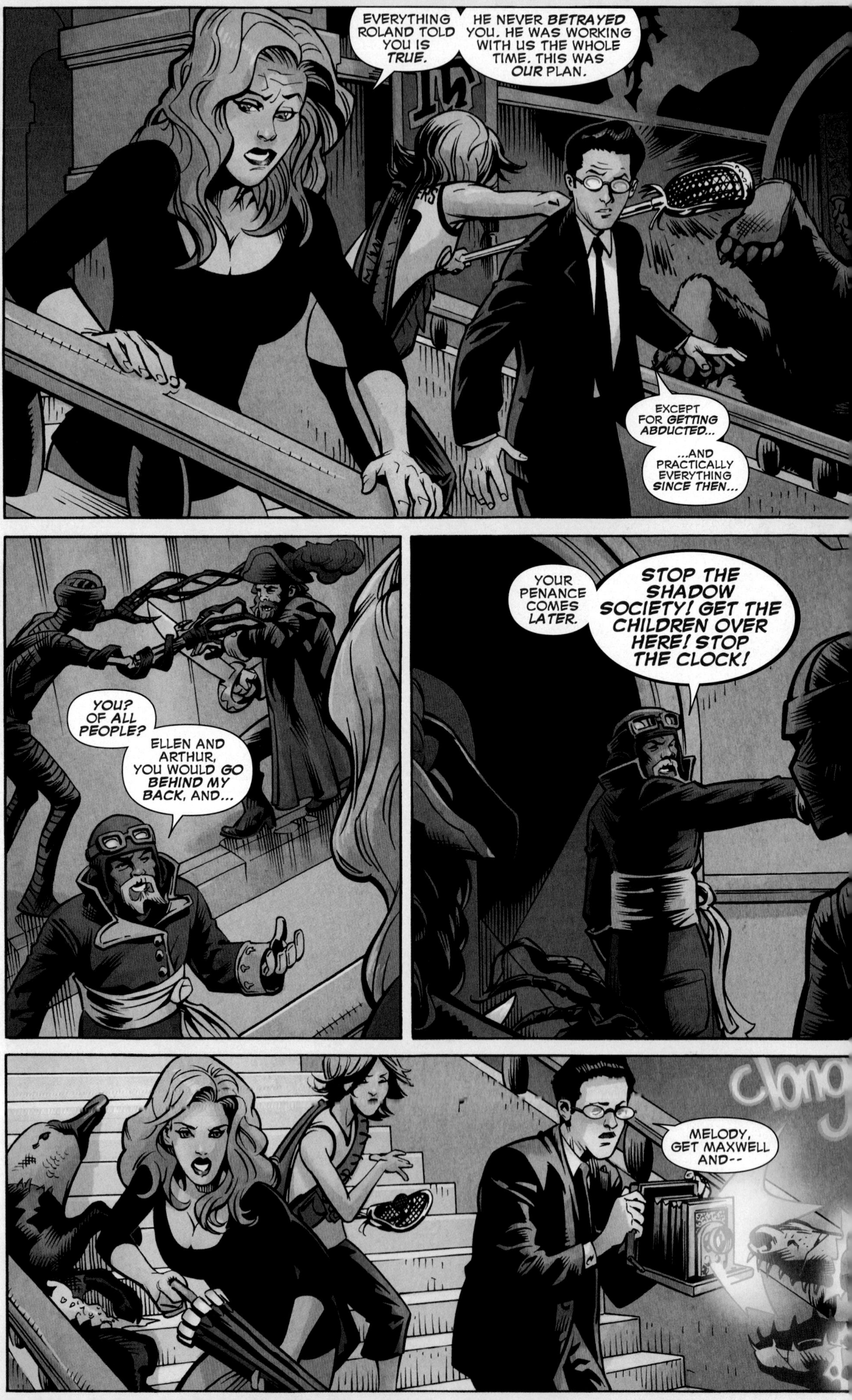
EVERYTHING ROLAND TOLD YOU IS *TRUE*.
HE NEVER *BETRAYED* YOU. HE WAS WORKING WITH US THE WHOLE TIME. THIS WAS *OUR* PLAN.
EXCEPT FOR *GETTING ABDUCTED*...
...AND PRACTICALLY EVERYTHING *SINCE THEN*...
YOU? OF ALL PEOPLE?
ELLEN AND ARTHUR, YOU WOULD *GO BEHIND MY BACK*, AND...
YOUR PENANCE COMES *LATER*.
STOP THE SHADOW SOCIETY! GET THE CHILDREN OVER HERE! STOP THE CLOCK!
MELODY, GET MAXWELL AND--

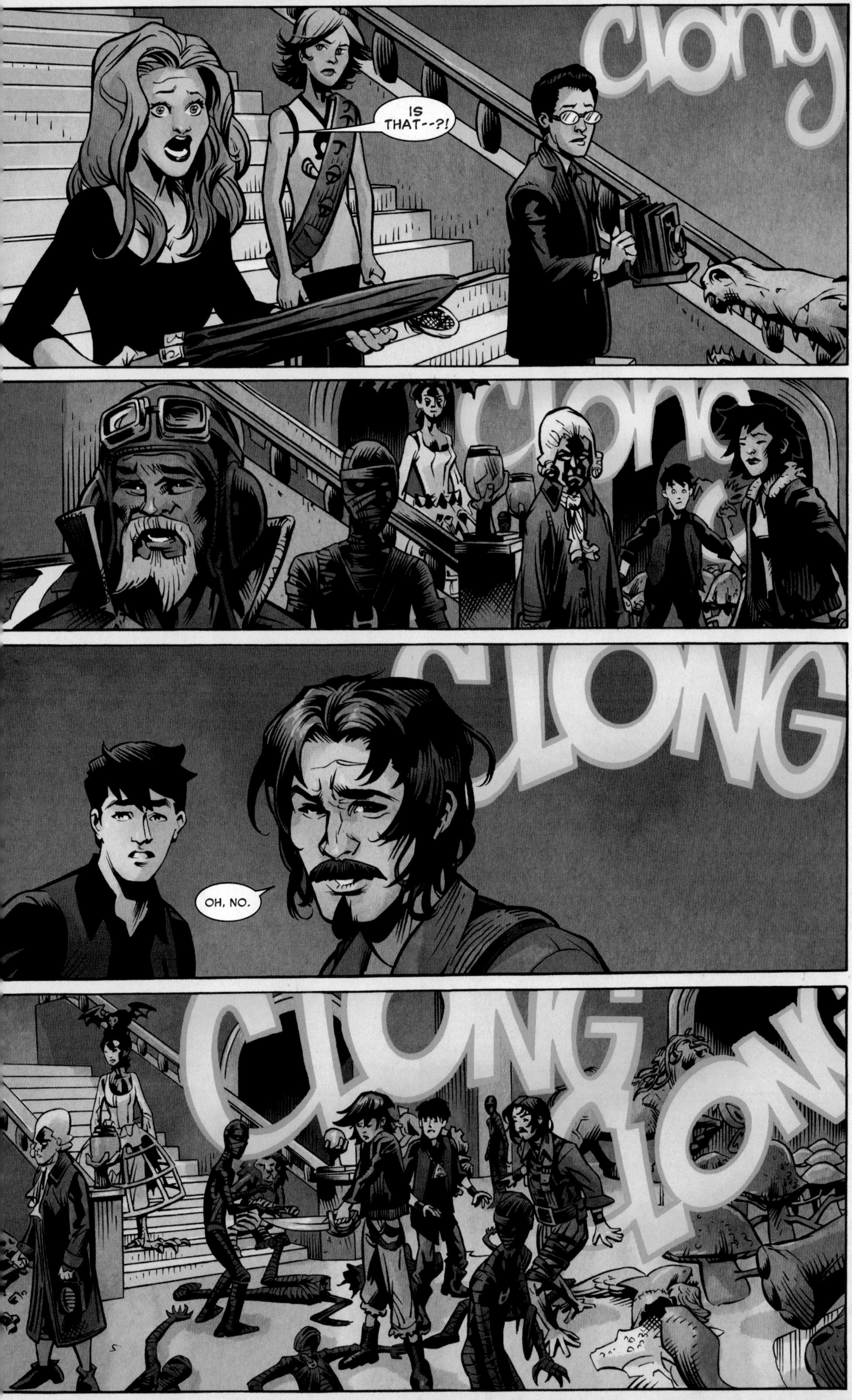
CLONG
IS THAT--?!
CLONG
CLONG
OH, NO.
CLONG-LONG

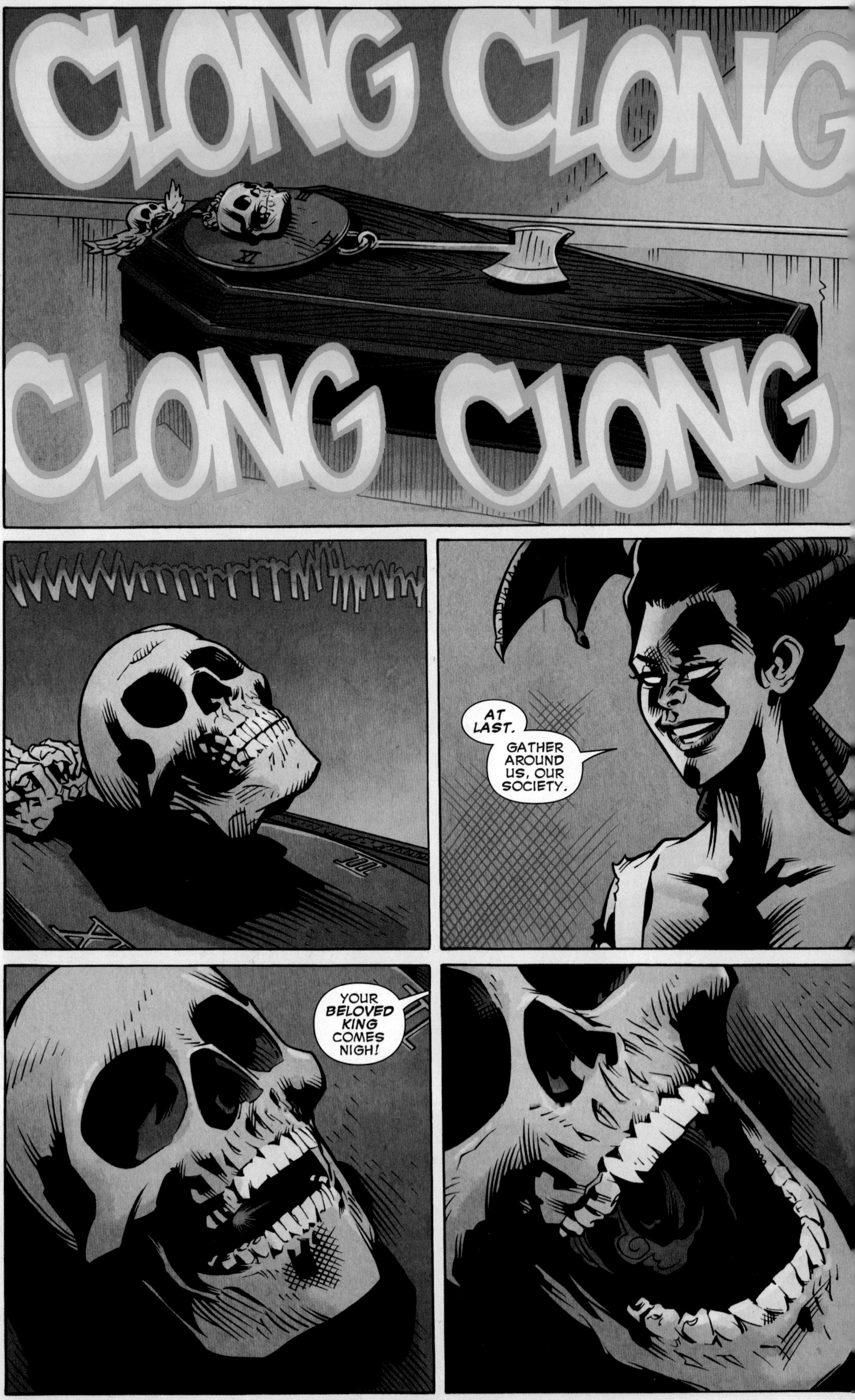
CLONG CLONG
CLONG CLONG
AT LAST.
GATHER AROUND US, OUR SOCIETY.
YOUR BELOVED KING COMES NIGH!

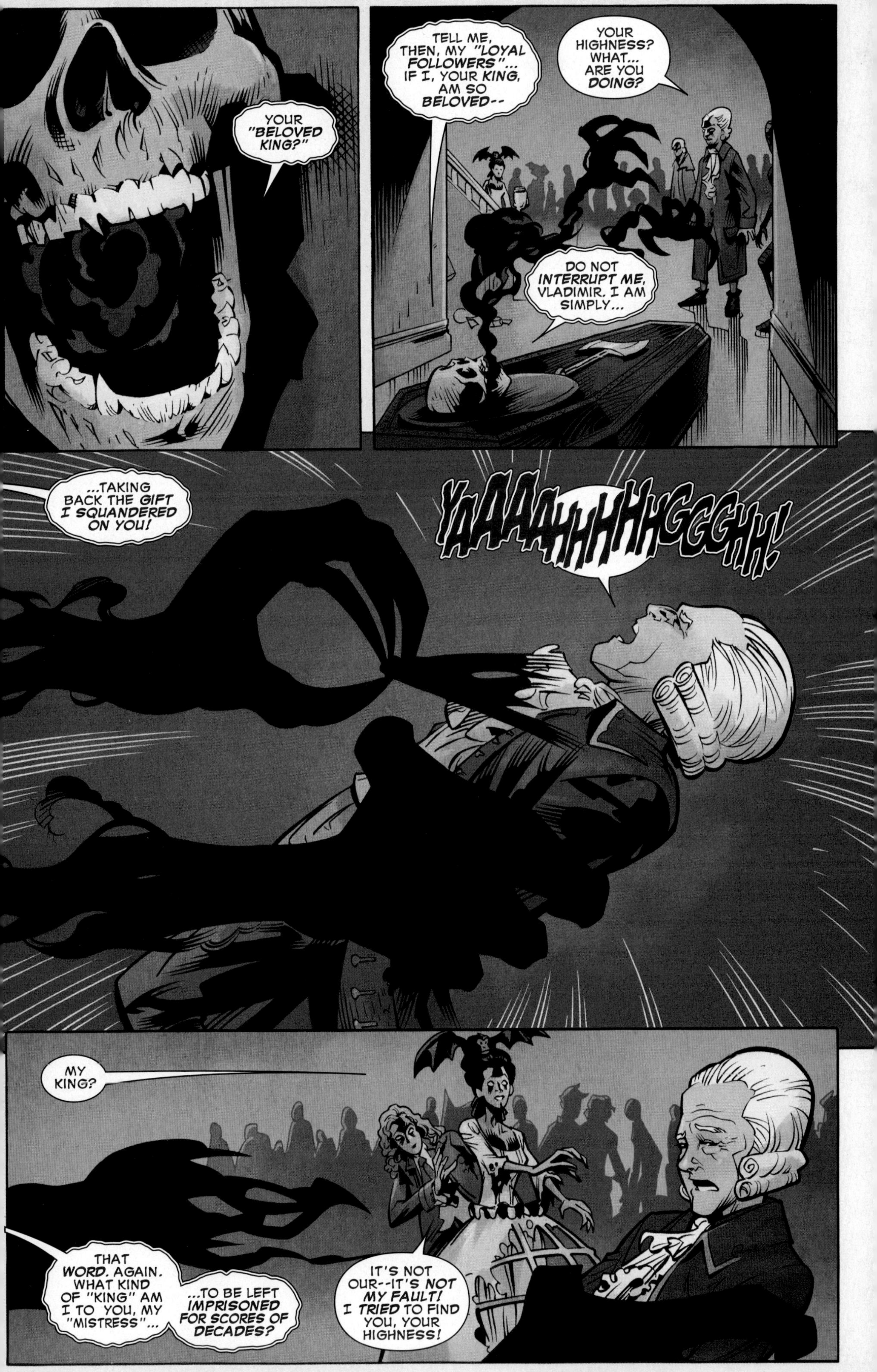
YOUR "BELOVED KING?"
TELL ME, THEN, MY "LOYAL FOLLOWERS"... IF I, YOUR KING, AM SO BELOVED--
YOUR HIGHNESS? WHAT... ARE YOU DOING?
DO NOT INTERRUPT ME, VLADIMIR. I AM SIMPLY...
...TAKING BACK THE GIFT I SQUANDERED ON YOU!
YAAAAHHHHGGGHH!
MY KING?
THAT WORD. AGAIN. WHAT KIND OF "KING" AM I TO YOU, MY "MISTRESS"...
...TO BE LEFT IMPRISONED FOR SCORES OF DECADES?
IT'S NOT OUR--IT'S NOT MY FAULT! I TRIED TO FIND YOU, YOUR HIGHNESS!

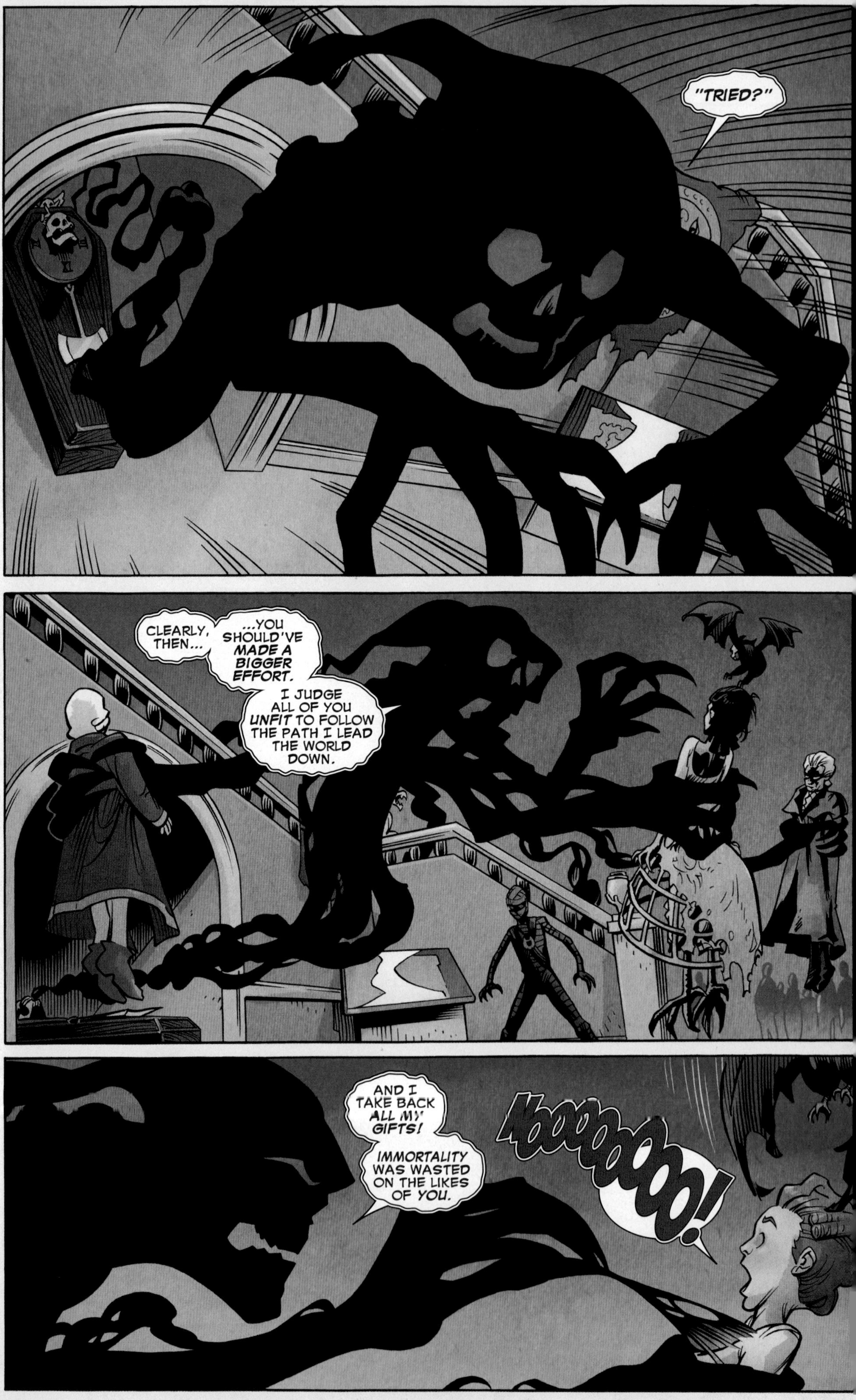
"TRIED?"
CLEARLY, THEN...
...YOU SHOULD'VE MADE A BIGGER EFFORT.
I JUDGE ALL OF YOU UNFIT TO FOLLOW THE PATH I LEAD THE WORLD DOWN.
AND I TAKE BACK ALL MY GIFTS!
IMMORTALITY WAS WASTED ON THE LIKES OF YOU.
NOOOOOOOO!

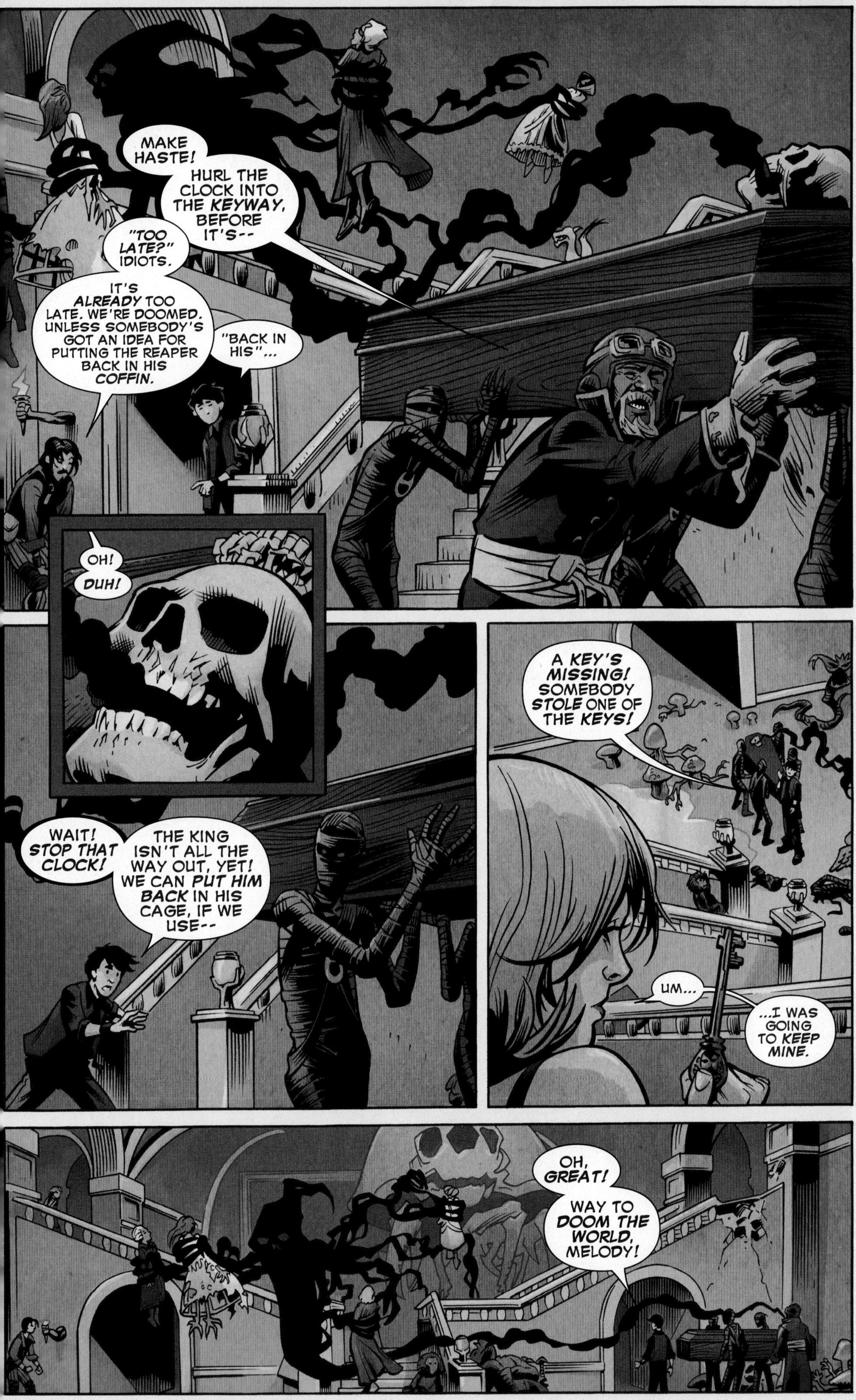
MAKE HASTE!
HURL THE CLOCK INTO THE *KEYWAY*, BEFORE IT'S--
"TOO *LATE?*" IDIOTS.
IT'S *ALREADY* TOO LATE. WE'RE DOOMED. UNLESS SOMEBODY'S GOT AN IDEA FOR PUTTING THE REAPER BACK IN HIS *COFFIN.*
"BACK IN HIS"...
OH! *DUH!*
WAIT! *STOP THAT CLOCK!*
THE KING ISN'T ALL THE WAY OUT, YET! WE CAN *PUT HIM BACK* IN HIS CAGE, IF WE USE--
A *KEY'S MISSING!* SOMEBODY *STOLE* ONE OF THE *KEYS!*
UM...
...I WAS GOING TO *KEEP MINE.*
OH, *GREAT!*
WAY TO *DOOM THE WORLD,* MELODY!

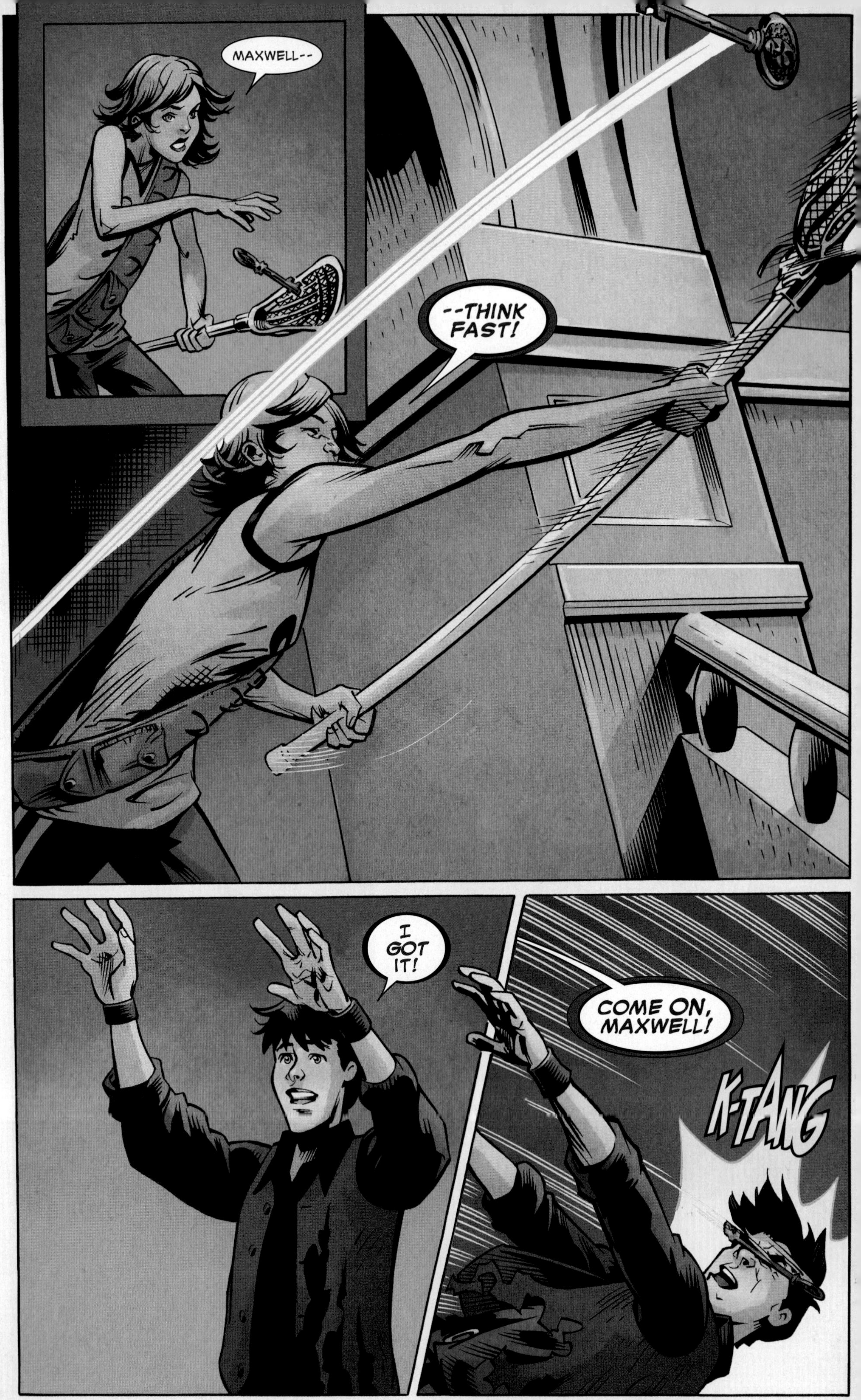
MAXWELL--
--THINK FAST!
I GOT IT!
COME ON, MAXWELL!
K-TANG

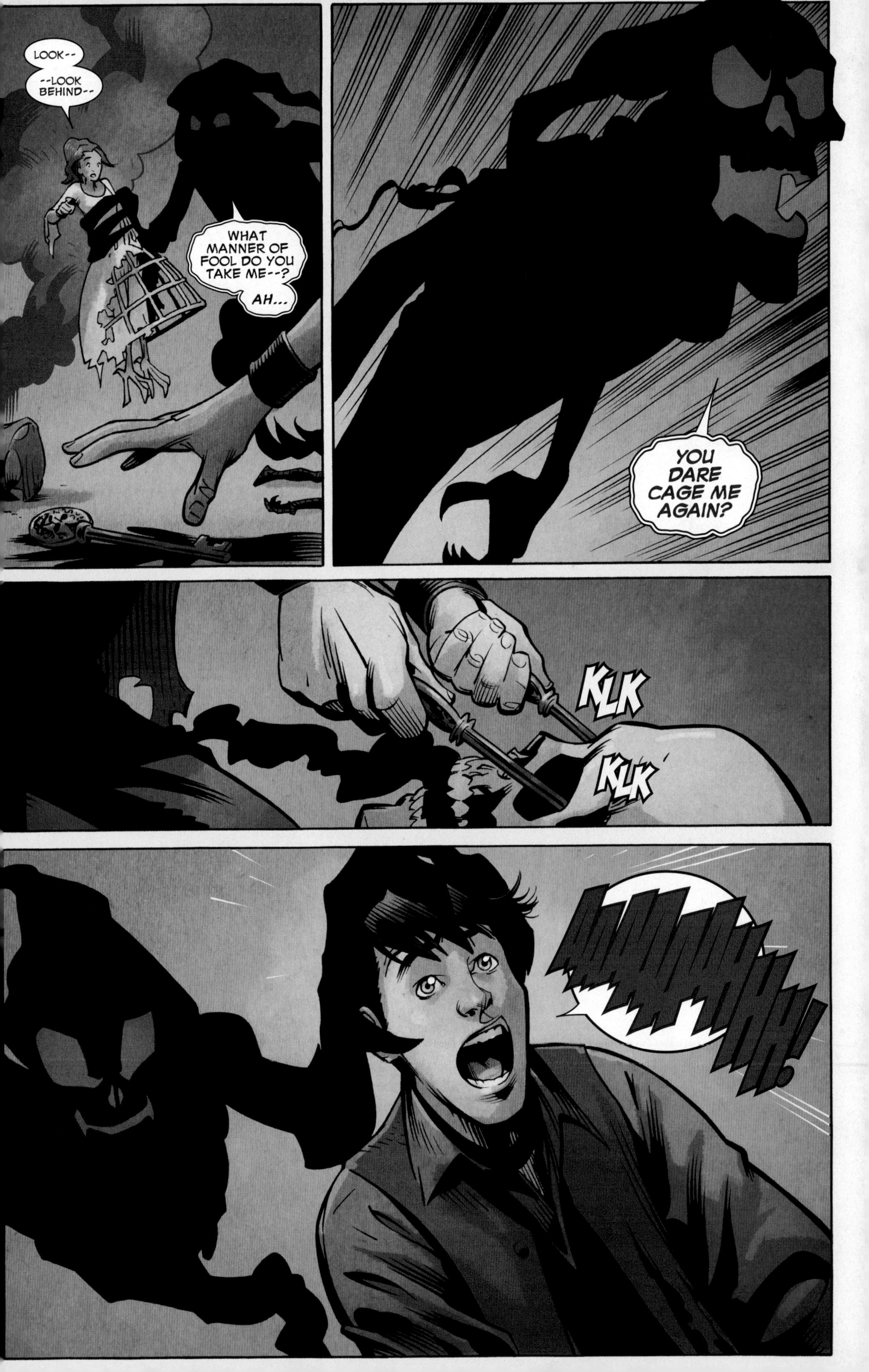
LOOK--
--LOOK BEHIND--
WHAT MANNER OF FOOL DO YOU TAKE ME--?
AH...
YOU DARE CAGE ME AGAIN?
KLK
KLK

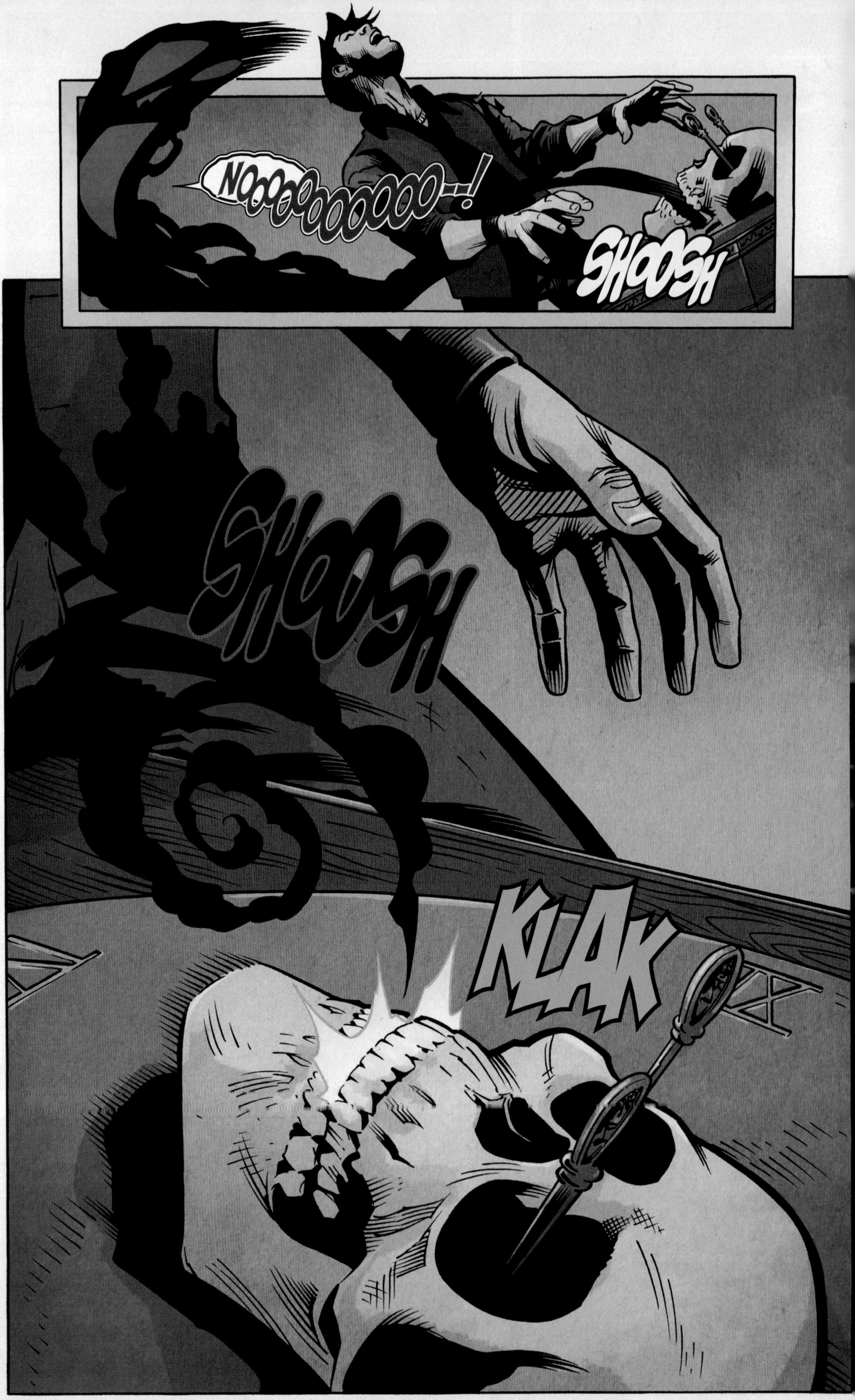
NOOOOOOOOOOOO--!
SHOOSH
SHOOSH
KLAK

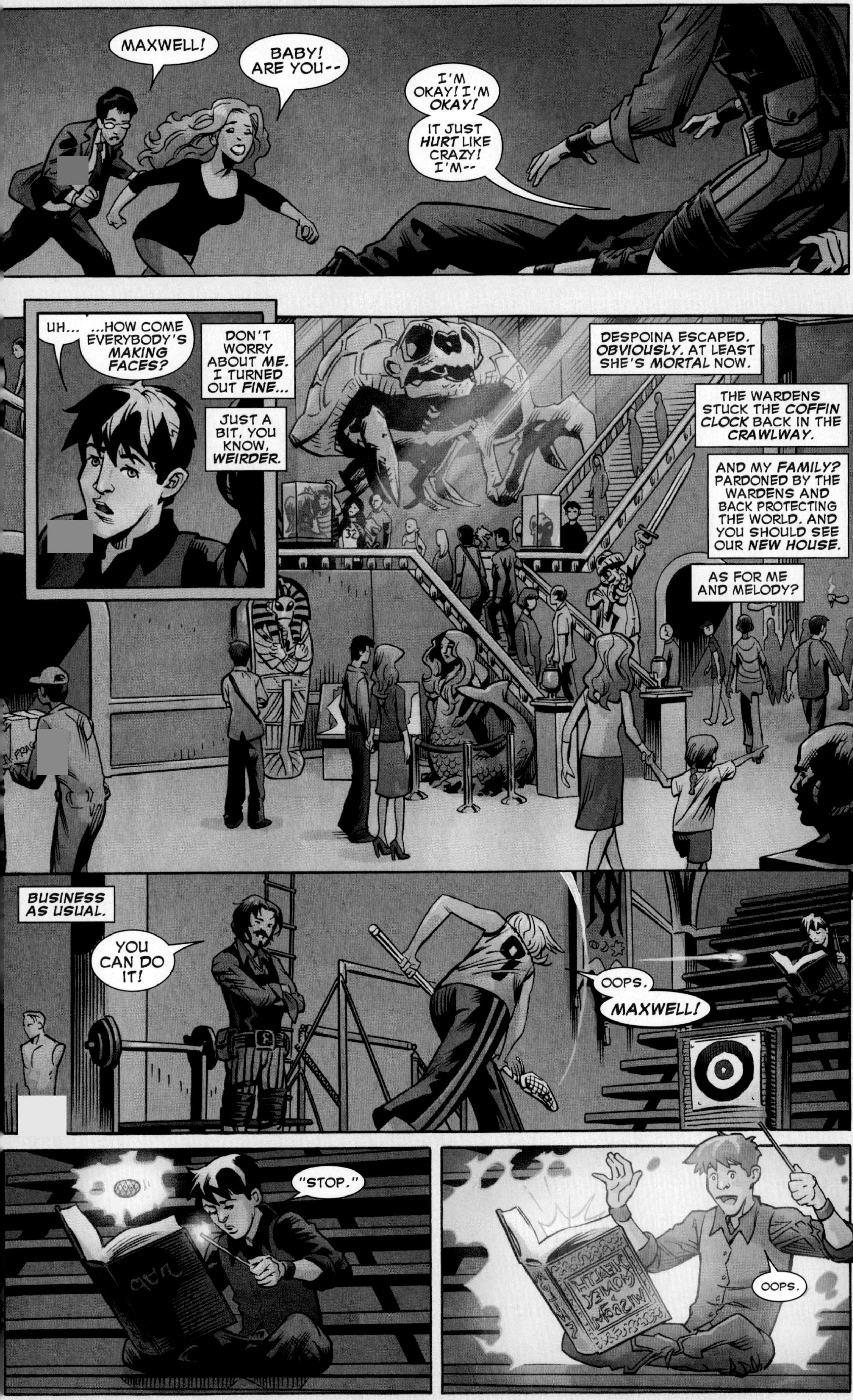
MAXWELL!
BABY! ARE YOU--
I'M OKAY! I'M OKAY!
IT JUST HURT LIKE CRAZY! I'M--
UH...
...HOW COME EVERYBODY'S MAKING FACES?
DON'T WORRY ABOUT ME. I TURNED OUT FINE...
JUST A BIT, YOU KNOW, WEIRDER.
DESPOINA ESCAPED. OBVIOUSLY. AT LEAST SHE'S MORTAL NOW.
THE WARDENS STUCK THE COFFIN CLOCK BACK IN THE CRAWLWAY.
AND MY FAMILY? PARDONED BY THE WARDENS AND BACK PROTECTING THE WORLD. AND YOU SHOULD SEE OUR NEW HOUSE.
AS FOR ME AND MELODY?
BUSINESS AS USUAL.
YOU CAN DO IT!
OOPS.
MAXWELL!
"STOP."
OOPS.

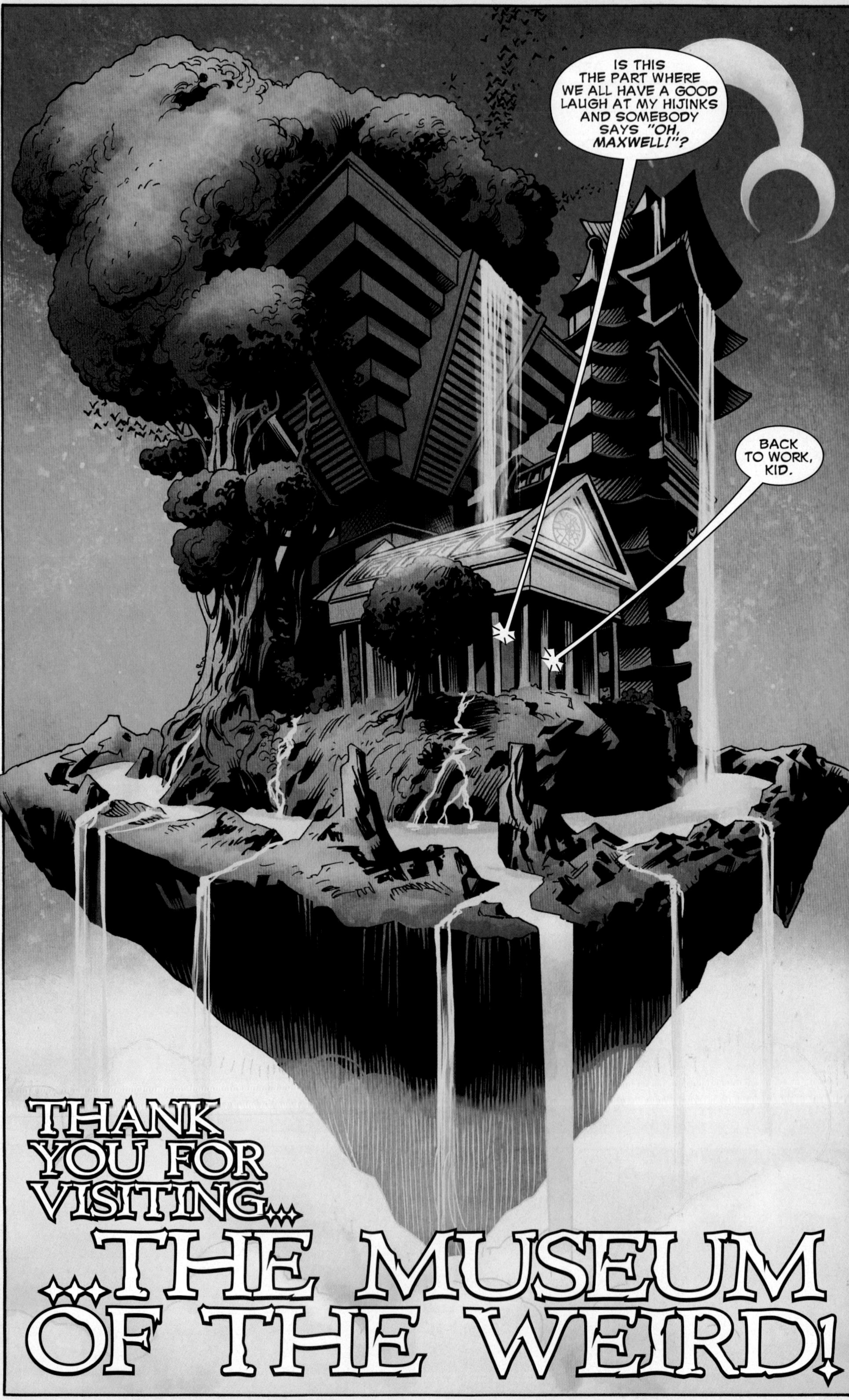
IS THIS THE PART WHERE WE ALL HAVE A GOOD LAUGH AT MY HIJINKS AND SOMEBODY SAYS "OH, MAXWELL!"?
BACK TO WORK, KID.
THANK YOU FOR VISITING...
...THE MUSEUM OF THE WEIRD!

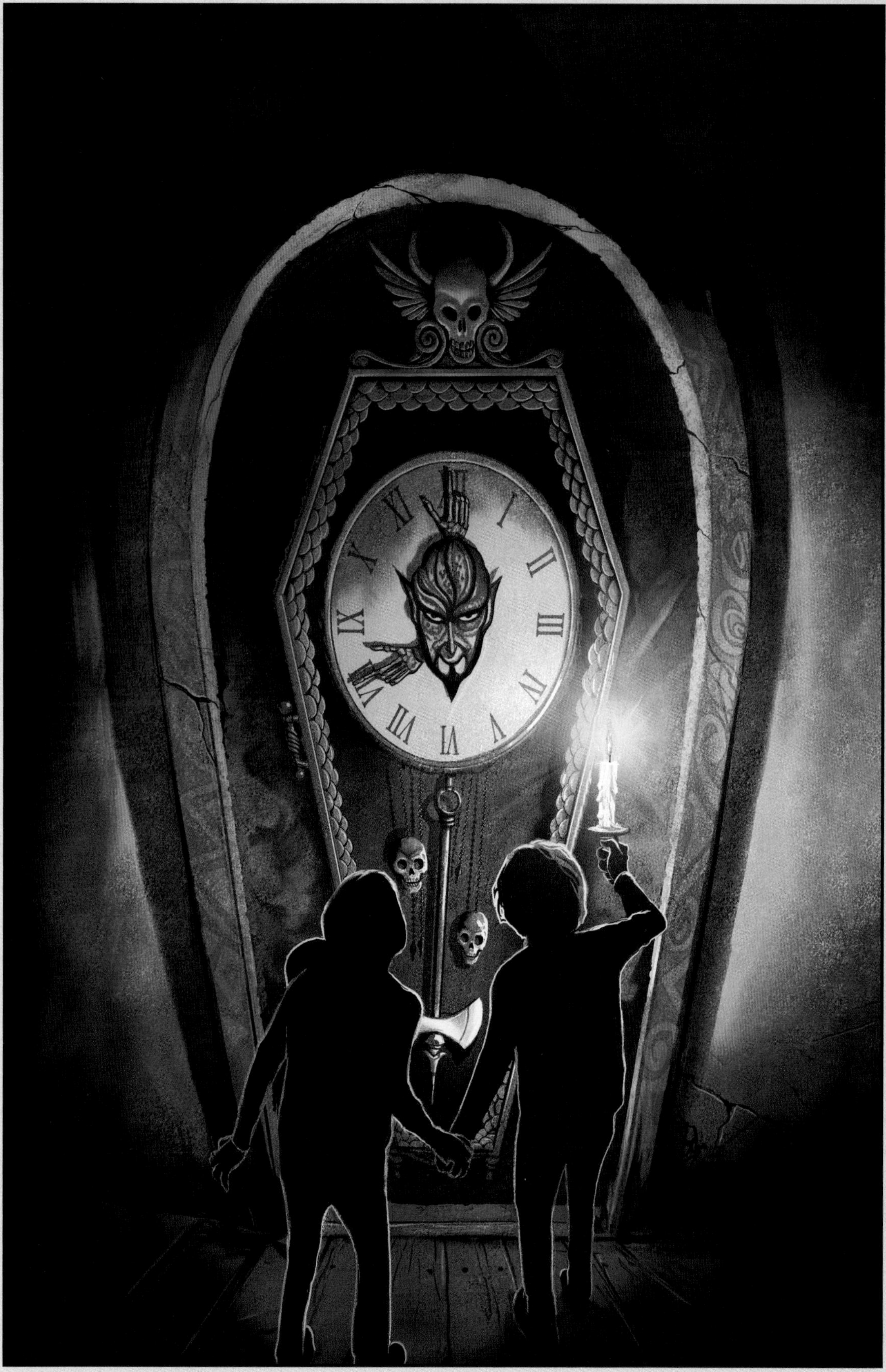

SEEKERS OF THE WEIRD #1 TEASER VARIANT
BY MICHAEL DEL MUNDO

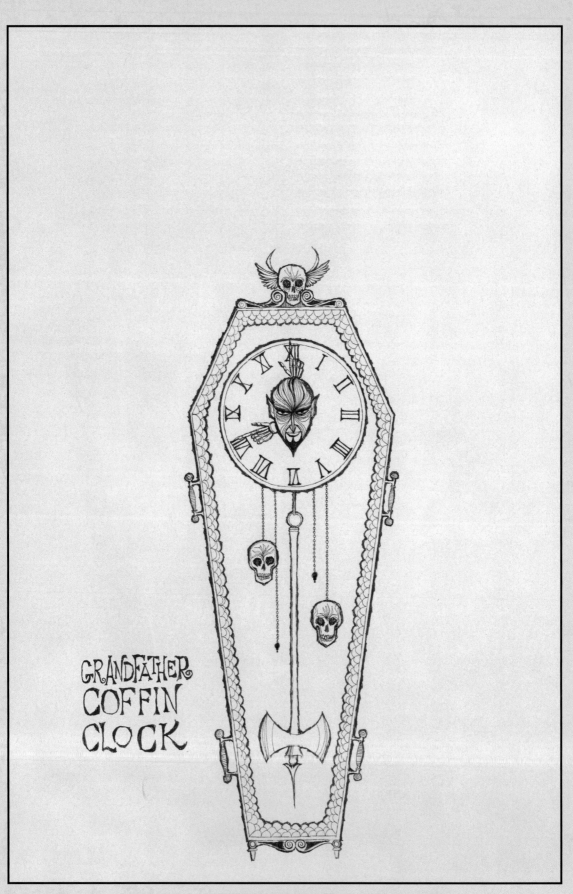

GRANDFATHER
COFFIN
CLOCK

SEEKERS OF THE WEIRD #1 VARIANT
BY ROLLY CRUMP

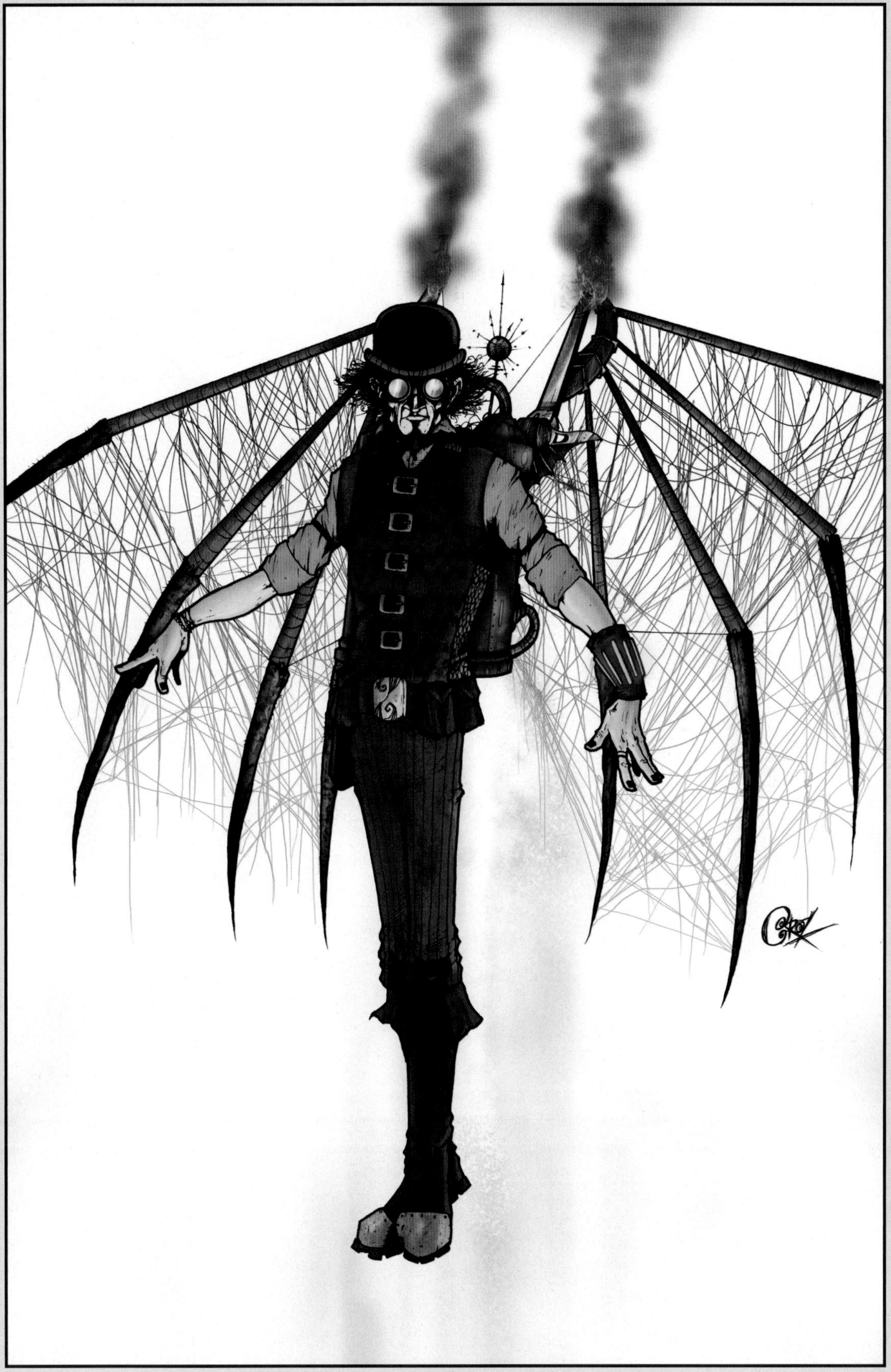

SEEKERS OF THE WEIRD #1 VARIANT
BY BRIAN CROSBY

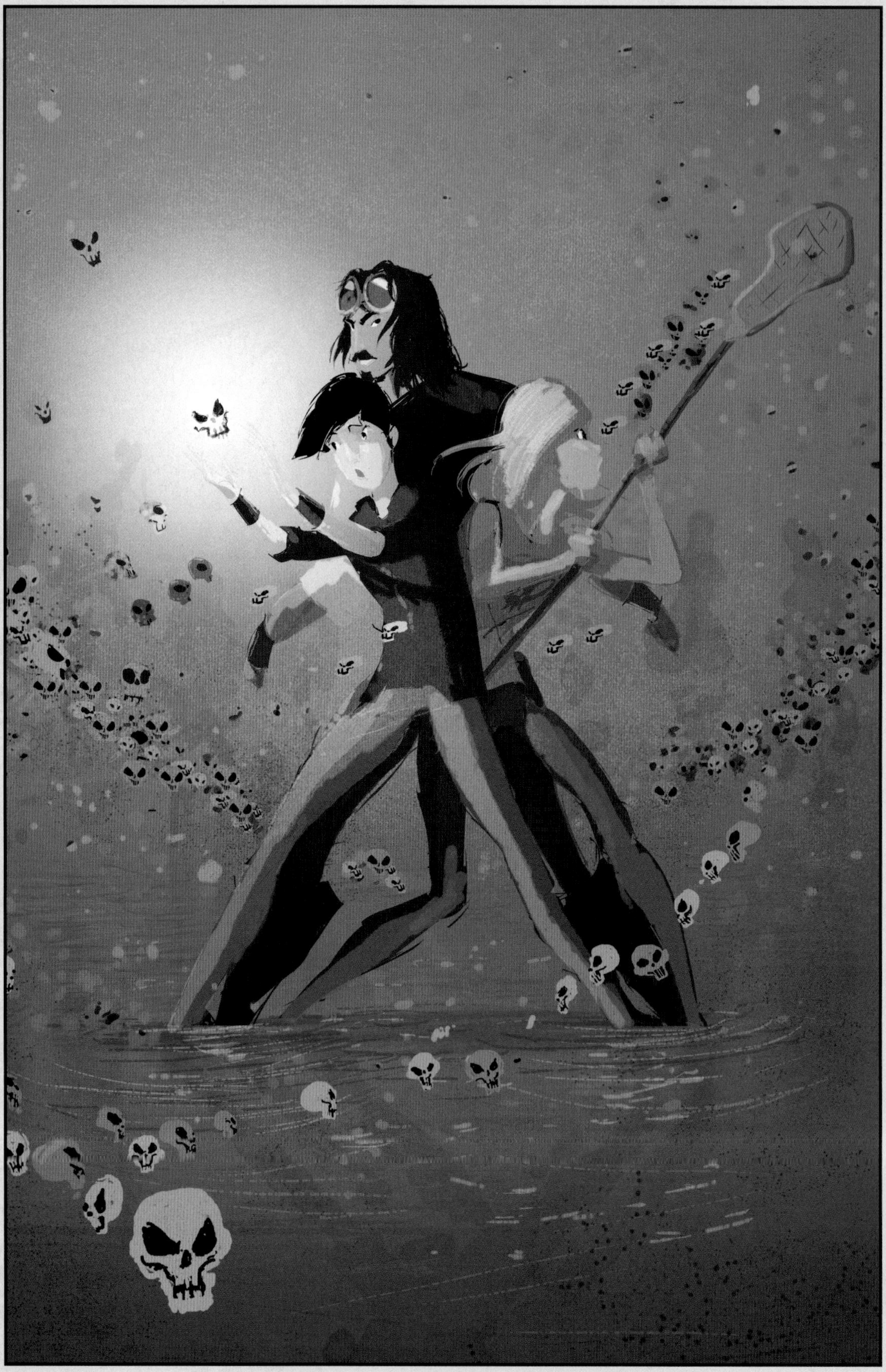

SEEKERS OF THE WEIRD #2 VARIANT
BY PASCAL CAMPION

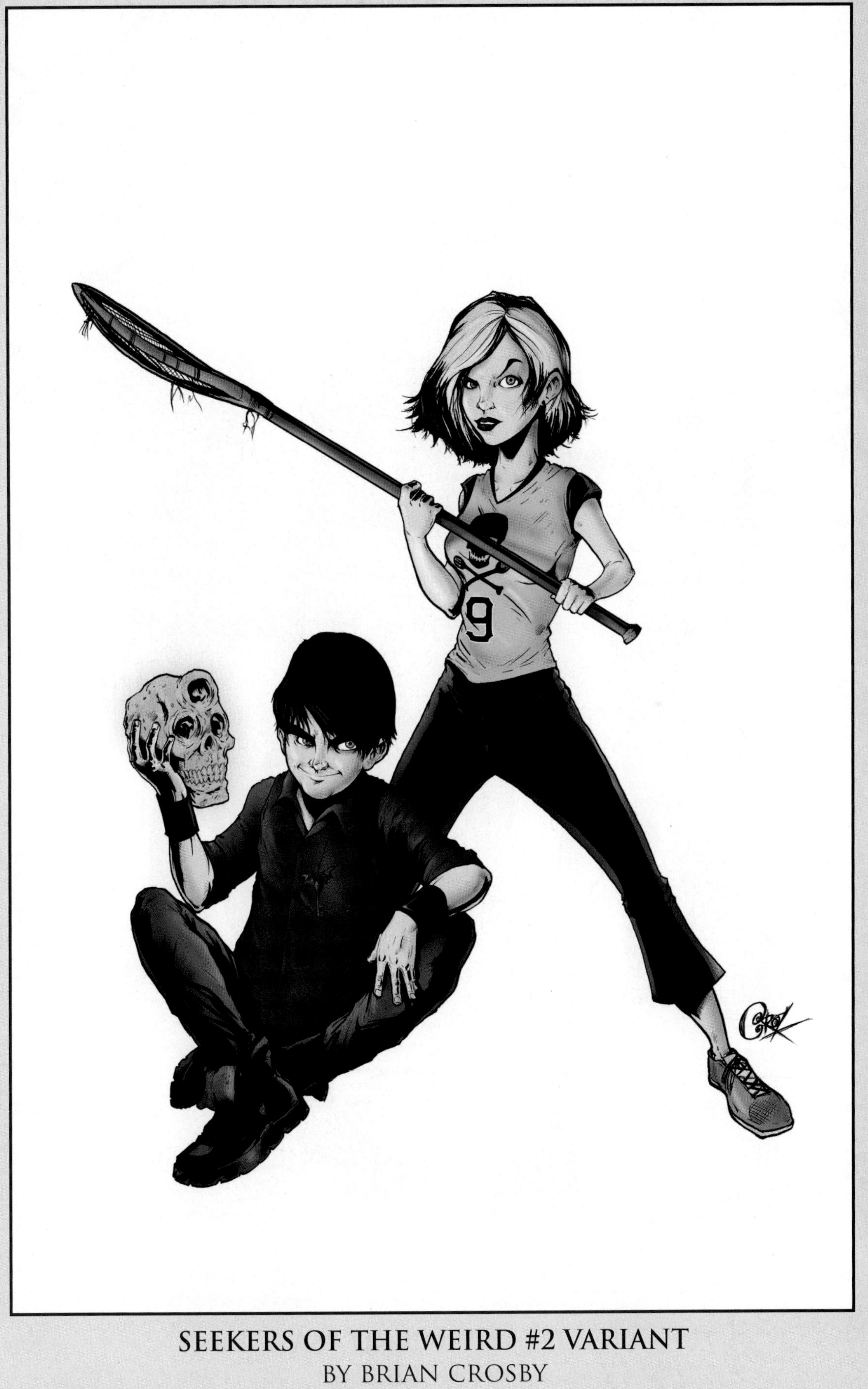
9

SEEKERS OF THE WEIRD #2 VARIANT
BY BRIAN CROSBY

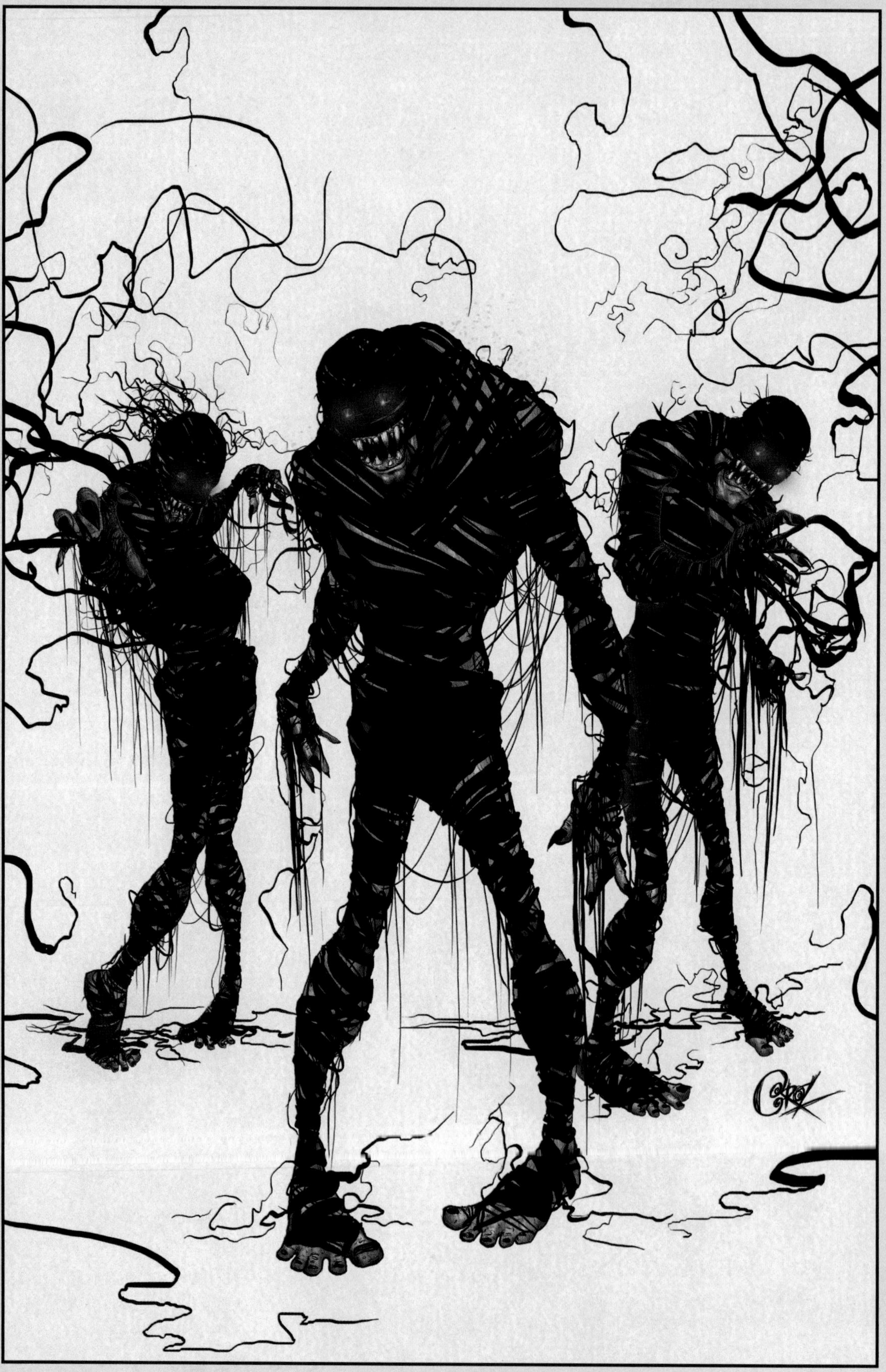

SEEKERS OF THE WEIRD #3 VARIANT
BY BRIAN CROSBY

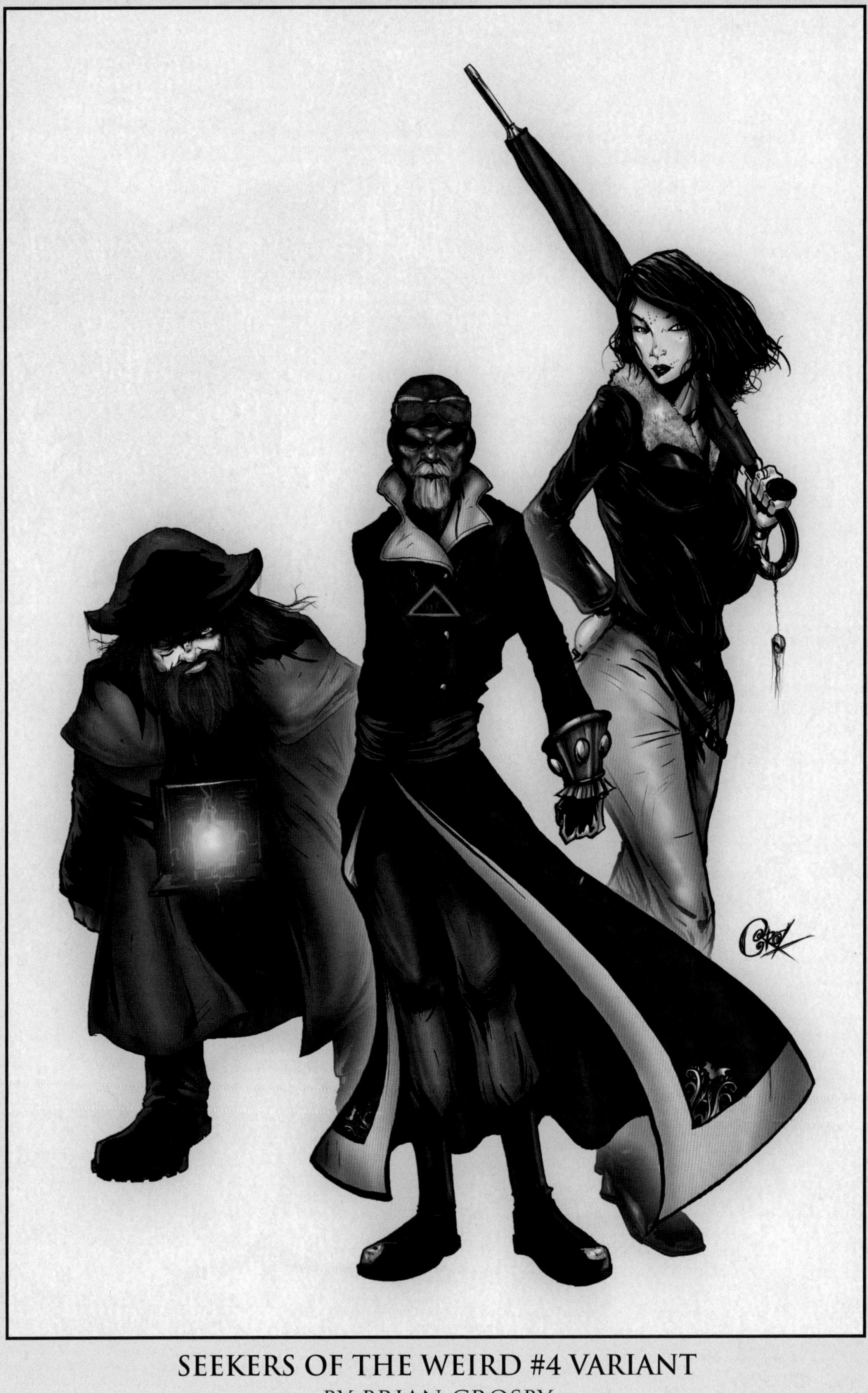

SEEKERS OF THE WEIRD #4 VARIANT
BY BRIAN CROSBY

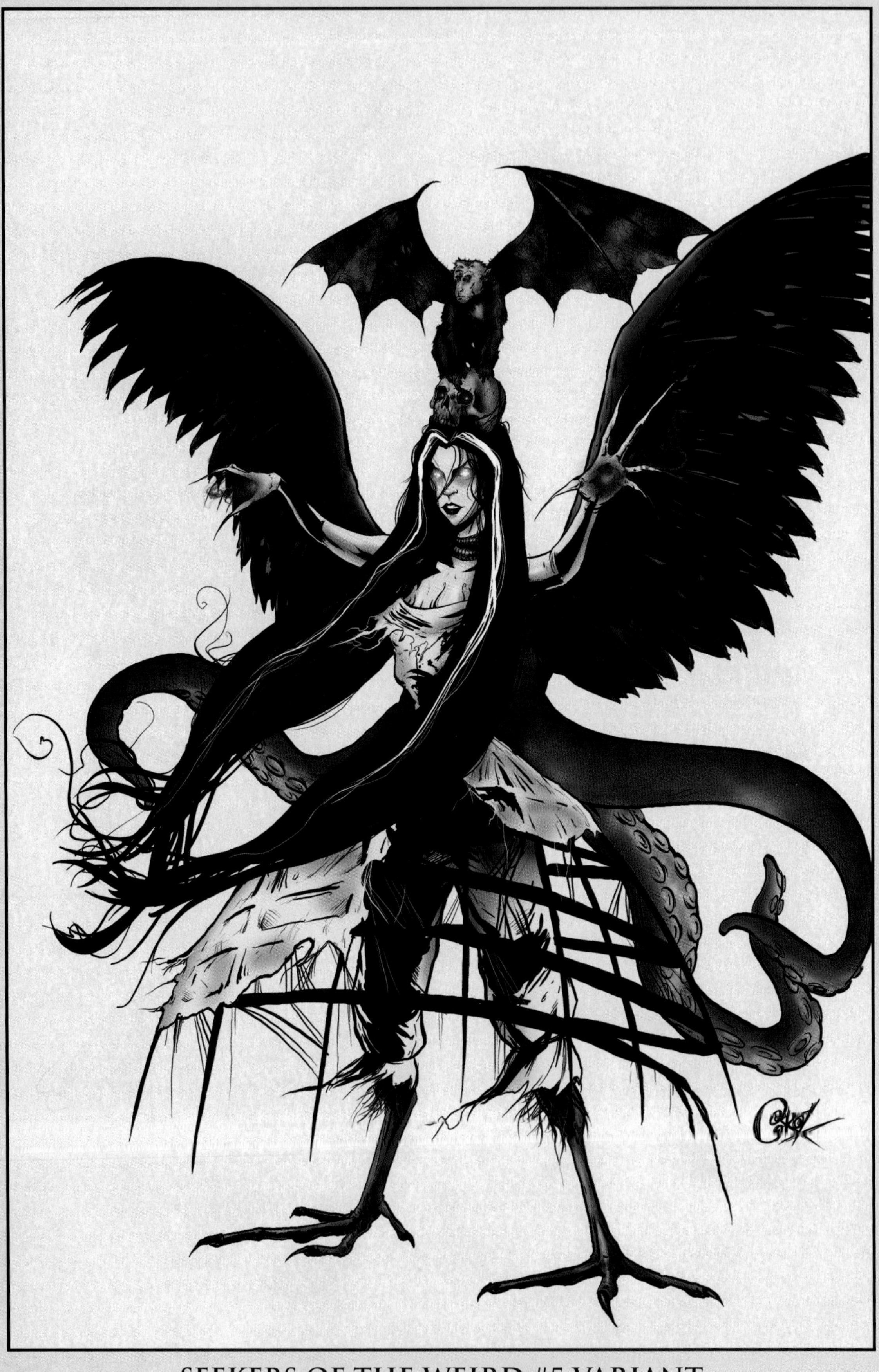

SEEKERS OF THE WEIRD #5 VARIANT
BY BRIAN CROSBY

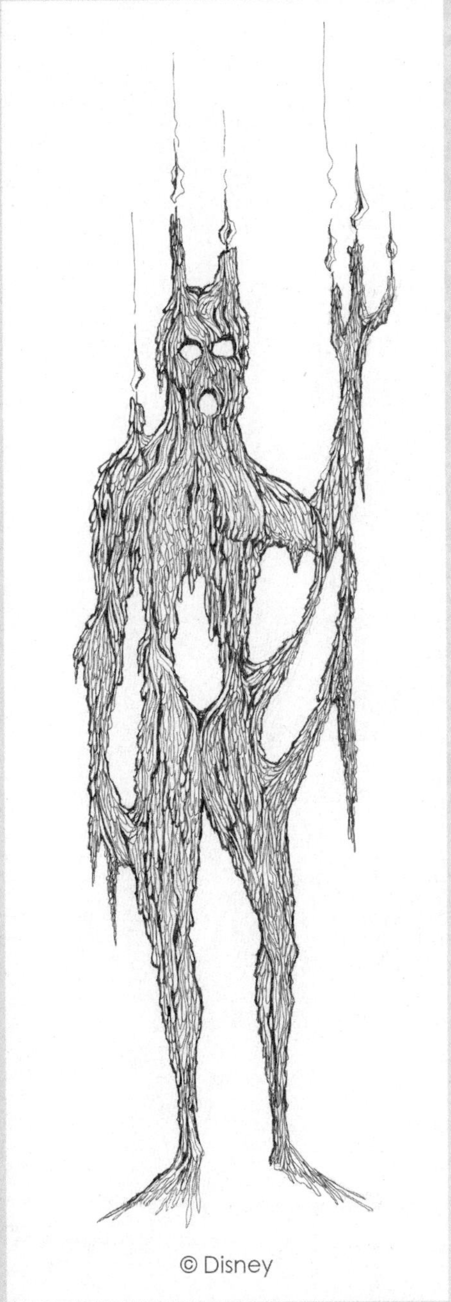
© Disney

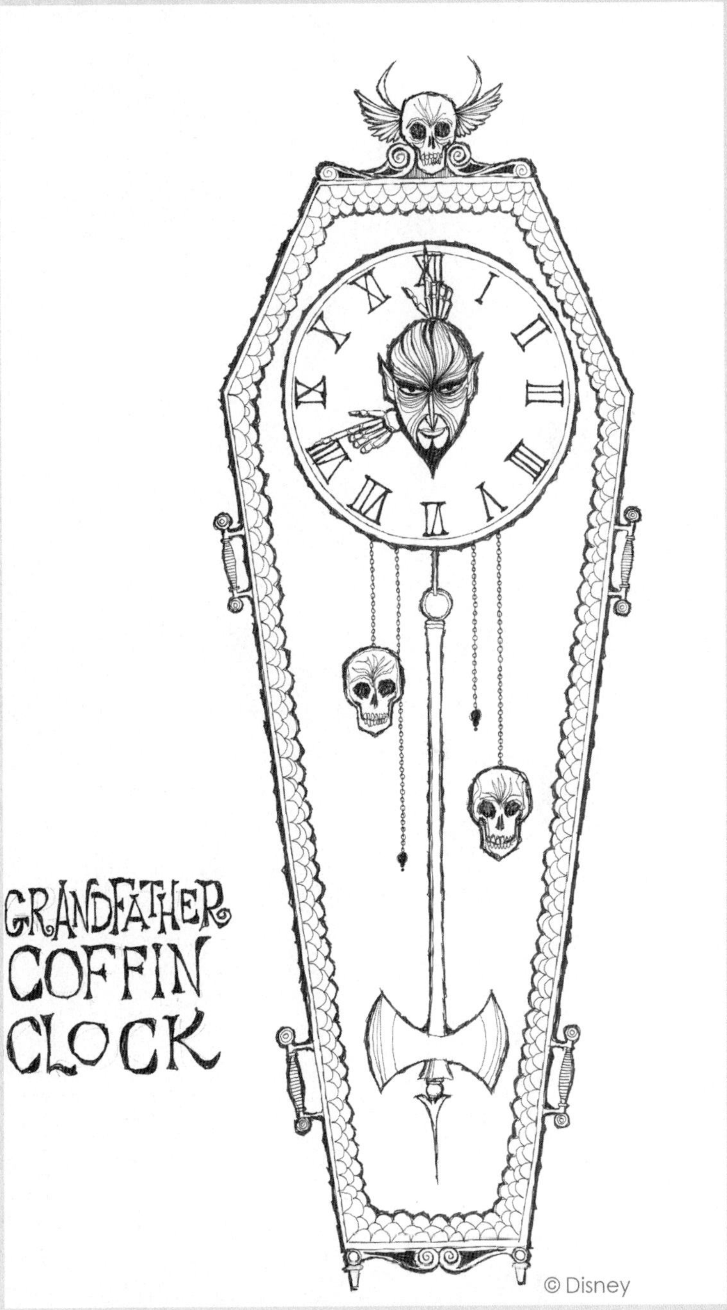
GRANDFATHER
COFFIN
CLOCK
© Disney

MUSEUM OF THE WEIRD DESIGNS
BY ROLLY CRUMP

ARTWORK COURTESY OF WALT DISNEY IMAGINEERING ART COLLECTION

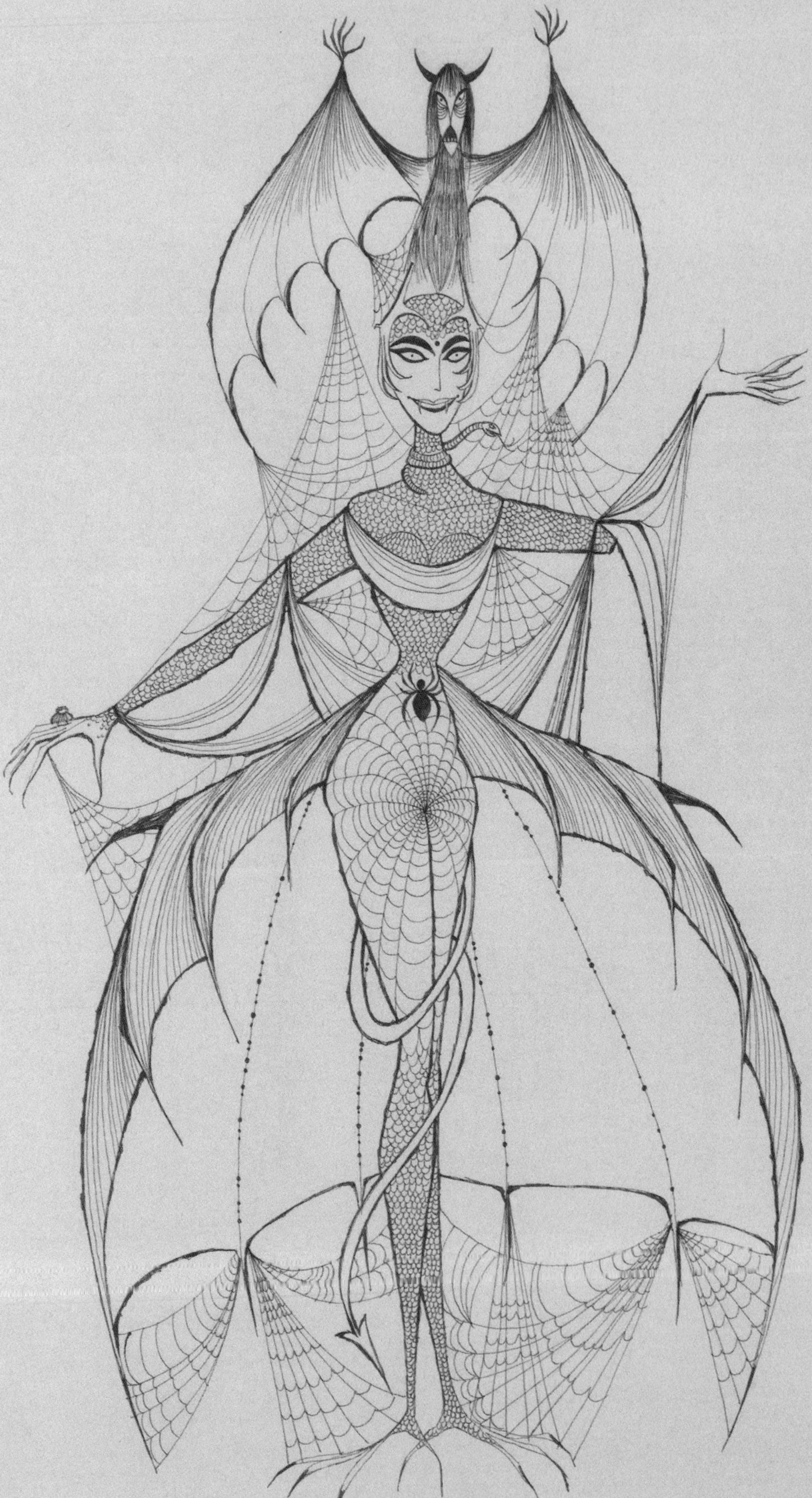

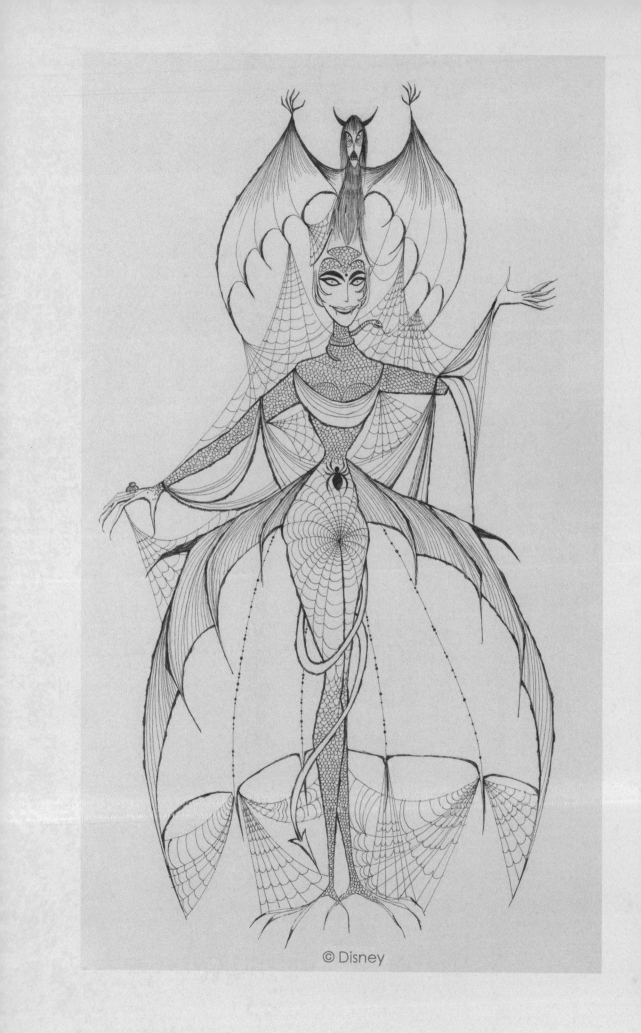

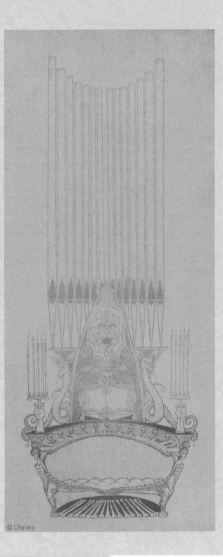

© Disney

SCULPTURE

© Disney

AQUARIUM WITH GHOST FISH

© Disney

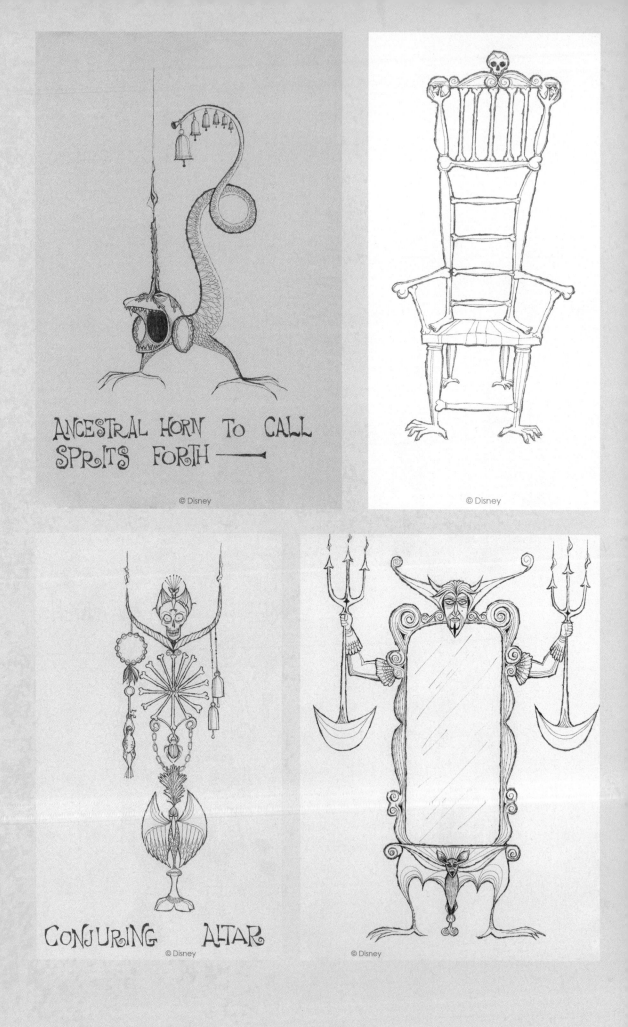

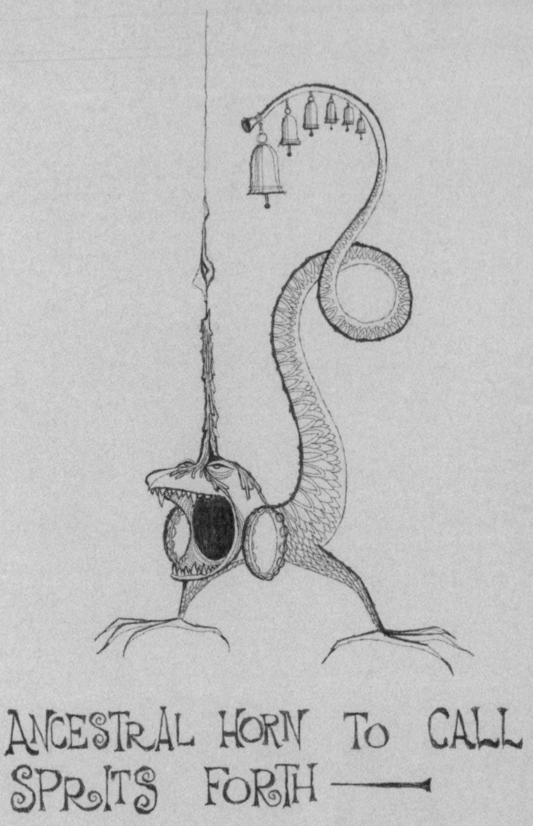
ANCESTRAL HORN TO CALL
SPRITS FORTH

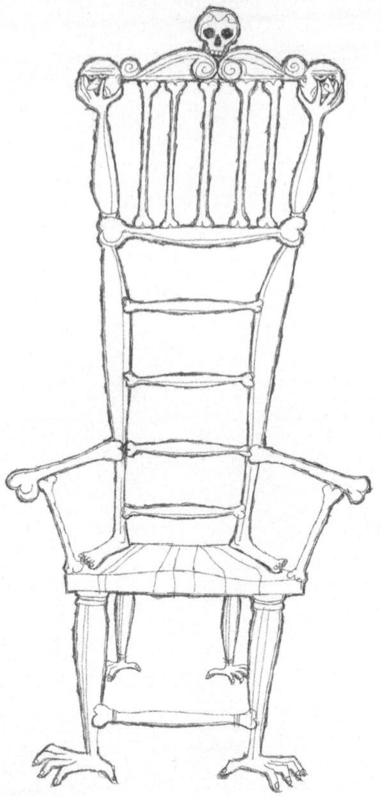

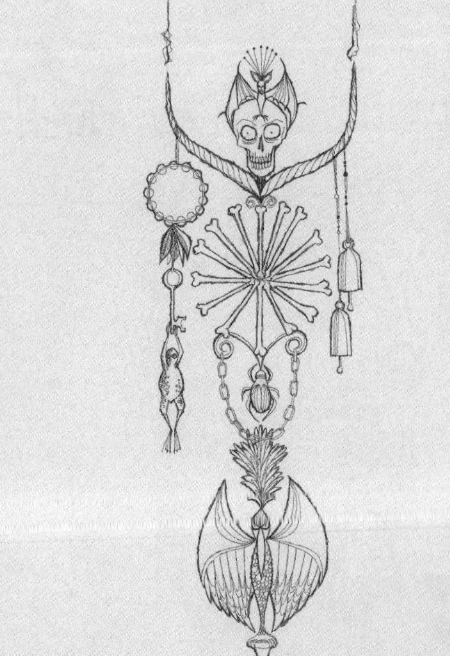
CONJURING ALTAR

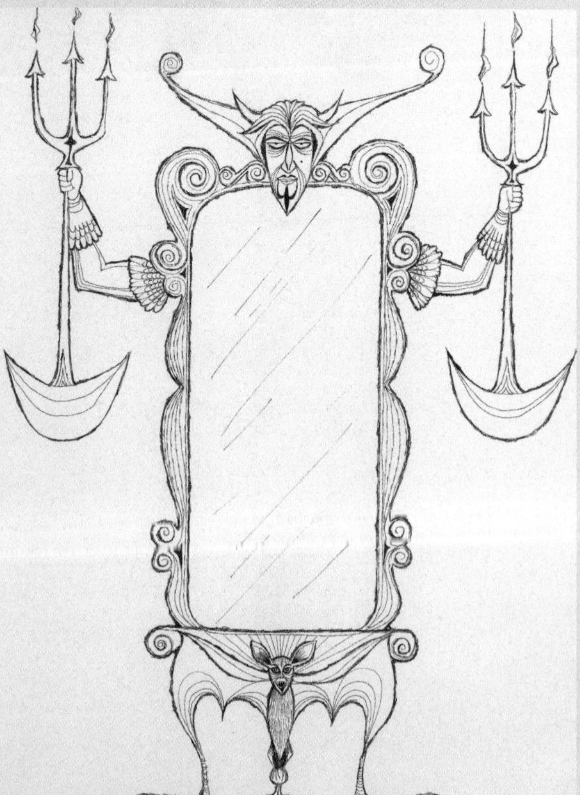

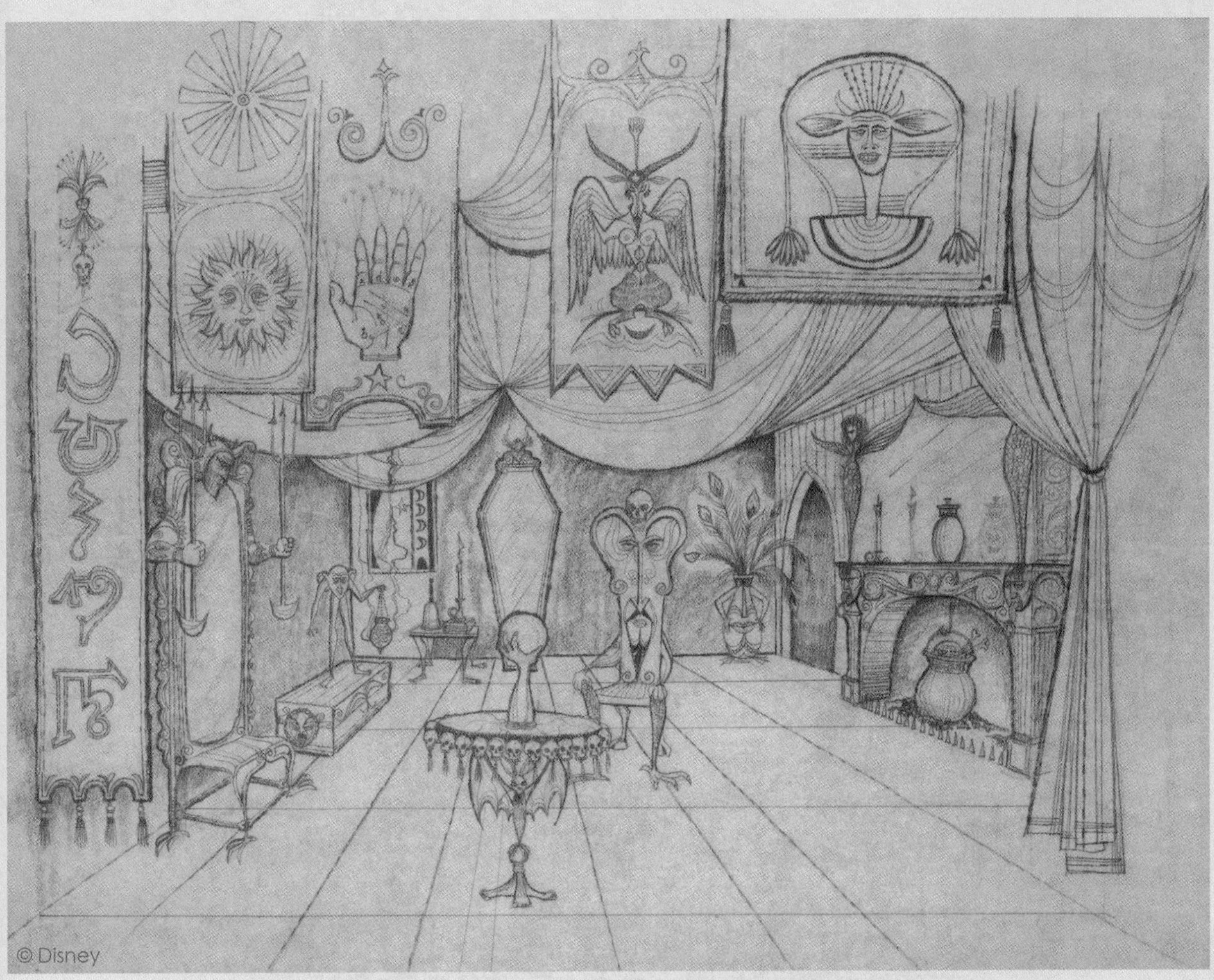
© Disney

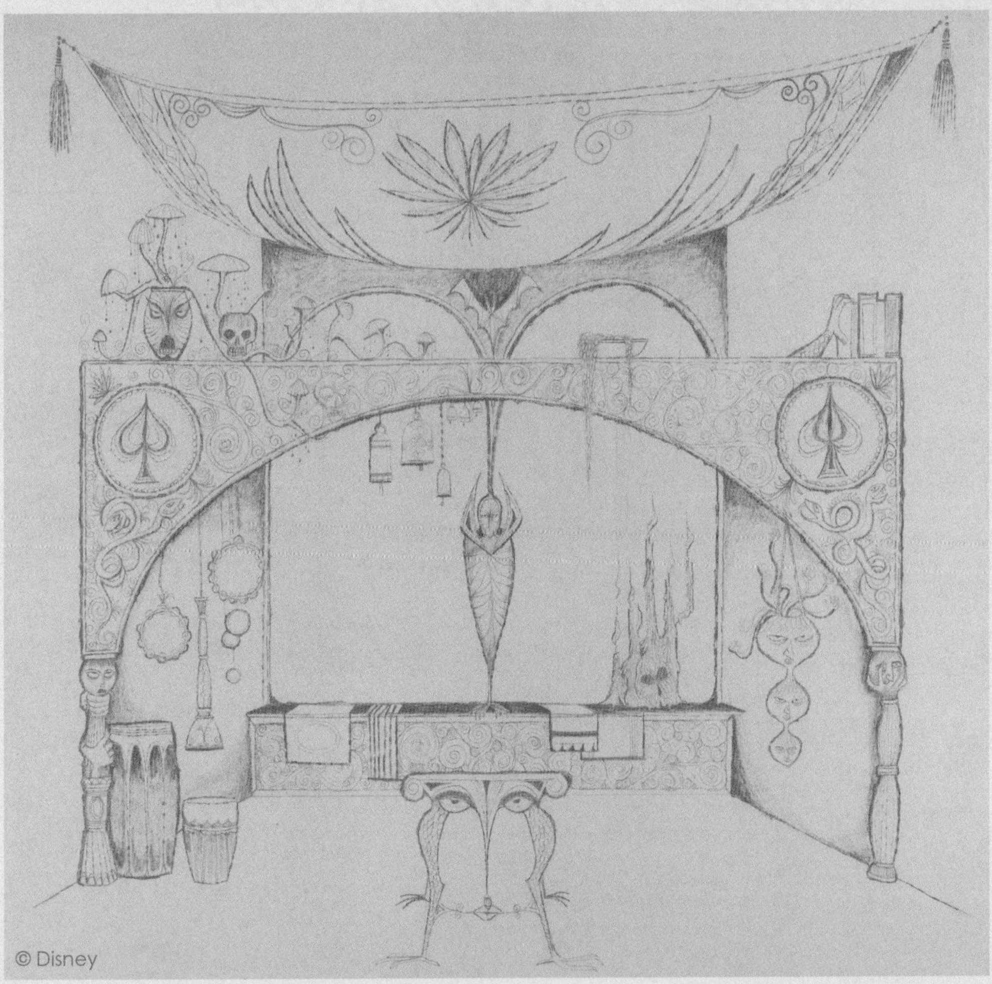
© Disney

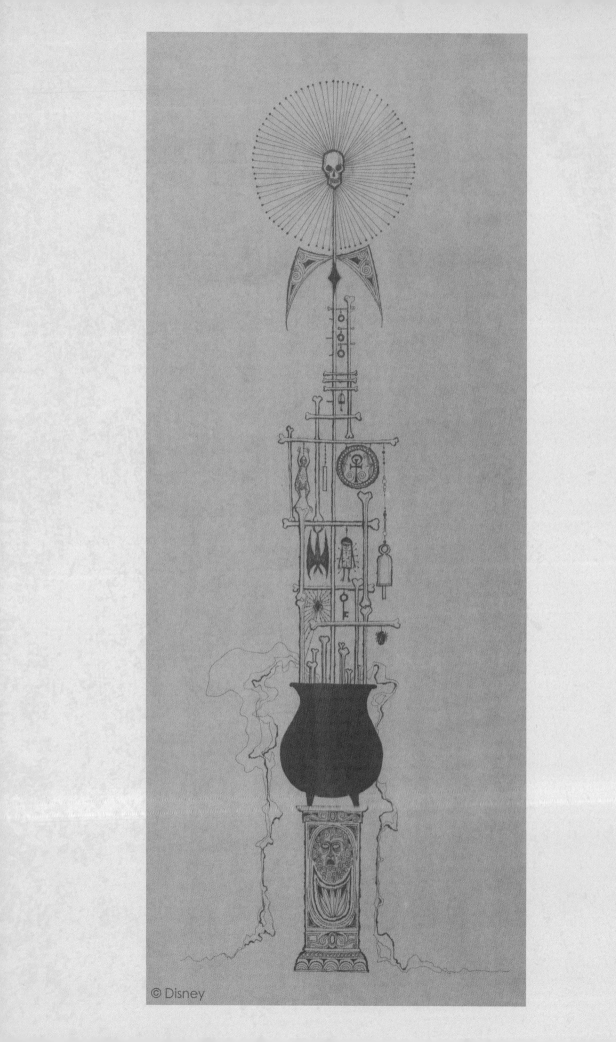

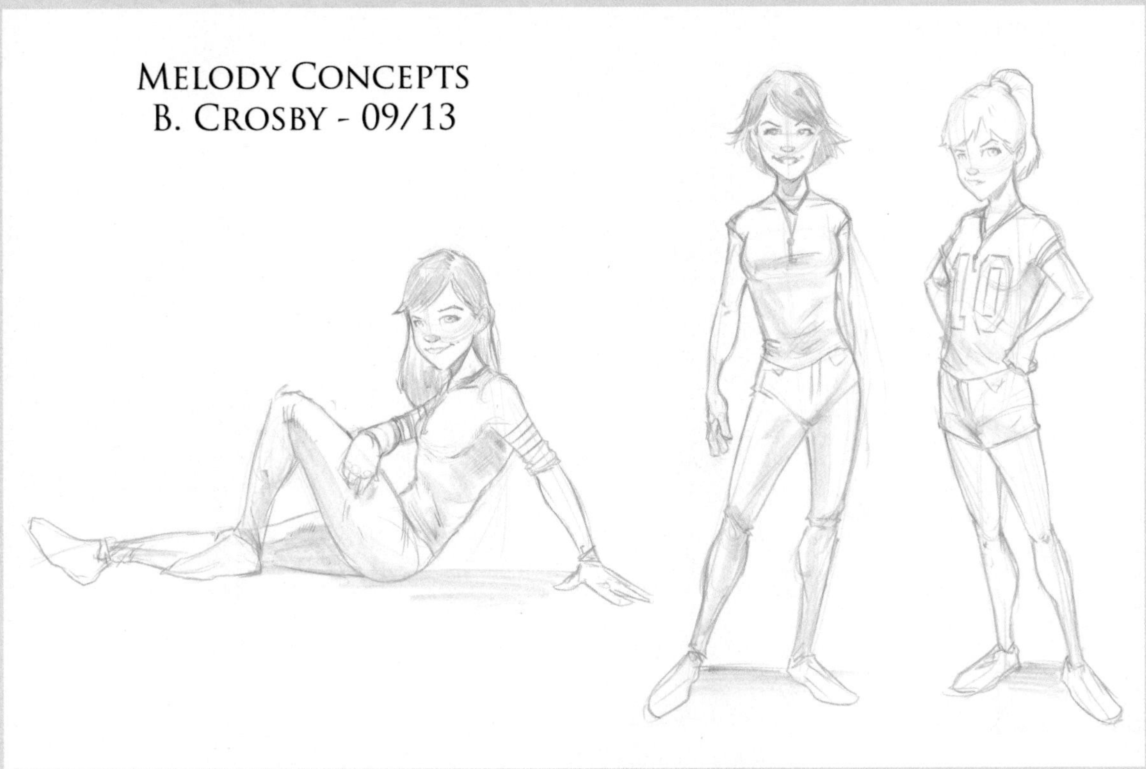
MELODY CONCEPTS
B. CROSBY - 09/13

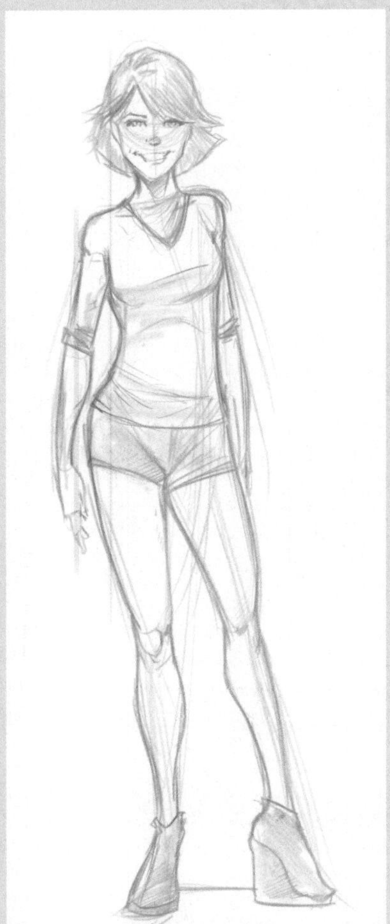

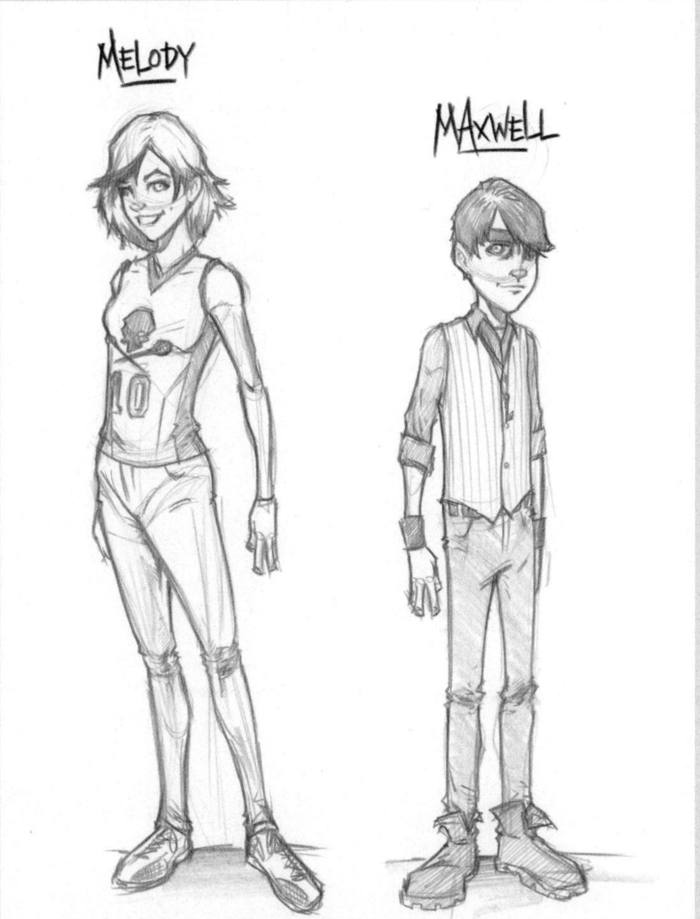
MELODY
10
MAXWELL

CHARACTER DESIGNS & CONCEPTS
BY BRIAN CROSBY

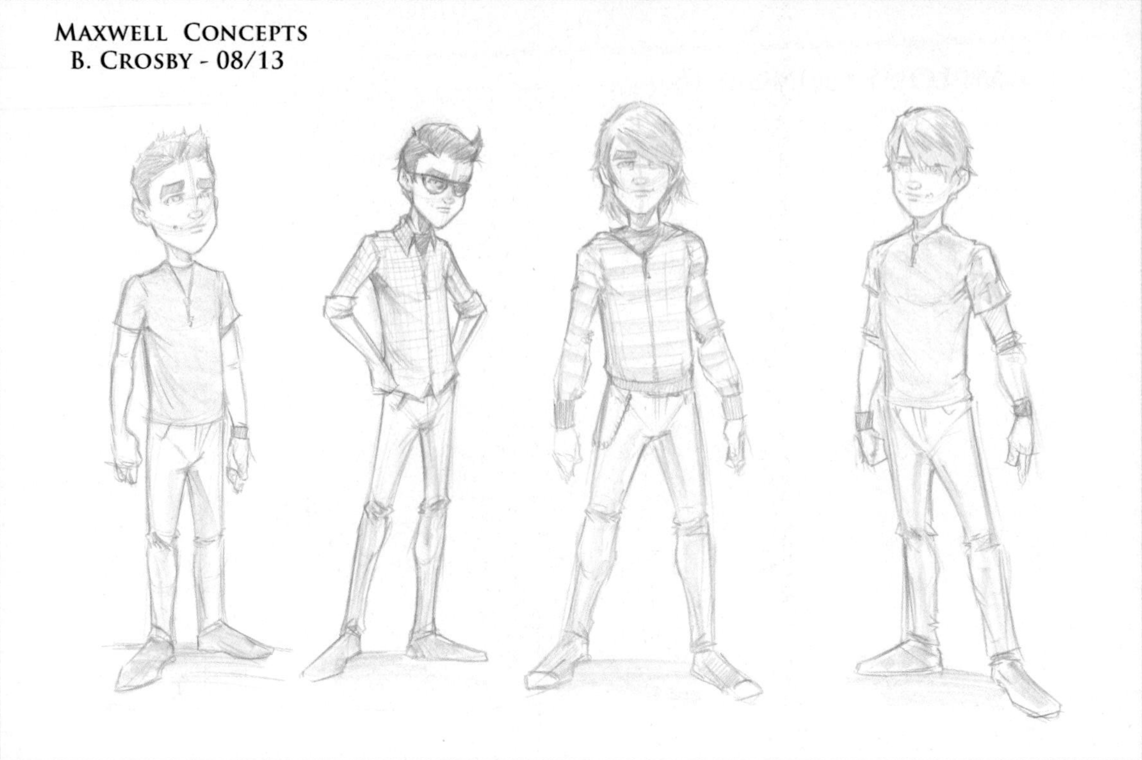
MAXWELL CONCEPTS
B. CROSBY - 08/13

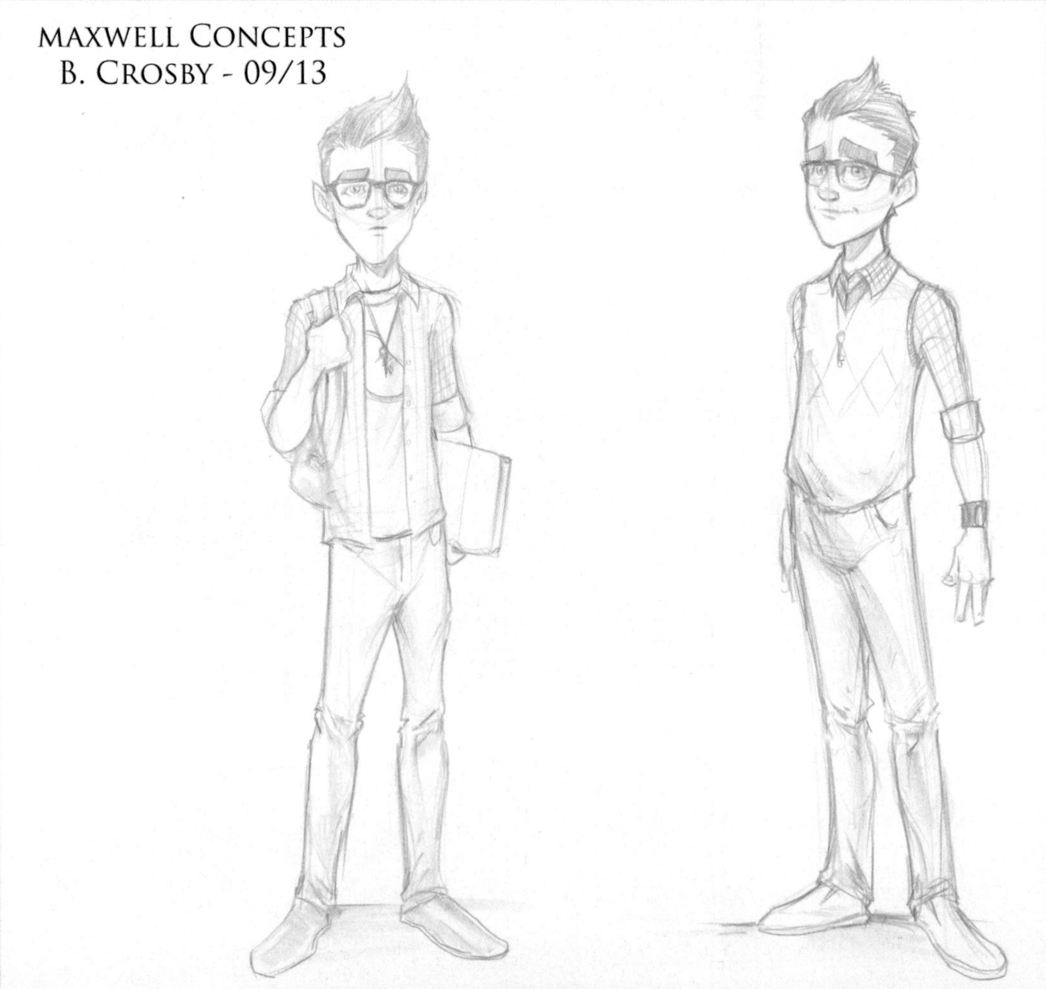
MAXWELL CONCEPTS
B. CROSBY - 09/13

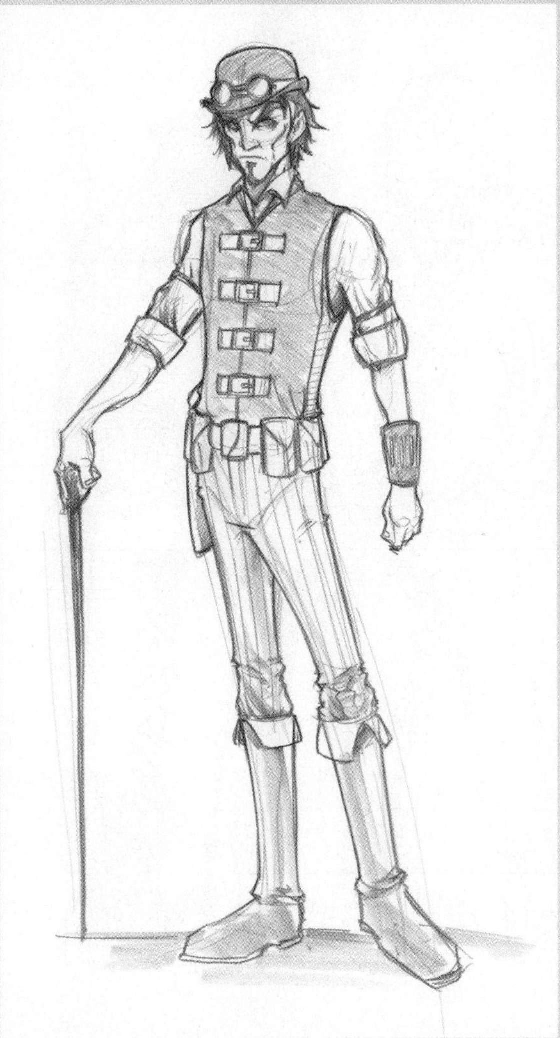

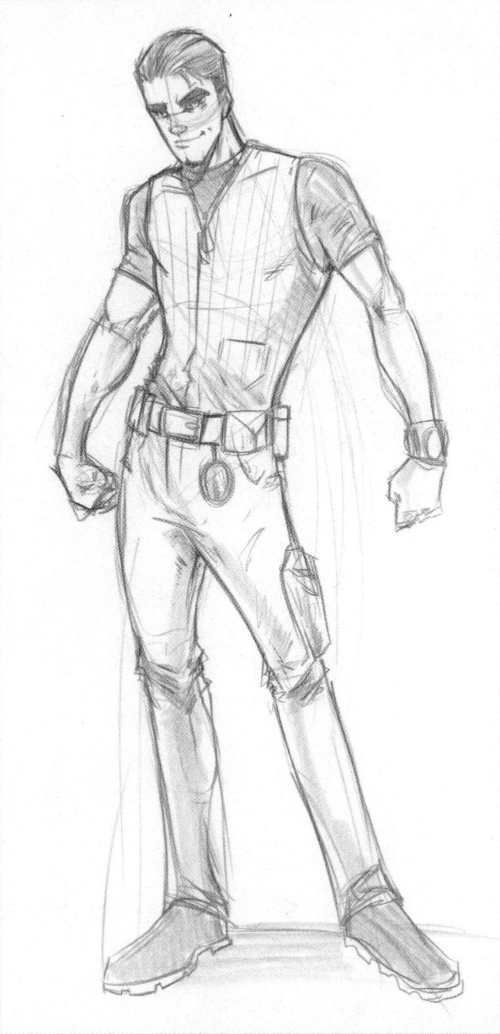

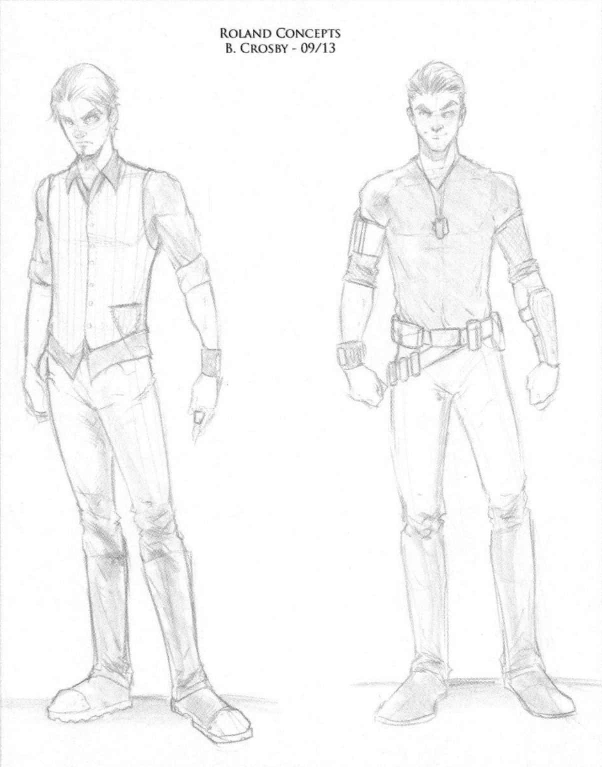
Roland Concepts
B. Crosby - 09/13

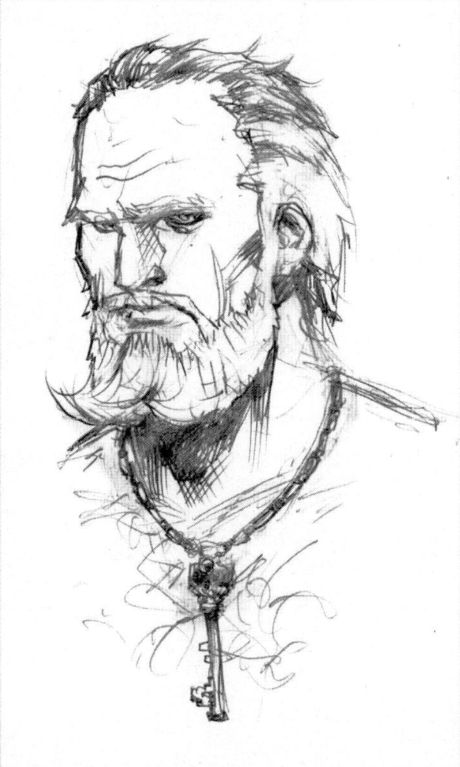

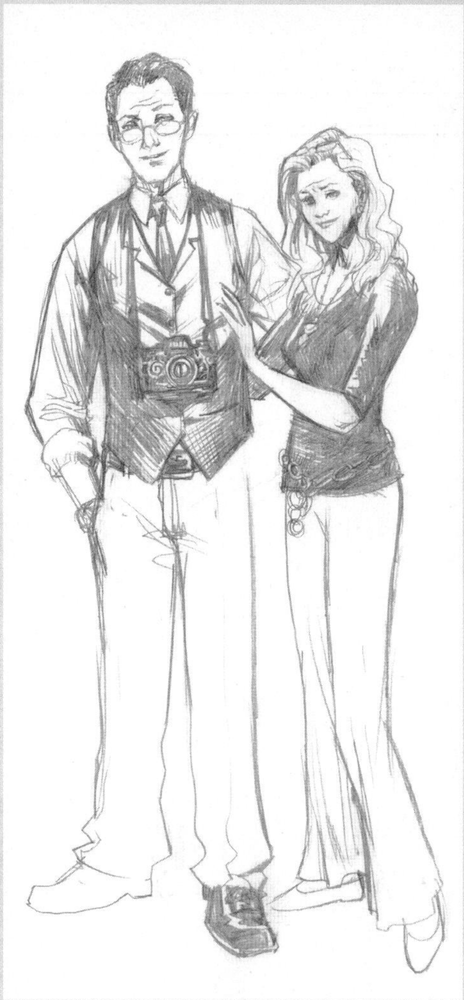

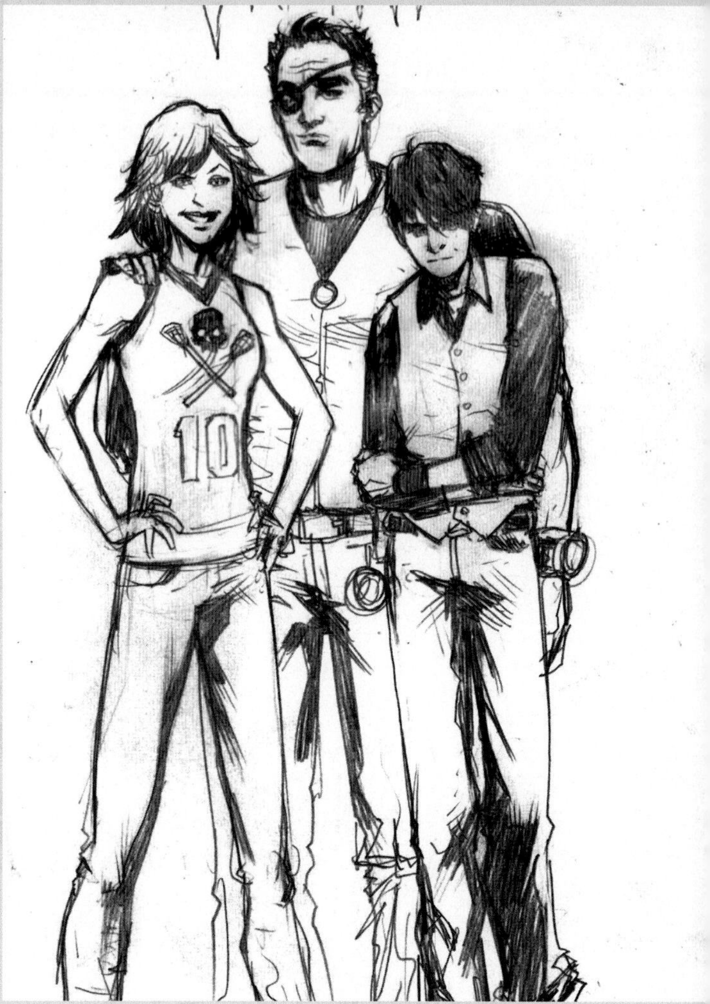

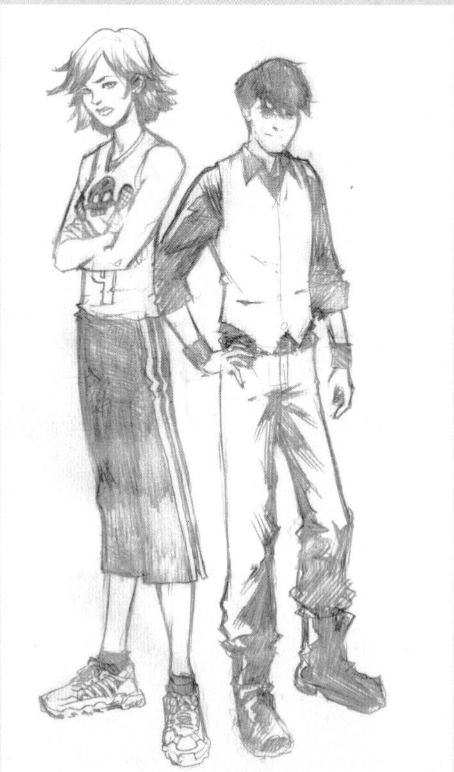
KEEP KIDS

CHARACTER DESIGNS & CONCEPTS
BY KARL MOLINE

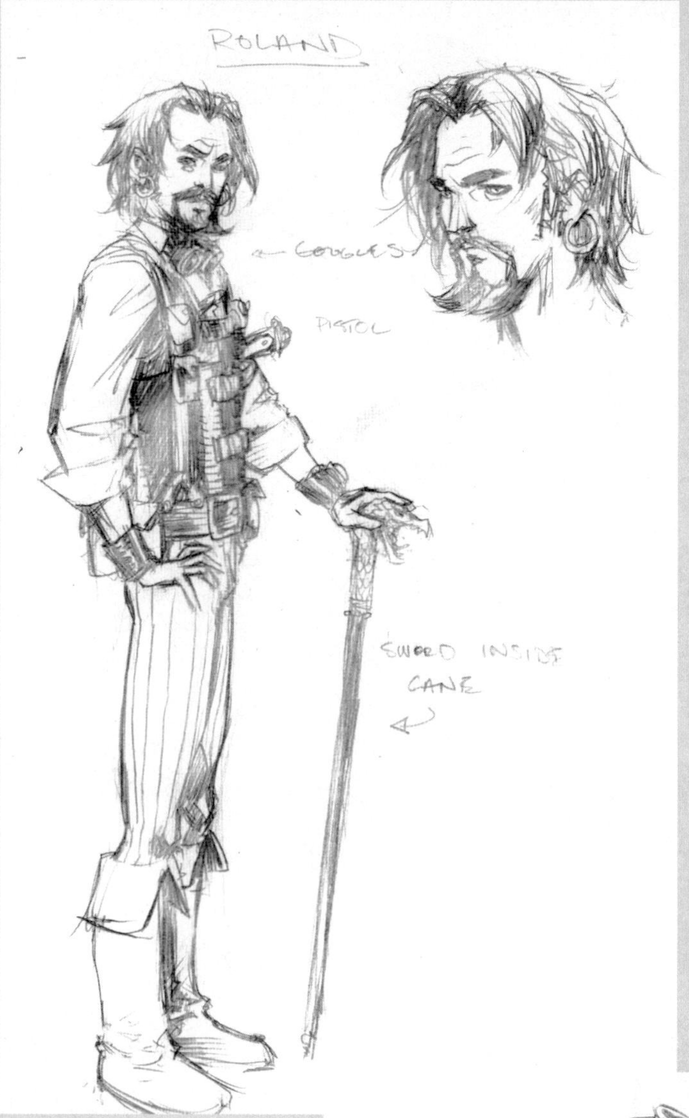
ROLAND
GOGGLES
PISTOL
SWORD INSIDE
CANE

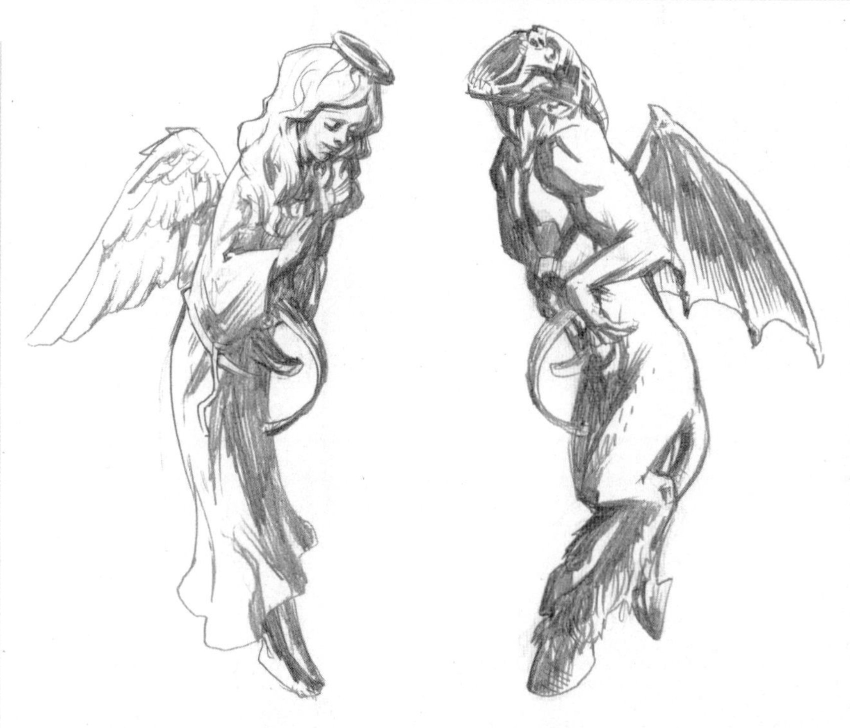

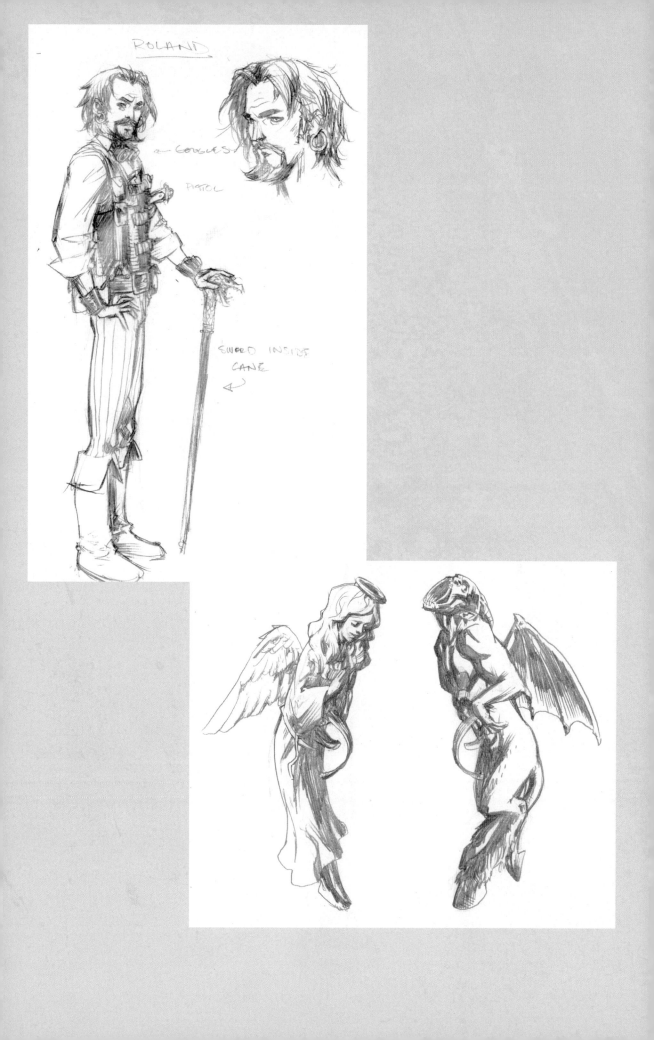

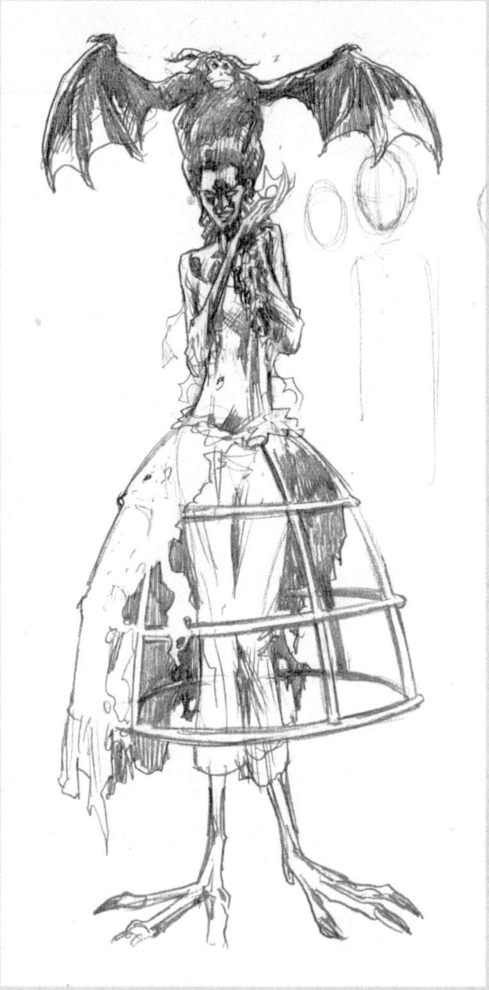
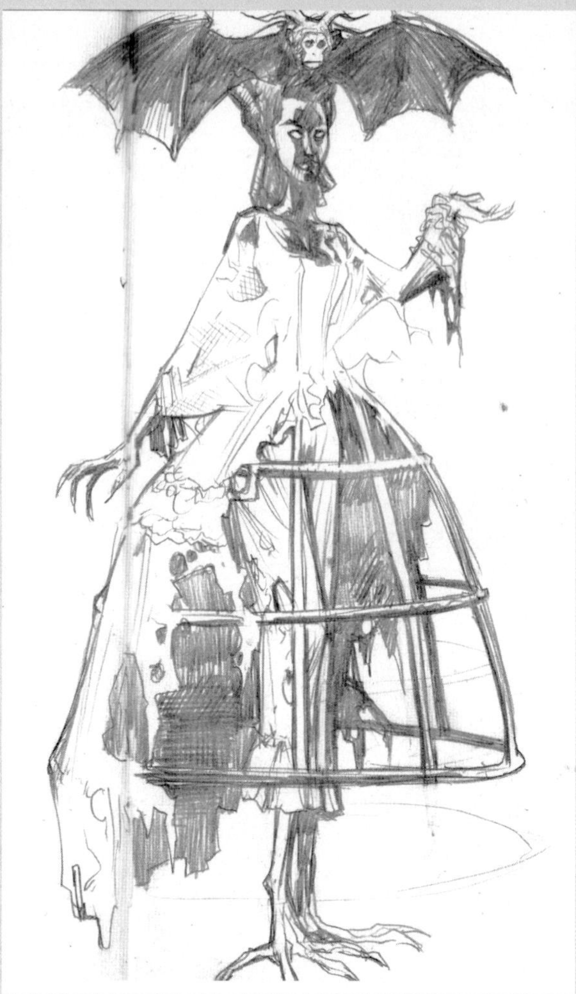
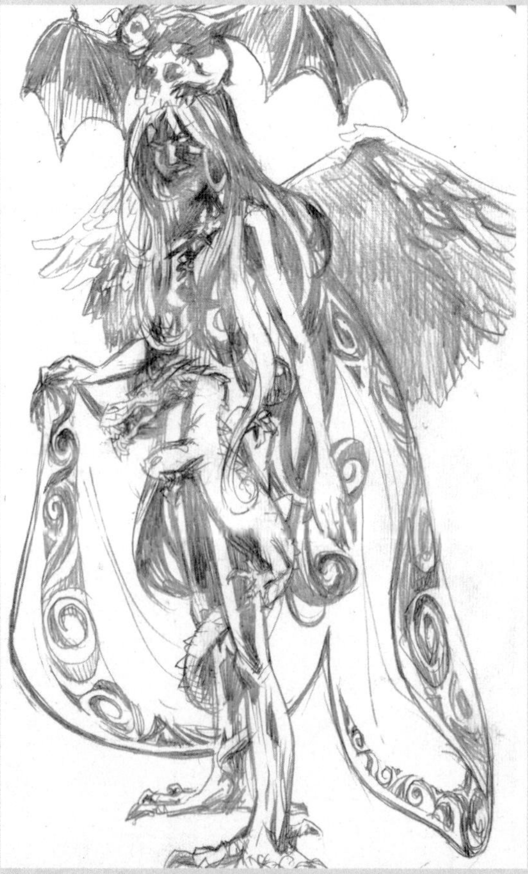

What's weirder than the story behind the story? How about the story behind that?

You see, as legend has it, the DISNEY KINGDOMS imprint began when – shortly after Marvel joined the Disney family – our Chief Creative Officer Joe Quesada attended a baseball game with a team of Walt Disney Imagineers and discussed potential project ideas over peanuts and Cracker Jacks. It was a true "What If?" scenario that asked what would happen if the House of Ideas worked together with the Imagineers to create action-packed worlds around Disney's greatest attractions. Fast forward a few years and—thanks to the effort's of Marvel's David Gabriel, who willed the DISNEY KINGDOMS imprint to life—that question has finally sprung to life in the pages of SEEKERS OF THE WEIRD!

But wait, there's another piece to this peculiar puzzle: The Museum of the Weird itself. The Museum, a collection of creepy curiosities unearthed from around the globe, was the creation of legendary Imagineer Rolly Crump. Rolly originally designed the odd artifacts for the Haunted Mansion, but once Walt Disney saw them, he knew they deserved to be spotlighted in their own home as a separate walk-through attraction in connection with the Mansion.

Unfortunately, due to Walt's passing, Rolly's amazing designs never came to full life in *Disneyland*© or the Magic Kingdom…but their existence was whispered about by Disney faithful for decades to come. The passion for the Museum compelled us – and our brilliant Imagineer allies Jim Clark, Brian Crosby, Tom Morris and Josh Shipley – to start questioning their untold story: Where did the items come from? Who discovered and gathered them? Who defends them…and who wants to exploit them?

The key to this epic is, of course, the mind of Rolly Crump. Our goal is to bring his unique, breathtaking and quirky cool visions to life in a fully realized world. Everything is built around being true and authentic to his revolutionary aesthetic and showcasing his amazing imagination to a whole new generation. Writer Brandon Seifert, penciler Karl Moline, inker Rick Magyar, artist Filipe Andrade colorist Jean-Francois Beaulieu, letterer Joe Caramagna and cover artist Michael Del Mundo have poured their hearts and souls into each issue…and we're all hoping you continue to join us for this wild and weird adventure!

Your Man @ Marvel,
Bill Rosemann

When I first told my friends that I was writing a book for Marvel, and they asked me what it was, there'd always be a pause before I replied. "It's a Disney book...for Marvel...about a Disney park attraction...that was never actually built...but isn't like, something made up! It totally got designed! You know. Partially."

Any way you slice it, DISNEY KINGDOMS: SEEKERS OF THE WEIRD is a weird series. Which I think is why it was such a good fit for me.

I broke into comics writing Witch Doctor, and it's one of the weirdest comics on the stands. I mean, come on: It's about magic and monsters, but it looks at them through a medical and biological point of view. But without just saying "magic is actually science!" No, magic is magic. But even if you're a vampire, blood is still going to clot while you try to feed on it—unless you do something about it. It's a supernatural book that uses terms like "vasodilator" and "pseudomorphs." Very weird book.

Editor Bill Rosemann had read Witch Doctor, and liked it. So when I contacted him at the tail end of 2012 and told him I'd desperately wanted to write for Marvel for my entire life, he said he was already keeping me in mind for the right project...such as this little book about a family called the Keeps...

They weren't always called the Keeps, of course. The plotting process for SEEKERS was extremely collaborative. Though the actual scripts were mine, the plot came not just from me but from Bill, assistant editor Mark Basso, and the Imagineers as well. And then, of course, there's Rolly. Rolly Crump, the legendary Imagineer whose brainchild was the Museum of the Weird.

Our top priority—well, under "tell a good story"—was to stay true to Rolly's bizarre designs for the Museum, and to figure out what they were and what they meant to the story. We had it as a goal to include every single thing Rolly designed for the Museum in the five issues of SEEKERS OF THE WEIRD. (And apart from the odd chandelier and such, I think we succeeded!) After the first issue was finished, the Imagineers showed it to Rolly. And he gave us his blessing. I can't really express what that meant to me.

It's also meant a lot to me to work with this creative team. I've been a big fan of penciler Karl Moline's art since he did Fray. I thought I had a firm idea of how good his work on SEEKERS would be. But no. It was way, way better. I've had to up my game just to keep up with Karl! A lot of the little details in this series— like the weapons the parents used in the first issue—wouldn't exist if not for Karl "leveling me up." On top of that we've got inker Rick Magyar, letterer Joe Caramagna and cover artist Michael Del Mundo all delivering dazzling work, and some of the best coloring I've ever seen in a comic from Jean-Francois Beaulieu. This is a weird book for sure. It's also turning out to be a great one.

Brandon Seifert
Portland, Oregon

At Walt Disney Imagineering, we believe that good ideas never die—they sometimes just need a little extra time to discover the right avenue to spring forth. This has definitely been true in the case of the well-known, yet never built Rolly Crump and Walt Disney concept for Museum of the Weird. Walt was so confident in this companion experience to his upcoming Haunted Mansion at *Disneyland©* that he and Rolly went on television during the *Disneyland©* Tencennial in 1965 to share it with the world. Unfortunately, Walt left us a little too early, in December of 1966. With the master dreamer gone, many ideas were...delayed.

When the Disney family came together with the Marvel family in 2009, many of us naturally began to wonder what type of collaborations could be possible. Some out of pure excitement, and to be honest, some out of fear. Fortunately for Disney and Marvel enthusiasts, there are some pretty serious crossover fans within both families who have been pondering and hoping for what this new relationship would bring. This is where DISNEY KINGDOMS was truly born. Much like how the silver screen has expanded the anecdotes and mythologies of Disney theme park attractions, our DISNEY KINGDOMS team at Walt Disney Imagineering had high hopes to join forces with the brilliant storytellers at Marvel to do the exact same thing through beautifully illustrated comic books.

DISNEY KINGDOMS: SEEKERS OF THE WEIRD is the first series in what we all hope will be a very long and fun relationship between Disney and Marvel fans. Walt Disney used to introduce us each week to exciting lands of Frontier, Tomorrow, Adventure, and Fantasy through the magic of television. If we may be so bold as to follow the example set by Walt Disney so many years ago, we will embark on endless new adventures through the experiences created by Disney theme parks, lands, attractions, characters and beyond! The future is filled with excitement, and will be further molded by your enthusiasm for DISNEY KINGDOMS by Marvel Entertainment and Walt Disney Imagineering.

Fasten your seatbelts, and enjoy the ride!

Josh Shipley
Creative Designer
Walt Disney Imagineering

MARVEL AUGMENTED REALITY (AR) ENHANCES AND CHANGES THE WAY YOU EXPERIENCE COMICS!

TO ACCESS THE FREE MARVEL AR CONTENT IN THIS BOOK*:

1. Locate the **AR** logo within the comic.
2. Go to Marvel.com/AR in your web browser.
3. Search by series title to find the corresponding AR.
4. Enjoy Marvel AR!

*All AR content that appears in this book has been archived and will be available only at Marvel.com/AR — no longer in the Marvel AR App. Content subject to change and availability.

SEEKERS OF THE WEIRD AR INDEX